The New Peace Linguistics and the Role of Language in Conflict

A volume in
Peace Education
Laura L. Finley and Robin Cooper, *Series Editors*

Peace Education

Laura L. Finley and Robin Cooper, *Series Editors*

Humanities Perspectives in Peace Education: Re-Engaging the Heart of Peace Studies (2021)
Nicole L. Johnson

Peace is Everyone's Business (2021)
Lowell Ewert and Frederick Bird

Experiential Learning in Higher Education: Issues, Ideas, and Challenges for Promoting Peace and Justice (2021)
Laura L. Finley and Glenn A. Bowen

Difficult Discussions: Issues and Ideas for Engaging College Students in Peace and Justice Topics (2020)
Laura L. Finley and Robin Cooper

The United Nations and Higher Education: Peacebuilding, Social Justice and Global Cooperation for the 21st Century (2020)
Kevin Kester

Gender, Sexuality and Peace Education: Issues and Perspectives in Higher Education (2018)
Laura L. Finley and Robin Cooper

Sustainable Peace in the Twenty-First Century: Bridging the Gap from Theory to Practice (2017)
Dilip Vasudeo Kulkarni

Peace Jobs: A Student's Guide to Starting a Career Working for Peace (2016)
David J. Smith

Peace Education Evaluation: Learning from Experience and Exploring Prospects (2015)
Celina Del Felice, Aaron Karako, and Andria Wisler

Teaching Peace Through Popular Culture (2015)
Laura L. Finley, Joanie Connors, and Barbara Wien

Peace and Conflict Studies Research: A Qualitative Perspective (2014)
Robin Cooper and Laura L. Finley

Understanding Peace Cultures (2014)
Rebecca L. Oxford

Peace Education from the Grassroots (2013)
Ian Harris

The Language of Peace: Communicating to Create Harmony (2013)
Rebecca L. Oxford

More Than a Curriculum: Education for Peace and Development (2013)
Johan Galtung and S. P. Udayakumar

Think, Care, Act: Teaching for a Peaceful Future (2011)
Susan Gelber Cannon

Building a Peaceful Society: Creative Integration of Peace Education (2011)
Laura L. Finley

Books, Not Bombs: Teaching Peace Since the Dawn of the Republic (2010)
Charles F. Howlett and Ian Harris

Spirituality, Religion, and Peace Education (2010)
Edward J. Brantmeier, Jing Lin, and John P. Miller

For the People: A Documentary History of the Struggle for Peace and Justice in the United States (2009)
Charles F. Howlett and Robbie Lieberman

Peace Education: Exploring Ethical and Philosophical Foundations (2008)
James Page

Transforming Education for Peace (2008)
Jing Lin, Edward J. Brantmeier, and Christa Bruhn

Encyclopedia of Peace Education (2008)
Monisha Bajaj

Educating Toward a Culture of Peace (2006)
Yaacov Iram

The New Peace Linguistics and the Role of Language in Conflict

Andy Curtis
Anaheim University

IAP
INFORMATION AGE PUBLISHING, INC.
Charlotte, NC • www.infoagepub.com

Library of Congress Cataloging-in-Publication Data

A CIP record for this book is available from the Library of Congress
http://www.loc.gov

ISBN: 978-1-64802-730-7 (Paperback)
978-1-64802-731-4 (Hardcover)
978-1-64802-732-1 (E-Book)

Printed in the United States of America

Dedication

To the memory of Mr. Manboadh/Syd Sookdeo, who died an unnecessary, accidental, and painfully un-peaceful death. RIP, Dad. To Mrs. Anjanee Sookram; the most tortured soul I have ever known. Glad you finally found some peace. RIP, Mum. To Liying, for everything over the last 25 years. To Jack, Jimena and Juan Sebastián—you are our future. We leave with the hope that your generations will do a better job of peacefully co-existing with each other and with the Earth than our generations have done. In that, our generations have failed yours. But we know you can do better. So, live long and prosper. Peace Out!

Contents

PART II

New Peace Linguistics Analyses of the Language of George W. Bush, Colin L. Powell, and Barack H. Obama

Abbreviations

BBC	British Broadcasting Corporation
BHO	Barrack H. Obama
BIA	Biden Inaugural Address
CALD	Cambridge Advanced Learner's Dictionary (of English)
CLP	Colin L. Powell
CNBC	Consumer News and Business Channel
CNN	Cable News Network
DJT	Donald J. Trump
JRB	Joseph R. Biden
M-W	Merriam-Webster Dictionary (of English)
NPL	New Peace Linguistics
NPR	National Public Radio
OFA	Obama Farewell Address
OED	Oxford English Dictionary
OIA	Obama Inaugural Address
PBS	Public Broadcasting Service
PL	Peace Linguistics
PPB	Peter Paul Buttigieg

The New Peace Linguistics and The Role of Language in Conflict, pages xiii–xiv

RGS	Rose Garden Speech
SCC	South Carolina Commentary
WoMDA	Weapons of Mass Destruction Address
WoTA	War on Terror Address

Acknowledgments

As I write in Chapter 1:

> nothing worth reading was ever really written by just one author, but in reality, co-constructed and co-created by all the people who help each author along the way, with feedback, words of encouragement, cups of tea and sympathy. All the people in the authors' personal and professional lives, from family and friends to editors and publishers, have played a role in shaping the authors' thoughts and feelings, their ideas and understanding, and how those are ultimately manifest as the words on the page . . .
> grasped from the ether before they float away.

Therefore, my heartfelt thanks go first to our foremothers and forefathers, abducted from the peaceful paddy fields of India, to be slaves of The Empire in British Guiana, then part of the underclass of England, for all the sacrifices you made, so we could live as free women and men. And to the Sookdeo-Sookram-Persaud-Hicks-Ross Family: Al, San and Camilla, Gab, Meg and Tony, for our family ties, and for bonds that cannot be broken.

Thanks also to Jay Lundelius et al. and Josh Dalton and Co., for extending our family; to Dwight Atkinson, for staying strong and long; to the Schofields—Bob, Deb, and the Songstress of Ireland—and to the Herringtons, Glenn and Michelle. Thank you for your friendship, for listening, and for years of caffeinated and ethanolic libations.

Had it not been for the Department of English Language Teaching and Learning at Brigham Young University-Hawaii taking a chance on a

The New Peace Linguistics and The Role of Language in Conflict, pages xv–xvi

non-Mormon like me, this book would not have been realized or written. Thanks then to my co-teacher Nancy Tarawhiti, my mentor Neil Anderson, and all the teachers in the Department of English Language Teaching and Learning at BYU-H, and to the two cohorts of students who completed the first ever university-level, credit-bearing courses on Peace Linguistics, in 2017 and 2018, for teaching me new ways to teach, new things to believe in, and for giving me hope for the future.

To Francisco Gomes de Matos and Rebecca Oxford, thank you for shining a light and for paving the way to a New Peace Linguistics. And to Kathi Bailey, David Nunan, Jun Liu and Mary Romney, thank you for teaching me how to lead, and more importantly, how to follow. For their feedback and input, thanks to Yan Yan (Lizzie), Gwan-Hyeok Im, Yue Peng (Luna), Rosemary Orlando and Val Ashford. And last but by no means least, thank you to Robin Cooper, George Johnson and everyone at Information Age Publishing, for having faith in me and in this work, after others had long-ago given up.

PART I

Introducing Peace Linguistics and the New Peace Linguistics

1

Introduction and Overview

In this chapter, we will consider the following questions in relation to different aspects of this book:

- Purpose and Goals: Why write and publish a book on Peace Linguistics now?
- Readership: Who was this book written for?
- The language used in this book: How was this book written?
- Chapter Summaries: What is this book about?

Some of the key points in this chapter include:

- Peace Linguistics Matters Because Peace Matters.
- The 'scientific' study of language and the 'systematic' study of language are not the same thing, especially with regard to gender and race.
- The Rwandan Genocide of 1994 is a catastrophic example of the destructive potential of language.

The New Peace Linguistics and The Role of Language in Conflict, pages 3–22

- This is the first book to be published on Peace Linguistics and the New Peace Linguistics.

Why a Book on Peace Linguistics?

As far as we know, this is the first book ever to be published on this topic, Peace Linguistics (PL). Previous books have certainly addressed the topic, but not at book-length. A valid question, then, is: Why a book on Peace Linguistics? To respond to that question, we need to take a few steps back, as paradoxically, we can sometimes see more from being further away. For example, the next time you have the opportunity to spend some time in a museum or art gallery, take a break from looking at the art and look at the people looking at the art. Having done this in museums and galleries around the world, over the last 30 years or so, I have been struck by how 'universal' is the sequence of behaviors. First, the observer of the artwork moves slowly closer and closer to the work—sometimes so close as to rouse a sleeping security guard from their slumber—at which point the observer takes a few quick steps back. Then, the observer often continues their back-stepping, but while keeping their eyes on the artwork. In my work, I have referred to this as 'stepping back, to get a better view' (Curtis, 2017d).

Let us now apply that stepping back approach to the question above: Why write a book on PL? Stepping even further back from that question, we can see two others: Why write about anything? Why go through the long and painful process of publishing a book? In the publish-or-perish world of The Academy, teachers at universities, colleges and even some schools nowadays are under pressure to publish. Those pressures may have little to do with contributing to the body of knowledge in a particular field, and more to do with securing employment, promotion, tenure, etc. However, as I chose to walk away from that world some years ago, and to work *pro bono* since 2011, those particular pressures no longer apply to me. Why then put myself through this process? In the preface to his book, *From Warism to Pacifism: A Moral Continuum* (2010), Duane Cady wrote: "This is as much a warning to the reader as a confession that I suspect that I am onto something that may be beyond my capabilities as writer and thinker. I am not apologizing for what follows." Cady went on to explain that he was "being frank" and inviting the reader to join him, "in a struggle to understand" and to make "sense of pacifism" (p. xv).

Like Cady (2010), I make no apology for what follows, though some of it may be deemed controversial, and like Cady, I felt compelled to write this book as part of my struggle to understand the role of language in conflict, which may help us to avoid such conflict, thereby resulting in more peace. I do not know if "I am onto something that may be beyond my capabilities as writer and thinker." But teaching the first courses on PL, then guest editing the first issue of a journal on PL, which resulted in my researching and writing this first book on PL, has certainly pushed my capabilities as a writer and a thinker, as a teacher and a learner, to their limits. And so, like Cady, I too invite you to join me in my "struggle to understand" and to make sense of today's war-torn world through the New Peace Linguistics (NPL).

To be clear, this book positions itself within the area of Applied Linguistics. However, *while all NPL may be applied linguistics, not all applied linguistics is NPL,* as there are a great many areas under the umbrella of applied linguistics, but with this book, and the other PL publications in recent years, PL is now poised—belatedly—to take its place next to those other areas. This is also a book that draws extensively on different forms of rhetorical analyses, referring to rhetoric in the sense of: "speech or writing intended to be effective and influence people; the study of the ways of using language effectively; clever language that sounds good but is not sincere or has no real meaning" (*Cambridge Advanced Learner's Dictionary, CALD,* 2021). However, even that relatively simple, straightforward dictionary definition of 'rhetoric' shows that there are different ways of understanding and analyzing rhetoric. Therefore, one of the ways in which this book can be distinguished from other books on applied linguistics and/or rhetoric is its focus on language, war and peace.

In their in-depth discussion comparing and contrasting the different genres or types of spoken and written texts, Brown and Yule (1983) stated that: "it is clear that spoken and written texts make somewhat different demands on language-producers" (p. 4). They also pointed out that the speaker has available to them "a full range of 'voice quality' effects" (p. 4), such as being able to speak more slowly or more quickly, more loudly or more softly, as well as "facial expression, postural and gestural systems" (p. 4). One of the main differences is that the writer has more time; to re-read their work, revise it, and repeat that cycle, to consult dictionaries and other texts, to find the *mot juste,* etc. As Brown and Yule (1983) explained, it is important to recognize that not only are there different demands made on the *language-producers* of written versus spoken texts, but different demands are also made on the *recipients* of those texts, i.e., the readers in case of written texts, and the listeners in the case of spoken texts.

It is also important to note that the texts analyzed in Part III of this book cross the spoken-written divide, as the speeches are written first, usually by professional speech writers, then perhaps read by the person who will deliver the speech, and possibly revised, so that the language of the text reflects the 'voice' of the speaker. The final version of the speech is then heard by a listening audience, some of whom, such as journalists, will also be taking notes, i.e., writing while listening. After the speech has been given, that is sometimes followed by a written version of the speech being made available, to the press, the general public, etc. Therefore, the criteria that might usually be applied to distinguish between written texts and spoken texts may not apply here. Brown and Yule (1983) conclude their detailed discussion of spoken and written texts by summarizing the process in which discourse analysts treat their data as "the record (text) of a dynamic process in which language was used as an instrument of communication in a context by a speaker/writer to express meaning and achieve intentions" (p. 26). That conclusion relates to the point made in Chapter 1, that 'communication' and 'language' are often used interchangeably, but they do not mean the same thing, as language is the *means* by which the *end*, communication, is achieved.

At this point, I should apologize for some potentially bad news: PL and this book on the New Peace Linguistics may not necessarily and not directly lead to the world being a more peaceful place. Sadly, there does not appear to be any book that has ever been published that has been able to bring about World Peace. On the contrary, some of the world's most widely read books, for example, *The Bible* and *The Quran*, have been used for centuries to justify so-called 'religious wars' (see Khan, 2010), resulting in death and destruction on an unimaginable and incalculable scale. However, NPL (including an 'assumed article', 'NPL' stands for 'the New Peace Linguistics') may be able to make some indirect contributions to World Peace, which leads us to the sub-question: Why Peace Linguistics? from which we can further derive: Why Peace? and Why Linguistics? Those questions are addressed in the following chapters, but it is worth addressing them briefly here as well, as they are fundamental to the field of NPL. Responding to the questions above, we can simply state that: *Peace Linguistics Matters Because Peace Matters.*

Around the world—as I write this and as you read it—there is conflict. From wars being fought between nations, to heated arguments between individuals. My claim is that all of those conflicts began with language. For example, one world leader—or anyone with armies and weapons at their disposal—saying something that is perceived to be hostile, aggressive or provocatory by another world leader. But there may be some good news about conflict, according to influential thinkers and writers such as Steven Pinker, described as "Harvard University psychologist and famed intellect" (Stetka, 2017). In his book, *The Better Angels of Our Nature: Why Violence Has Declined* (2011), Pinker claimed that, "humans are now living in the most peaceful era in the history of our species" (Stetka, 2017). Some support for Pinker's claim has been reported. For example, Therése Pettersson and Kristine Eck (2018) studied data collected by the Uppsala Conflict Data Program between 1989 and 2017, and found that, regarding "organized violence": "2017 saw a decrease for the third consecutive year to a level 32% lower than the latest peak in 2014" (p. 535). Pettersson and Eck concluded that: "The overall decrease in fatalities lends support to the claim that conflict deaths are in decline and that the world is increasingly peaceful" (p. 535). However, such claims have also been challenged.

According to the medical reporter for the *Scientific American*, Bret Stetka, "there is plenty of evidence supporting Pinker's claim" as: "Most scholars agree the percentage of people who die violent war-related deaths has *plummeted* through history; and that *proportionally* violent deaths decline as populations become increasingly large and organized" (Stetka, 2017, emphases added). However, Stetka also reported on a 2017 study that challenged Pinker's claim that we are now living "in the most peaceful era in the history of our species." The 2017 study was carried out by two professors of anthropology, Dean Falk and Charles Hildebolt, who compared "annual war deaths for 11 chimpanzee communities, 24 hunter-gatherer or other nonstate groups and 19 and 22 countries that fought in World Wars I and II, respectively" (Stetka, 2017).

Based on their comparative data, Falk and Hildebolt (2017) concluded that: "the larger the population of a group of chimps, the lower their rate of annual deaths due to conflict... [which] was not the case in human populations... [who] have evolved to be more violent than chimps" (Stetka, 2017). Such apparently contradictory conclusions can be explained by considering relative population sizes in terms of proportions or percentages, as Falk and Hildebolt found that, although, "There is a strong trend for larger [human] societies to lose smaller percentages of their members to war... *the actual number of war deaths increases with growing population sizes*" (Stetka, 2017, emphasis added). Therefore, according to the longitudinal data gathered and analyzed by Falk and Hildebolt: "the overall battle-death toll in modern organized societies is *exponentially higher* than in hunter-gatherer societies surveyed during the past 200 years" (Stetka, 2017, emphasis added). Such findings may be taken to imply that human beings are naturally predisposed to violence, or that we are somehow, as a species, programed to respond to conflict violently.

One way to make sense of such research findings lies in looking closely and carefully at the language used to present and interpret the results. In the Pinker vs. Falk and Hildebolt findings, one of the key phrases is the reference to "the past 200 years." Given the fact that even the longest average human lifespans are currently well-below one hundred years, surveying the past two centuries may obscure large-scale, widespread violence *in our lifetimes.* For example, the Institute for Economics and Peace found that: "Despite living in the most peaceful century in human history, the world has become less peaceful over the last decade" (Ventura, 2018). Another example is the 2019 25th anniversary of the genocide in Rwanda, when the country mourned for 100 days, as that was the number of days it took, in 1994, for the slaughter of 800,000 men, women and children to take place—one-tenth of the population of the country at that time (see, for example, de Castillo, 2019). More than five people killed every minute of every hour of every day. For 100 days. This is where the limitations of language—facts and figures, words and numbers—can be seen, as no sounds or syllables can convey the horror of such an event, and language was key in those killings.

The critical importance of language in the Rwandan Genocide was described in Rebekah DeZalia's chapter 'Being Rwandan: The Use of Language, History, and Identity in Post-Genocide Rwanda' (2014). DeZalia explained that, during colonial rule: "the Belgians combined existing narratives with their Hamitic myth to validate their rule through the Tutsi minority" (p. 157). Later, in postcolonial Rwanda, "the Hutu used their version of this historical narrative . . . to justify their dominance over the Tutsi and . . . to promote this violence on a level never before seen in the country" (p. 157). One of the most specific and most disturbing examples of the power of language in such circumstances was the word 'cockroaches', used by the majority Hutu to describe and dehumanize members of the country's ruling-minority Tutsi population (O'Grady, 2016). The word was repeatedly used on radio programs, which was the main form of public broadcasting in Rwanda that time, and became an essential part of the build-up to the eventual genocide. In 'The Language of Genocide', William Donohue (2011) analyzed two 1994 broadcasts from the Rwandan Genocide as examples of what he referred to as "the Identity Trap." That particular trap explains "how various linguistic conventions combine to establish a social context that builds up the speaker's social identity while denigrating the 'enemy's social identity, which provides the rationale for escalating conflict against that enemy" (p. 13). More recently, Kennedy Ndahiro, the editor of the Rwandan daily newspaper *The New Times,* published a piece in *The Atlantic* titled "In Rwanda, we know all about dehumanizing language" where and when "years of cultivated hatred led to death on a horrifying scale" (Ndahiro, 2019). (See also Curtis & Oxford, 2021; Oxford & Curtis, 2021).

We have, thus far, looked at a number of answers to the opening question above: Why (write) a book on (New) Peace Linguistics? That question relates to the importance of 'Linguistics', which has long been defined as 'the scientific study of language' and which I am proposing should be 'the systematic study of language'. Whichever descriptor is chosen, 'scientific' or 'systematic', again, stepping way back, a question that follows then is: Why study anything? There are, of course, many possible answers to that question, which form the basis of education systems around the world, but one answer is: By studying things we learn more about them, so we can better understand them. In civilized societies, that better understanding is an end in and of itself, and an essential part of the idea that being an educated person is an inherently good thing to be. However, as Peace Linguistics is part of the field of Applied Linguistics, beyond a greater understanding being an intrinsically worthy goal of study, applying NPL can also contribute to a better understanding of how language is used to manipulate people, to the point of encouraging them to murder their neighbors with machetes in the middle of the night, as they did in Rwanda in 1994.

There were, of course, many conditions and factors that led to the Rwandan Genocide, going back more than a century, to 1918, when: "Both Germany and Belgium turned the traditional Hutu-Tutsi relationship into a class system . . . [and] The Belgians used the Tutsi minority to enforce their rule" (PBS Frontline, 2014). The minority Tutsis, who were only 14% of the population, were favored by the colonial, European powers over the Hutus, who were 85% of the population. For example, the Tutsis received a "western-style education", and in 1926, the Belgian colonizers introduced, "a system of ethnic identity cards differentiating Hutus from Tutsis" (PBS Frontline, no date)—dividing-and-conquering by sowing the seeds of a conflict, which first manifested itself in the large-scale killing of Tutsis in 1963, and again a few years later, in 1967. As well as Germany and Belgium, the USA and the U.N. Security Council also played key roles in not preventing the 1994 genocide. When such unimaginable and catastrophic events take place, there are many causes and more than enough blame to go around. But looking at how such conflicts took place, to better understand how they may be avoided in the future, is one of the major focuses of Peace Studies, including Peace Education and Peace Research. In the same way, looking at how language is used by those in power, who are in a position to start, to stop, or to prevent wars and other forms of large-scale conflict, is one of the major focuses of NPL.

As this is the first book on this topic, there is also the question: Why a book on (New) Peace Linguistics *now*? One reason that distinguishes our current times from previous times is the growth of the Internet, which has brought with it many benefits. But as with all technological developments, there is also a downside, including the all-day, everyday news-cycle that many of us now live with/under. As a result of that cycle, we can now go online and see death and destruction, around the world, around the clock. All of those news reports use carefully chosen language to present those reports, and as stated earlier, one of the premises of NPL is that all conflict starts with language. Therefore, a greater understanding of the roles of language in conflict, in presenting conflict and in avoiding conflict, may be especially important in today's 24/7 news-cycle. Another factor linked to the growth of the Internet is the growth of so-called 'social media'—'so-called' because it can be extremely, anti-socially damaging and destructive, (Brown, 2018). Thanks to messaging platforms such as Twitter, anyone with access and an account—from world leaders to homeless people (Cary, 2011)—can write and send messages to millions of people, all over the world, in just a few moments. For example, on November 18, 2016, the day of a presidential election in the USA, 40 million Twitter messages, or 'tweets', were sent in a single day (Isaac & Ember, 2016). Therefore, as a result of the saturation news cycle and (anti)social media, we may now be living through one of the most language-intensive times in human history, making language-based areas of enquiry such as NPL potentially more important today than at any time before.

Having made a case for NPL, it is also worth considering the name, because what we call things matters. As one of the goals of NPL is to better understand the language of those in power, the name 'Power Linguistics' was suggested, and work has been published on 'the linguistics of power and the power of linguistics' (Garrard, 2016). However, Garrard's work is focused on using language corpora, which is: "a large sample of text or collection of texts in one or more languages, and sometimes in machine-readable format, that can be subjected to a range of large-scale analytical methods" (Garrard, 2016, p. 136). Therefore, Garrard's 'power linguistics' is more breadth-based than the in-depth analyses of specific texts of NPL (see also Holtgraves & Lasky, 1999, on 'Linguistic Power and Persuasion'). Other naming suggestions include 'War Linguistics' or 'Conflict Linguistics', rather than 'Peace Linguistics', as the damage is being done by wars and other kinds of (armed) conflict, not peace, and there is a well-established disciplinary domain of 'War Studies'. However, if we deliberately and consciously focus on desired outcomes, then most people would choose peace over war. Therefore, 'Peace Linguistics', like 'Peace Studies' is the chosen title, reflecting that desired outcome of less war and more peace.

Historically, the term 'Peace Linguistics' has been in use for decades, although until recently it was mostly focused on how language could and should be used in ways that avoid conflict. In contrast, NPL is focused on analyses of how language is actually being used, and how it is being used by some of the most powerful people in the world, such as presidents of the USA. It is, though, important to note here that this book is a first step on what may turn out to be a long and winding road, which may result in some kind of trickle-down effect, starting with the language of world leaders. But eventually: "NPL could help avoid or de-escalate conflicts between individuals, between small, medium and large groups [and] . . . conflicts between nations, by helping the participants understand the central role of language in those conflicts, and systematically analyzing the language being used" (Curtis, 2018g, p. 104).

To further employ the well-worn metaphor of the journey, given that this is the first book on Peace Linguistics, it is a first step, and as such, it is unlikely that we will get it all right first time. As one of my mother's friends, an older lady from our home-country of Guyana, used to say to us, when we came home from school, in England in the 1970s: "Don't nobody get nothin' all right first time, darlin'. You gotta start somewhere. And you gotta keep goin." Therefore, my hope is that this book will be the start of a wider discussion about many different aspects of language, war and peace, including how applied linguists may be able to help make the world a less conflict-covered and less war-torn place to live (or to die). (In this book, 'language aspects', 'language features', 'language strategies' and 'language moves' are used interchangeably.) Furthermore, as a book about language as it relates to sensitive areas (and in some contexts, taboo topics) such as death and destruction, war and peace, I am hoping that some readers will see this book as controversial in its claims, and disagree with some of the positions I take. That constructive criticism is how knowledge advances, although preferably not through the tearing down of what came before, but through building on those foundations.

Who Was This Book Written For?

One of the many challenges of writing a book on a topic on which no books have been written before is the question of audience or readership. Once an academic or scholarly field has been established, then any book written within that disciplinary domain can claim to be of interest to anyone working in that field. That is not the case for NPL. Another challenge in developing NPL as an area of enquiry is its inherently interdisciplinary nature. From the perspective of connecting different domains of knowledge—which might have become artificially separated and disconnected from each other as a result of formal systems of education—the interdisciplinarity of NPL is a benefit, as it enables multiple perspectives, leading to multifaceted understandings. However, the institutions that claim to be 'makers of knowledge', such as universities, are focused on faculty members developing highly specialized, i.e., narrow, fields of expertise, leading to the creation of intellectual silos, defined as: "an isolated grouping, department, etc., that functions apart from others especially in a way seen as hindering communication and cooperation" (*Merriam-Webster*, 2021). Therefore, people working in the fields of Peace Studies, including Peace Research and Peace Education, appear to have had very little contact (if any at all) with people working in the fields of Language Studies, including Language Research and Language Education. This book, then, was written to help bridge those gaps, by being of use to those experts in Language Studies who have little or no knowledge of Peace Studies, and vice versa, i.e., of use to those experts in Peace Studies who have little or no knowledge of Language Studies.

Two other broad groups emerged during my teaching, researching and writing about NPL. One group is comprised of those who have been using the term 'Peace Linguistics' for some time now, but whose work has included little actual linguistics, i.e., language analysis. However, that work has generated many useful ideas and suggestions for avoiding the kinds of language that lead to conflict, and using instead the kinds of language that lead to peaceful communicative outcomes. The other group is made up of those researchers and writers who have been engaged in work that could be described as 'Peace Linguistics', as they include language analyses, but who have not been using that term. As highlighted above, what we call things matters—a fact that may even be one of the fundamental premises underlying all work carried out under the umbrella of Applied Linguistics. Therefore, both groups—those who have been using the term 'PL' with little of the 'L', and those who have been doing 'PL' but without connecting the 'P' and the 'L' as closely together—may also find this book useful.

Another challenge of writing the first book on a topic is the fact that student textbooks cannot be written for a field that is just coming into existence. However, the first Peace Linguistics courses were taught at Brigham Young University-Hawaii (BYU-H) in 2017 and 2018, and that course is growing. For example, instead of PL being an elective at BYU-H, it is now a required course, with prerequisites, and the course is continuing to attract students who are Peace-Building majors, Language Education majors, and from other disciplines as well, such as Anthropology. The (N)PL course at BYU-H may spread beyond that beautiful, remote island, beyond BYU, and beyond the USA, to the rest of the world. Therefore, this book was written with the next generation of NPL *teachers* in mind, and with an awareness of future NPL *students.* That is why dozens of activities—labeled 'ReActs' (as a portmanteau of 'Reader Activities', and to encourage readers to react to the chapters)—have been created and distributed throughout the book to help both groups, future NPL teachers and future NPL students, apply what they have learned. The ReAct tasks are also designed to make the political personal, connecting the public language of politically powerful people with the private, individual language of intra-personal communication. To further help future teachers and students of NPL, there are also dozens of annotated suggestions for further readings, at the ends of the chapters, which are in addition to the hundreds of references listed at the end of the book, which can also be used as resources.

There are dozens of applied linguistics associations who may find this work of use. For example, the Association Internationale de Linguistique Appliquée (AILA, or the International Association of Applied Linguistics), which was founded in 1964 in France, has more than 8,000 members worldwide, in more than 30 countries, in North America, South America, across Europe, Asia and elsewhere (https://aila.info/). In addition, there are centres such as CAL, the Centre for Applied Linguistics, based in the USA, and other applied linguistics centres in other countries. In addition to those kinds of professional organizations and research centres, there are institutes that focus on Peace Studies, including the Peace Research Institute in Oslo, which celebrated its 60th anniversary in 2019 (https://www.prio.org). There is also, for example, the International Peace Institute, with offices in the USA, Europe, the Middle East and North Africa (https://www.ipinst.org), and the UNESCO Mahatma Gandhi Institute of Education for Peace and Sustainable Development (http://mgiep.unesco.org/). Such associations, organizations and institutes may also find this book useful, as well as many university programs. For example, many universities in Canada now offer degree-level Peace and Conflict Studies programs. As with all new fields, there may well be more individuals and groups that will find this book useful, and we look forward to hearing from them.

How Was This Book Written?

In this book, as in many books, most of the wh-questions about the book itself—why the book was written, who was it written for, who was it written by, and so on—are addressed along the way. However, there are rarely notes on *how* the book came to be in the hands (or on the screen) of the reader in its present form. Perhaps there is an assumption that books follow a similar (or even the same) process: write, receive feedback, revise, rinse-repeat, and publish. However, as any published author will tell you, every book, like every author, follows a process that is different. Also, all books (except for picture books) only exist because the language in which they were written exists. No language, no books. But for books that are all about language, then notes on the language in the book are required, and can be helpful for the reader. Therefore, in this section, we will briefly consider how this book came to be, in its present form.

First, the references, citations and sources. This book cites more than 700 sources in the list of references, and in the recommended readings at the end of each chapter and in Appendix A, which is a lot for a book of this size. However, the first book on any topic is by definition a starting point, marking a moment in history, and is therefore usually subject to (much) closer scrutiny than the books that follow. The first book often becomes a historical document, which the following books in that field build on, and which are compared to and contrasted with that first book. If the first book's author did their job correctly, then that book will stand the test of time. But the field must move on beyond that starting point, and eventually establish its own identity that is distinctive, and which may turn out to be markedly different from its origins. Such is the nature of creating new knowledge.

An important part of doing a 'good job' and scholarly 'due diligence' is erring on the side of caution, and over-referencing rather than under-doing it. Also, part of the higher level of first-book scrutiny sometimes involves challenging many (or even all) of the author's claims, especially the more controversial ones. And this book is full of such claims, from my challenging of the widely held belief that, if we could all just be at peace, personally, then peace would reign and wars would end, to my critical analyses of the texts of certain world leaders, by those who support them. Those are two of the main reasons—closer first-book scrutiny in general, and the challenging of specific points that may be vigorously disagreed with—for the (over-ly)extensive citing of sources, and for extensive use of verbatim quotes, so as to avoid the charge of me putting my words into the mouths of others.

Another way in which this book differs from typical scholarly works is the number of references to online sources and non-academic sources. One reason for there being so many of those sources in this book is a concern about accessibility of sources. For example, at the time of writing (Fall/Autumn 2021), the flagship journal, *Applied Linguistics,* published by Oxford University Press, was charging approximately 50 USD for one day/24-hour access to one single article, which appears to be the industry norm. There are many educators in many countries for whom 50 USD represents a week or more of their teaching income. Also related to income, almost none of the vast profits generated from such price tags goes to the authors themselves. Academic publishing may, then, be one of the few areas of work in the so-called 'first world/rich world, developed countries' wherein the people who make the products (the published academic journal papers) receive no financial remuneration whatsoever, while almost 100% of the profits go to those who control the industry. Lastly, in terms of opening up economic access to reliable, up-to-date, online (re)sources, most of the newspapers cited allow readers access to a number of free articles, before asking the reader to pay a subscription fee, and even then, those fees are a fraction of what academic journal publishers are charging for even limited access.

The question of broadening accessibility via the Internet does, however, raise the question of reliability. Therefore, one of the goals of this book has been to balance accessibility and reliability, by ensuring that the online sources are trustworthy, for example, only using verifiably *bona fide* new agencies, such as the BBC, and other similar agencies. Unfortunately, there is no such thing as 100% unbiased reporting, as even non-profit new organizations like the BBC are funded by the UK Government, and are therefore subject to whatever governmental restrictions are put upon them. Also, even though the academic world likes to portray itself as being completely objective, especially where 'hard data', i.e., numbers, are involved, such objectivity is impossible, as research is carried out by human beings, who are no less conflicted, biased and opinionated than the rest of the non-researching population. We just do our best to set aside those thoughts and feelings and let the data lead us, rather than the other way around. In relation to reliability, for every online source accepted many more were rejected and excluded, for example, if the source could not be verified, if it is unclear who wrote the piece, if extreme opinions are being presented as facts, etc. The third aspect of online sources carefully considered, in addition to accessibility and reliability, is currency or 'currentness', in the sense of how up-to-date is the information presented, as it typically takes years to get an article published in the top journals in the field, and sometimes even longer for books, for example edited collections with multiple contributors.

In recent years, attacks on such basic concepts as facts and truth, on which civilizations can claim to be built, have escalated exponentially (Holmes, 2016; Loofbourow, 2016; Thomas, 2017), to the extent that the *Oxford English Dictionary* 2016 word of the year was 'Post-Truth'. As the *OED* announced on their website: "Post-truth has gone from being a peripheral term to being a mainstay in political commentary, now often being used by major publications without the need for clarification or definition in their headlines" (languages.oup.com). The *OED* went on to explain the reasons for their word-of-the-year choice, including the fact that, although "the concept of post-truth has been in existence for the past decade" the *OED* had seen "a spike in frequency this year in the context of the EU referendum in the United Kingdom and the presidential election in the United States. It has also become associated with a particular noun, in the phrase post-truth politics" (languages.oup.com). That leads us neatly to the extensive use of dictionary definitions throughout this book, especially the *Collin's Advanced Learner's Dictionary*, for the simple reason that anyone who knows English is a learner of English, whether or not it is their first language or mother tongue. Every living language is an organic entity, constantly growing and changing, so it can never be fully, completely and absolutely learned.

For those of us who have spent most of our professional lives doing language for a living on a daily basis, we seek solace in the dictionary, as an anchor in some kind of perfect storm of language; a place where words have specific, agreed-upon meanings—regardless of whoever decides that their opinion is, in fact, a fact. Unlike Humpty Dumpty in Lewis Carroll's *Through the Looking Glass* (1871), a word cannot mean just what someone chooses it to mean. Only talking eggs get to do that, not real people. However, that is not to say that dictionaries are 100% objective either, as one of the world's most well-known dictionaries, the *OED*, has its own bizarre history, as documented in Simon Winchester's book, *The Professor and the Madman: A Tale of Murder, Insanity, and the Making of the Oxford English Dictionary* (2005). In that book, Winchester explained that the compilation of the *OED*, which began in 1857 and which took more than 20 years to complete, was overseen by the Scottish philologist and lexicographer, Professor James Murray (1837–1915), who was the editor of the *OED* for 36 years, from 1879 until his death. Shockingly, Murray found that more than 10,000 of the earliest entries had been written by a William Chester Minor (1834–1920)—who at the time of writing his 10,000-plus entries was a 40-year long-term resident (1870–1910) living in a London psychiatric hospital. Dictionaries have histories too. However, no matter how psychiatric or otherwise odd the history of a dictionary may be, they are cited extensively in this book as a reliable, publicly-accessible and in most cases, freely-accessible, source of knowledge, not only about current word-meanings, but how those meanings have changed over time, to reflect changes in society and even in civilizations.

Keeping with the theme of explaining the language used in a book about language, in this book both the first names and the family names are sometimes given, which is not the academic norm—but why not? We do not, in our daily lives, usually refer to people by their family name; indeed, in many cultures, using a person's first name is the norm, as long as the interlocutors know each other, and it is not a situation in which professional titles are required, such as Dr. So-and-So or Professor This-and-That. There are cultures in which, as a sign of respecting seniority, first names would be considered inappropriate and overly familiar. However, in the academic world, the first-name obfuscation is more about lending a veneer of objectivity to the work. One of the reasons for me terminating my generous medical scholarship while working in hospitals in the UK in the 1980s (and moving to the rich and glamorous world of English Language Teaching!) was the use of misleading language. For example, "I took a test tube" would elicit gasps of (mock) horror from my health science professors, who would use their red pen to cross out the phrase and write: "My dear boy, I assume you meant to write 'a test tube was taken' as who took it matters not in the least." Of course, in healthcare—as in everywhere else—who does what to whom (as well as why, when, where and how) matters a great deal. And so, it came my time to leave.

The simple fact of the matter is that every researcher who ever was (is and will be) was a person long before they reached the academic heights of being a researcher—and after they shuffle off that heavy mantle, back to being a regular person must they return. (Earth to Earth, Ashes to Ashes, etc.). Therefore, to recognize and celebrate these researchers' humanity, their origins and their endings, first names are included as much as possible. And regarding the importance of what we call things, of names and naming, the United States of America is abbreviated in this book as 'USA', not 'US'. Partly because the USA is one of the only countries in the world of which the name is also a pronoun, i.e., 'us.' More importantly, it turns out that abbreviating 'USA' to 'US' appears to be a largely US thing, i.e., in other countries—especially my colleagues in South America, Latin America and North America, who bristle at being called 'American', especially in recent years—'USA' is used rather than 'US'. Therefore, in this book, the international country-name abbreviation used is 'USA', except when used as an adjectival modifier, for example, 'the 46th US President'.

Seasons are used as chronological indictors, and as this book was written in Canada, the seasons referred to herein are those in North America and Europe. The last note on the language used in this book is the use of 'we'. In the same way that the third person "a test tube was taken" hides the agent of the action, the name on the front of this book is also an obfuscation of sorts. In my experience, nothing worth reading was ever really written by just that one author, but in reality, co-constructed and co-created by all the people who help each author along the way, with feedback, words of encouragement, cups of tea and sympathy. All the people in the authors' personal and in their professional lives, from family and friends to editors and publishers, have played a role in shaping the authors' thoughts and feelings, their ideas and understanding, and how those are ultimately manifest as the words on the page. Therefore, as my own small but I hope meaningful way of acknowledging the many hundreds of poor souls who have patiently listened to me talk, laugh and cry about this book over the last many years (see Acknowledgments), please know that you are here, each time you see 'we'.

What Is This Book About?

Writing a book is not recommended. After 20 years of writing books, and especially after the last 1,000 days and these 100,000 words, I know whereof I speak. It may seem strange to recommend to readers to be wary of writing a book—while you are, at this very moment, reading one. But the toll that book-writing can take on your health and your relationships (with yourself and with everyone around you) can be considerable. If you are fortunate, some of that damage can be undone, but some may be permanent. For writers like myself, when you write a book like this, a little piece of you dies. You pour so much of your physical, mental, emotional and spiritual energy and time into the book—time and energy you can never get back—to make it something original, unique; something that matters, that helps make a lasting positive difference in our world. On the upside, writing a book like this can involve a sort of localized 're-birth,' in which parts of you, hitherto hibernating, slowly (and sometimes painfully) come back to life. In my case, writing a book about peace has required me to revisit every violent episode of my life (of which there have been many) but writing through those traumas may be one of the most effective ways to move past them, and begin to heal.

Given the toll that this kind of book-writing takes, an important and obvious question arises, but one which is very rarely asked in public, especially in the academic world, where the publish-or-perish imperative makes the question of why write a book redundant. In that world, professors write for the same reason they do research—because they have to. There are many other reasons for researching and writing, but the simple fact is that, for most professors, there is no choice. However, having walked away from the safe and secure forever-employed world of tenured university teaching a decade ago (to devote my time to working *pro bono*, as a free agent, for non-profit language education organizations around the world), those imperatives have not applied to me for a long time. Therefore, the first part of Chapter 1 considers the question of why anyone would write a book, especially on two topics about which (as far as we know) book have never been published before, in this case, under the title of 'Peace Linguistics' (PL) and proposing a 'New Peace Linguistics' (NPL). The second part of Chapter 1 explains with whom this book was written in mind, although we hope there will be many audiences that we had not considered who will find this book helpful and of practical use.

The third question addressed in Chapter 1—another one rarely considered publicly and in writing—relates to *how* this book was written, in terms of the language used herein. As this is a book all about language, it is necessary to start with a brief consideration of the language used, given the fact that, as we discuss in the following chapters, language is not neutral but a powerful human-made tool, which is often taken for granted in the way we take the oxygen we breath for granted. Human life depends on both—oxygen and language—but because we are immersed in them, from the moment of our birth to the moment of our death (earth to earth, ashes to ashes, etc.) we stop noticing that the lives we have lived up to this moment, up to this word, would have been impossible without these two precious, life-giving resources. And like all human-made tools, language can be used either for destructive or constructive purposes, depending on the language we choose to use, and how we choose to respond.

Chapter 2 looks at the relationships between language and conflict as being at the heart of NPL. For some readers, that may seem like something of a contradiction in terms, as 'peace' is often considered to be the opposite of 'conflict', especially armed conflicts such as war. However, the names 'Peace Linguistics' and 'the New Peace Linguistics' are positive, aspirational and outcome-focused, and based on the premise that a better understanding of the opposite of peace can help us avoid negative outcomes of conflict, up to and including all-out war. However, before furthering our understanding of the role of language in conflict, it is necessary to first consider what we mean by 'language', as like the word 'peace', 'language' can mean different things to different people (spoken/written, verbal/non-verbal, etc., see Gregerson & MacIntyre, 2021). Chapter 2 also explores how language studies, especially applied linguistics, have been largely overlooked or undervalued in spite of the essential role of language in conflict-transformation and in peace-making.

Chapter 3 presents explanations of what PL is, what it is not, and why PL matters. The shortest answer to that last point is that *PL Matters Because Peace Matters.* And whether or not we are living through the most conflict-torn times in human history, we are living through some of the most language-intensive times in the last 10,000 years or so (give or take a couple of centuries), since the beginning of the Neolithic Period (and not counting the Stone Age). Starting with one of the most recently published definitions of PL, that definition is carefully and comprehensively deconstructed in ways that have not taken place in the 40 years since the term PL first appeared in the literature. Unfortunately, in spite of those decades, most people—whether in language education or in peace education—have never even heard of PL, much less ever made use of it. Different kinds of 'warist discourse' are also discussed in Chapter 3, as are the relationships between rhetoric, politics and poetry.

The last chapter in Part I, Chapter 4, consider more questions, this time about the similarities and differences between the previous iterations of PL and NPL, starting with a small but important update to the definition of PL in order to define NPL. As the centuries-old phrase puts it, whatever new discoveries we make, we stand on the shoulders of giants, lifted up by all those who came before us, so we can see new horizons and new possibilities. With that in mind, much of Chapter 4 is about the work of peace language educators such as Francisco Gomes de Matos, Rebecca Oxford and many others; recognizing and acknowledging the importance of their work. Also considered are the limitations of, for example, giving advice on how language could and should be used peacefully, rather than analyses of language as it is actually being used, which is where NPL comes in.

By basing itself on systematic, in-depth analyses of the language of the people who have the power to bring about peace or to start wars, NPL is becoming a distinct field in its own right, within applied linguistics, in this case, applied to the question of how we, the people, make sense of the language of those in power. Lastly, the four Part I chapters are presented in chronological order. Alternatively, the first chapter could have started with where we are now, with NPL, and worked backwards to the origins of PL. Instead, we have chosen to begin at the beginning, by considering the meaning of fundamental concepts such as 'peace' and 'language' and the relationships between the two, and from there to introduce PL, then build on that, to introduce NPL, and its relationship to PL.

Part II is made up of three chapters which build on the foundation laid in Part I, starting with an NPL analysis of the speech given to the nation, and to the world, by US President George W. Bush on September 2001. After a brief introduction to and overview of the language and the linguistics of othering, we analyze the speech given by the President of the USA on September 20, 2001—nine days after the 9/11 terrorist attacks. As well as bringing a shocked and mourning country together, to comfort and reassure them, President Bush also used divisive them-and-us language, and created false dichotomies of the you're-either-with-us-or-you're-against-us kind, the damaging effects of which large parts of the world are still dealing with today. The second spoken text to be NPL analyzed is the speech given by the US Secretary of State in 2003, Colin Powell, which dragged the USA into a war with Iraq that was eventually shown to be based largely on false premises—premises that may even have been deliberately falsified. However, regardless of the truthfulness or falsity of the claims that war was necessary to prevent weapons of mass destruction being used against the

USA and its allies, what Powell said and how he said it was so convincing that more than 100,000 lives were lost; souls that could have been saved. Furthermore, tracking Powell's comments about that avoidable war over 16 years, from 2003 to 2016, shows how language can be used by those in power to deny knowledge, to not take responsibility, and to blame others, including the victims of the war.

The second and third chapters (Chapters 6 and 7) in Part II are based on the (first) Inaugural Address and on the Farewell Address of the 45th President of the USA, Barrack Obama, given in 2009 and in 2017, respectively. An NPL analysis of Obama's 2009 address found a number of language strategies employed, including condensing a great deal of meaning and multiple messages into relatively little language, as well as language that can draw some audiences in, but push some away, story-telling techniques, and other language of interest to NPL practitioners. In Chapter 7, based on an NPL analysis of Obama's 2017 Farewell Address, connections are made across speech events over time, in the form of 'echoing' or 'call-backs'. Those occur when a speaker connects their text to previous speech events of the same kind or similar, for example, connecting a presidential inaugural speech to that same president's farewell speech. Chapter 7 also explores the use of military and medical metaphors, 'warist discourse' and re-representations of history.

Part III is made up of five chapters, the first of which is an NPL analysis of a single spoken sentence uttered by Donald J. Trump (DJT) in 2015 in South Carolina, when he was campaigning to be the next president of the USA. Although only a single sentence, albeit it a very long and winding one, that 2015 line revealed at least ten aspects of language use that NPL practitioners need to be aware of and on the lookout for, including, for example, the myth of 'the self-made man', negative stereotyping based on race, and labeling entire cultures and civilizations as 'killers'. In Chapter 9, an NPL analysis of a speech given by DJT, during a 2019 press conference, found another ten or more uses of language more likely to lead to conflict outcomes than peaceful outcomes. For example, presenting life as a mutually exclusive dichotomy, in which there are only winners and losers, describing people and places as 'infestations' and 'invasions', and invoking images of mythical, satanic beast, such as 'monsters' to refer to 'the Other'.

Chapters 10 and 11 are based on NPL analyses of two written texts, which generated a total of more than 20 more language features, the first of which is a 2018 letter from DJT to the leader of North Korea, Kim Jong-un, cancelling a peace summit. The language used in that letter that is of particular interest to NPL practitioners include self-aggrandizing and egocentric expressions, and the issuing of threatening and accusatory warnings.

The second written text is a foreign policy statement from DJT, released in 2018, explaining and excusing the USA doing and saying nothing about the brutal, pre-meditated murder of the journalist, Jamal Khashoggi. In the policy statement, some of the NPL language strategies uncovered include obfuscating rather than communicating, scaring the audience and feeding off their fear, claiming that war is not only good for, but a vital part of, an economy—*as long as the war is somewhere else*—and blaming the victim, in this case, the murder victim. The last Part III chapter looks through an NPL lens at the Inaugural Address of the 46th President Joseph R. Biden, given at the start of 2021, and which included examples of using language to call for unity, to recognize wrongs and to commit to making positive changes. The last chapter of the book briefly reviews some of main points that emerged in the previous chapters, and looks forward to potential developments in the NPL field in the future.

Earlier drafts of this manuscript included separate chapters on Linguistics, Applied Linguistics, Sociolinguistics, Discourse Analysis, Text Analysis and Rhetoric, and on Peace Studies, Peace Research and Peace Education. However, as there are already many comprehensive texts available on each of those areas, we decided to focus this first book on PL and NPL. Therefore, instead of separate chapters on the areas listed above, Appendix A gives details of a dozen books on Linguistics and Applied Linguistics, and on Peace Studies and Peace Education (six in each of those two main areas), which have been helpful for people working in Peace Studies and Peace Education, who have had limited exposure to Linguistics and Applied Linguistics, and vice versa, as one of the goals of this book is to help bridge those two broad disciplinary domains. In Appendix B, there are links to the official government records of the U.S. Whitehouse Archives, together with some notes on those original source materials.

2

Language and Conflict

The Heart of the Matter

In this chapter, the following propositions are examined:

- Language is *the* source of conflict
- Language is *a* source of conflict
- There can be language without conflict
- There cannot be conflict without language
- Therefore, language is an essential prerequisite for starting and for ending conflict

A key question is then addressed: What do we mean by 'language'? and the relationships between conflict, language and PL are laid out. Also, the centrality of language studies and applied linguistics in understanding conflict and peace appears to have been largely overlooked, or at best, only mentioned in passing. That may be one reason why PL is still completely unknown by most language educators and by most peace educators.

The New Peace Linguistics and The Role of Language in Conflict, pages 23–35

Getting a Little Philosophical

In the title of his book about the Austrian neurologist and founder of Psychoanalysis, Sigmund Freud (1856–1939), Alfred Tauber describes Freud as a 'Reluctant Philosopher' (2010). Like Freud, when it comes to language, I too consider myself, at best, a 'reluctant philosopher', although this is not a book about the philosophy of language, or the language of philosophy. Although both of those areas of enquiry are important, philosophizing is not what (N)PL is about. Another reason for not basing this book on such philosophical approaches to understanding language is because there are already many fine writings in those areas, including Martin Heidegger's *On the Way to Language* (1971), in which he wrote "Language is the House of Being" (p. 1), the meaning of which is still being discussed decades later (Sundvall, 2018). However, perhaps because of the intimate and unbreakable connections between language and thought (except perhaps in cases of, for example, Alzheimer's patients like my mother), there are times when it is necessary to go deep(er) and to get a little philosophical. For example, because this book is based on a number of propositions or statements of belief, about language and conflict, which might look or sound like philosophical positions, it is important that those propositions be laid out clearly and concisely from the beginning.

The first of these propositions states: 1. *Language is the source of conflict,* which can be extended and expanded upon to state: *Language is the source of **all** conflict,* which might be considered an extreme position to take. However, a less extreme and less controversial statement would be: *Language is the source of **most** conflict.* The third and mildest version of the statement would be: *Language is the source of **much** conflict.* Leaving aside attempts to quantify the amount of conflict caused by language, we can also consider the definite versus the indefinite article in the first proposition: 1. *Language is **the** source of conflict,* i.e., the only source of conflict, versus *Language is **a** source of conflict,* i.e., one source of conflict, among a number of sources. There are many potential sources of conflict, from firing a bullet from a gun into another person, to launching a nuclear missile from one country at another. However, in this book, I will argue that, before that gun was fired and before that missile was launched, words were exchanged, that led to an escalation of anger, fear, hatred, etc. In that sense, language was the starting point of both of those catastrophic outcomes. A second proposition states that: 2. *There can be no conflict without language,* from which we can derive third and fourth proposition: 3. *Although there can be language without conflict, there cannot be conflict without language,* and 4. *Language is an essential prerequisite for starting and for ending conflict.*

REACT 2.1: *Which of the four propositions or statements above do you agree or disagree with? Rate your responses with one of the four options: Strongly Agree, Agree, Disagree or Strongly Disagree. How would you explain your rating?*

The language-conflict statements above may be seen as controversial, and understanding them depends on what we mean by 'language' and what we mean by 'conflict'. In this section, we will, therefore, consider what is meant by those two key terms, for the purposes of this book, starting with 'language', then going on to 'words'. It is possible to state that: *Words are the basis of language,* and that: *Language is based on words.* Both statements could be equally true, and using some of the language-logic applied above, two questions arise: *Can language exist without words?* and: *Can words exist without language?* Cases can be made for the truth or falsity of both of the word-language and language-word statements above, and for positive or negative answers to both questions. However, in the interests of limiting the philosophizing, we will not be presenting those cases or answering those questions. Instead, we will adopt the position that 'Word' and 'Language' are interdependent concepts, each needing the other, while acknowledging "the technical difficulty of defining the linguistic concept of 'word'" (Dedaić, 2003, p. 1).

What Do We Mean By 'Language'?

The use of games in language learning is well documented (see, for example, Wright, Betterridge & Buckby, 2006). Taking a page from that area of educational gaming, we could start by playing The Languages Game, in which players compare and contrast the different languages they know. But with a small change to the spelling and grammar, we can make it The Language is... Game, which is based on us articulating what we understand by that word, 'language'.

REACT 2.2: *How would you complete the following sentence (in 20 words or fewer)? Language is...*

Although the question of what language is might, at first blush, appear to be relatively straightforward, like much in the field of language and applied linguistics, it is not. In fact, before we can even get to the question of what language is, we can find ourselves sinking into the philosophical quicksand around the question of what is a word. For example, Luca Gasparri and Diego Marconi (2015) started by explaining: "The notions of word and word meaning are problematic to pin down" (p. 2) which is, in part, because of the fact that words like 'word' can have many meanings, depending on who is using the word, to communicate what to whom, as well as the contexts in which the message is being sent and received. Gasparri and Marconi went on to distinguish between linguistic definitions of 'word', "which attempt to characterize the notion of word by illustrating the explanatory role words play" (p. 2) and definitions that "attempt to elucidate the notion of word by describing the metaphysical type of words" (p. 2). From there, Gasparri and Marconi introduced their readers to the notions of lexicon, lexical entries, and lexemes, which are, "the smallest linguistic expressions that are conventionally associated with a non-compositional meaning" (p. 2). For example, the words 'ran', 'runs', and 'running', are various forms of the lexeme 'run' (usually written lexemically as 'RUN').

In Christian cultures, an appreciation of the power of words can be traced back to Biblical times, as stated in the King James Bible: "In the beginning was the Word, and the Word was with God, and the Word *was* God" (John, 1:1, emphasis added). Partly because of that Biblical reference, in the 1900s, there was a large-scale, intellectual grappling with the meaning of 'word', resulting in the work of linguists such as Sir Alan Henderson Gardiner (1879–1963), a well-known English Egyptologist of the day. In his book, *The Theory of Speech and Language* (1932), Gardiner wrote that: "Words in themselves do not mean anything" (p. 1), and he concluded that: "The sentence, not the word, is the unit of actual speech" (p. 1). Gardiner distinguished 'words' from 'language', as words are "language *meaningfully applied* to some state of things and *purposely addressed* to some listener" (Gardiner, 1932, p. 1, emphases added). Although Gardiner was thinking of spoken language, rather than written, as he refers to a listener, the importance of meaningful application and purposeful address still apply.

Going to the other end of the explanatory scale, from the most technical to the most general meaning, if we look, for example, in an online English dictionary such as the *Cambridge Advanced Learner's Dictionary* (*CALD*, 2021), we can find more easily understandable definitions of 'word'. But even there, there are a dozen basic meanings of 'word', starting with "a single unit of language that has meaning and can be spoken or written" (*CALD*, 2021). And this does not consider the meanings and uses of 'word' in popular culture, such as: "A versatile declaration… [used] to indicate that something has impressed you favorably" (*Urban Dictionary*, 2021). But for now, we can use the *CALD* single-unit-of-language definition, as we wade further into the muddy waters of language and its many meanings. Moving beyond the phrasal and sentential units of meaning, we can go from the micro-level of words to the macro-level of language. But here too we risk sinking into the quicksand. An example of the challenges of answering the seemingly straightforward question of what is language can be seen in the book title, *What Is This Thing Called Language?* (2013) by David Nunan. One way of answering that question is to look at the etymological origins of a word; to see how the meaning of a word has changed over time, as those changes are related to changes in the ways we understand the concepts signified by the word.

The origins of the word 'language' appear to date back to the late thirteenth century word 'langage', which meant: "words, what is said, conversation, talk" (Harper, 2021), from Old French, with the same focus as Gardiner's (1932), on spoken language. Before that, in the twelfth century, 'langage' meant: "speech, words, oratory; a tribe, people, nation" (Harper, 2021), from the Vulgar Latin 'linguaticum'. That reference to "a tribe, people, nation" reflects the importance of the relationships between the three major concepts of Language, Culture and Identity. Returning to the present day, the *CALD* gives the following definition of 'language': "a system of communication consisting of sounds, words, and grammar." The online *Oxford English Dictionary* (*OED*, 2021) gives a similar meaning for 'language': "The method of human communication . . . consisting of the use of words in a structured and conventional way." Reiterating the relationships between language, culture and identity, the *OED* expands its definition to include 'language' as a "system of communication used by a particular country or community." However, although 'communication' and 'language' are often used interchangeably, they are not the same thing at all, as language is the *means* used to achieve the *end*, which is communication.

Before we return to the rhetorical question asked in Nunan's 2013 book title (*What Is This Thing Called Language?*) it is important to note that the same question was also asked as a book title several decades earlier, by Robert Dixon (1965), in his book, *What is Language? A new approach to linguistic description.* Dixon presented his theoretical approach to language, and considered the philosophical perspectives on the language of Plato, Aristotle, Wittgenstein, and others. Several decades after asking his question, Dixon moved from the subject matter of language to himself as the subject, in his book, *I Am a Linguist* (2010), in which he writes: "In essence, language is the most precious of human resources. Each individual language functions as an emblem for the ethnicity of its speakers" (p. 23). Dixon's comment again highlights the importance of the relationships between notions of language, culture and identity, and presents the idea of language as a "precious resource", which implies that it should be used carefully, and perhaps sparingly, as resources can be exhausted. Fortunately, language may count as an environmentally friendly renewable resource, like solar, wind or water. Attempts to describe and define 'language' can also be found some decades before Dixon (1965). For example, in 1933, Dorothea McCarthy stated that: "Language is the medium by which higher intellectual processes are revealed" (p. 329). Although that may be true, the language used by McCarthy, in referring to the "vast gap between man and the lower animals" (1933, p. 329) reflect some of the now seemingly arrogant assumptions of the 1930s, about the inherent supremacy of the human species, because we have language; assumptions which have since been challenged (see, for example, Hogenboom, 2015).

By the early years of the new millennium, researchers had extended the question of what is language to a series of questions, as explored in the paper by Hauser, Chomsky and Fitch (2002), who ask, about language: 'What Is It, Who Has It, and How Did It Evolve?' (pp. 1569–1579). Hauser *et al.* (2002) proposed a distinction between what they refer to as "the faculty of language in the broad sense (FLB) and in the narrow sense (FLN)" (p. 1569). The former (FLB), "includes a sensory-motor system, a conceptual-intentional system, and the computational mechanisms for recursion", whereas the latter (FLN) "only includes recursion and is the only uniquely human component of the faculty of language" (p. 1569). As with many such definitions, Hauser et al.'s (2002) appears to be written by experts in the field for other experts in the field and not for outsiders, thereby illustrating how language can be used for excluding as well as for informing (Curtis, 2017c). By 'recursion', linguists mean that a structure such as a phrase or a clause can be re-used as part of a larger phrase or clause, which in theory means that an infinite number of sentences can be created from a finite number of words.

After such technically precise but generally unhelpful definitions and descriptions (in the sense of not helpful to non-experts), such as those given by Hauser *et al.* (2002), we can more fully appreciate Nunan's refreshingly non-technical description in *What Is This Thing Called Language?* (2013), in which he explains that language is, "the stuff that surrounds us" (p. 1). However, we are rarely consciously aware of language, like the oxygen we breathe (as noted above), which also surrounds us, and which is also essential for life, but which we cannot see, hear, touch, taste or smell, so we take it for granted—even though we would die without oxygen. Indeed, it is precisely because we are so immersed in the languages and cultures of our birth and/or our surroundings that we no longer notice them in the way we do when we are exposed to or immersed in languages and cultures that are new to us, such as when we travel to far-off lands for the first time.

For Nunan, "Language is ubiquitous." (2013, p. 6), and "context is often critical to comprehension" (p. 7), and it may even be the case that complete comprehension is impossible without some understanding of the context. Nunan also stated that: "ultimately language is about meaning, and the creation of meaning" (p. 7), and he concluded that, in spite of the fact that we spend so much of our lives listening, speaking, reading, and writing, "most of us remain largely ignorant [at the conscious level] of this phenomenon that defines us as humans" (p. 200). Whether or not language is unique to humans depends on how language is defined, but the ways in which we humans use language—especially when we use it as some kind of weapon—may indeed be unique to our species.

Although the notion of 'words as weapons' is not new, there has been growing interest in the deliberate 'weaponizing' of words. For example, in 2012, Justin Strawhand, writing for the *Huffington Post*, published a piece, 'A History of Weaponized Language', in which he concluded with a challenge to the field of linguistics and a question: "Modern linguistics has done much to deny the notion that words possess any intrinsic meaning, yet the question remains: what of words especially designed to kill, to maim, to segregate, and to destroy?" In 2017, writing for *The New York Times*, John Herrman asked: "If Everything Can Be 'Weaponized,' What Should We Fear?" and he stated that: "The fabric of civilian life is now wrapped in a linguistic fog of war." In 2019, an article, 'The Weaponization of Words', by poet, author and writer for *The London Times*, Joe Nutt, was published. According to Nutt: "It wouldn't be difficult to compile a list of words that have been weaponized . . . I suspect one of the first was racist—a word so effectively nailed down in the US that it has become an unanswerable charge" (Curtis 2018c).

Wayne State University, in Detroit, Michigan, even has its own 'Word Warriors', who according to their website, want: "to help rejuvenate the language we love [English] by advocating for words of style and substance that see far too little use" (wordwarriors.wayne.edu). Although the goals of the students at Wayne State University may be entirely peaceful, putting 'word' and 'war' together does bring to mind the phrase 'a war of words', defined as: "A prolonged, often acrimonious, debate" (*OED*, 2021). As we will see in Part II of this book, there are many ways in which language can be used which constitute words of war, words at war, and words as war.

This discussion of language brings us inevitably to an even bigger question: Where did human language come from? In *The Seeds of Speech: Language Origin and Evolution* (1996) Jean Aitchison asked: "So how did it all begin, this powerful, weird communication system of ours?" (p. 4). In answer to her own question, Aitchison admitted: "Frustratingly, we do not know. The origin of language is crisscrossed with controversy and befogged in mystery" (p. 4). And in relation to the on-going unknowns about language learning and teaching, Nunan admitted that: "Despite the hundreds of researchers who have devoted their professional lives to investigating language acquisition and use, we still know relatively little" (2013, p. 6) about how we learn language(s) (Curtis, 2017d). That may be seen, on the one hand, as a disheartening comment on the results of all that research, or on the other, as a recognition of the tremendous complexity of this thing called 'language'.

Before wrapping up this section, we need to acknowledge an area of applied linguistics and language education known as Language Awareness, as this kind of awareness can be an important aspect of Peace Linguistics. One of the first books about Language Awareness was published in 1974, *Language Awareness*, edited by Eschholz, Rosa, and Clark. That book was an important contribution to the field for a number of reasons, including the fact that the book contains an essay by Malcolm X (born Malcolm Little), 'Coming to an Awareness of Language' (pp. 1–8), in which he describes his journey from illiteracy to literacy, and the positive impact that had on his short but influential life (he was assassinated in 1965, at the age of 39). In the inaugural issue of the journal *Language Awareness*, published in 1992, the editors asked the question: 'Language awareness: Wat is dat?' (Editors, 1992, pp. 1–3). And regarding the challenges of defining 'language', the editors expressed their position that: "Language is a murky notion" (p.2). The editors also explained that Language Awareness has to do with "becoming conscious of one's own and others' use" of language, and "with developing a sensitive relationship" with language (p. 2), which is one of the goals of NPL. For example, Mahalingappa, Rodriguez, and Polat (2021) present ideas on how to promote peace through social justice using critical language awareness.

Conflict, Language and Peace Linguistics

REACT 2.3: *To continue the language game we started playing at the beginning of this chapter, how would you complete the following sentence (in 20 words or fewer)? Conflict happens when...*

The intra-personal and inter-personal aspects of conflict can be seen in the development of the word 'conflict' and its meanings, starting in the early fifteenth century, when the word meant "armed encounter or battle," from the Old French, and before that from the Latin *conflictus*, meaning "a striking together" (Harper, 2021). One of the fifteenth century meanings of 'conflict' was "internal mental or spiritual struggle," and by the 1850s the meaning had become "incompatible urges in one person." Both of those last two meanings focus on the intra-personal nature of conflict, but by the 1870s, 'conflict' was being used to mean a sense of "discord of action, feeling, or effect, clashing of opposed principles, etc." Today, the meanings of 'conflict' include, "an active disagreement between people with opposing opinions or principles" (*CALD*, 2021) and perhaps reflecting the political climate of recent years, one of the examples of how 'conflict' is used is: "His outspoken views would frequently bring him into conflict with the president" (*CALD*, 2021). The contrasting relationship between 'conflict' and 'peace' can be seen in the second *CALD* definition of 'conflict': "fighting between two or more groups of people or countries", together with the following example: "They had worked for peace during the long era of conflict", alluding to the presence of peace being conditional on the absence of (armed) conflict.

In 1957, a new journal was launched; originally titled simply *Conflict Resolution*, the name was eventually extended to the *Journal of Conflict Resolution.* In the inaugural issue, the editors emphasized the "fruitfulness of an interdisciplinary approach" to studies of conflict, and the individual, institutional and international nature of conflict (see also Curtis, 2018d) between "members of a family, between labor and management, between political parties, and even within a single mind, as well as among nations" (Editors, 1957, p. 2). The journal editors' comments made it clear that conflict can happen anywhere, at any time, to anyone, and for those of us who have spent most of our professional lives involved in the teaching and learning of languages and cultures, it is hard to imagine that conflict could be conceptualized, articulated or discussed without a central focus on language.

As we saw at the beginning of this chapter, one of the fundamental premises of this book is that, at the very least, language is central to conflict, and at most, there can be no conflict without language. This lack of focus on language in conflict is not just an accidental oversight (as has been suggested to me by some of my colleagues in the Peace Studies world), or the conclusion of a language-obsessed applied linguist (which I am), whose world revolves around language (as mine does). For example, one of the first researchers to explicitly address this apparent disconnect between language and conflict was Sue Wright, in her slim (65-page) but important edited volume, *Language and Conflict: A Neglected Relationship* (1998), comprised of three short essays (one by Wright, one by Dan Smith, and one by Paul Chilton).

It is tempting to conclude that, in the decades since Wright's titular observation, awareness of that language-conflict relationship has been less neglected. But before we look at whether or not that is the case, it is worth first considering some of the points made by Chilton and her co-authors who argued, more than 20 years ago, that: "the political influence, significance and effect of linguistic borders, and the discourse manipulation of language are factors in conflict which should not be ignored" (back cover). There may be multiple meanings of "the discourse manipulation of language", one of which could refer to the manipulation *of* the language itself, but there is also manipulation *by* language, i.e., using language to manipulate people. Chilton, in his essay, 'The Role of Language in Human Conflict' (1998, pp. 2–13), stated that: "Of all the social variables that can be said to be involved in the causation and maintenance of war, *language is the most diffuse and the most difficult to define*" (p. 2, emphasis added).

Chilton's comment relates to the discussion above, of the challenges of clearly and concisely answering the question: What is Language? About the reasons for that particular challenge, Chilton explained that: "because language is profoundly implicated in all human social activity... [it therefore]... cannot be easily isolated as *a specific causal factor* in violent conflicts" (p. 2, emphasis added). Chilton also concluded that the all-pervasive nature of language was the main "reason that social scientists, including peace researchers, have been hesitant in investigating the contribution of language to the outbreak of armed conflicts" (p. 2), which highlights the need for the field of Peace Linguistics to grow and develop into its next iteration, the New Peace Linguistics.

The hope of NPL practitioners is that this long-neglected language-conflict relationship was eventually noticed and recovered, or least rehabilitated. However, that may not be the case, for example, the *Little Book of Conflict Transformation: Clear Articulation of The Guiding Principles by A Pioneer in The Field,* by John Lederach (2003). At around 80 pages in total, it is indeed a little book (and part of a series titled *The Little Books of Justice and Peacebuilding*). And Dr. Lederach (born 1955) is indeed famous, as a Professor of International Peacebuilding at the Joan B. Kroc Institute for International Peace Studies, at the University of Notre Dame, in the USA, with a track-record of conflict mediation going back 30 years. It is, then, disappointing to see that books like Lederach's appear to fall into a category that might be referred to as 'LiP', which stands for 'Language in Passing', or 'LisP', which stands for 'Linguistics in Passing', for example: "be attentive to language, metaphors, and expressions that signal the distresses of identity" (Lederach, 2003, p. 28). While encouraging such language awareness is good advice, such limited, even superficial, references to language are what I mean by 'LiP and 'LisP', and which could also be referred to as 'Linguistics Lite', in which 'lite' describes a low-calorie, less substantive version of whatever is being referred to.

'Language in Passing' and 'Linguistics in Passing' (LiP and LisP, respectively) also relate to the notion of paying lip service to something, in the sense of indirectly acknowledging the existence of language and/or linguistics, but doing so in ways that do not reflect the importance of either language or linguistics in studies of conflict or peace. For example, in the *International Journal of Peace Studies*, Funk and Said's (2004) paper is titled, 'Islam and the West: Narratives of Conflict and Conflict Transformation'. In spite of the centrality of language in the role of narratives of all kinds, in their very lengthy (13,000-word) paper, language is only explicitly referred to just three times. And even then, language is only mentioned in passing: "English courses at the local American Language Center" (p. 12); "Islam provides a language that addresses politics as well as social relations and worship" (p. 12); and "the second story provides a hint of what might be gained from moving beyond facile, stereotypical language and judgments" (p. 22). Presenting such a detailed discussion of narrative, with so few and such superficial references to language, when narratives cannot exist without language, appears to overlook the importance of the linguistic aspects of narrative. There are many examples of papers in Peace Studies which are based on explorations of narratives (see for example, Israeli, 2011; Karaman-Kepenekci, 2010; Tanaka, 2005), but with few explicit references to language, and even fewer to linguistics, applied or otherwise. To NPL practitioners, the message being communicated by such 'LiP', 'LisP' and 'Linguistics Lite' papers in leading peace studies journals appears to sound something along the lines of: Yes, of course language, and the study of language and meaning, is important—so important, in fact, that we are going to take it for granted, and only refer to it in passing. 'Huh?' say the NPL practitioners.

In contrast to the LiP/LisP/Lite papers, Naomi Head's paper, Transforming Conflict: Trust, Empathy, and Dialogue (2012), acknowledged that, "the critiques of positivism paved the way for the 'linguistic turn' in IR" (p. 37) (International Relations), and that the "focus on language [that] emerged from a philosophical preoccupation with Western metaphysics" (p. 37), as well as "the constitutive role of language, desires and beliefs" (p. 37). Head also stated that: "the language and rhetoric of deception runs through much of American political commentary" (p. 46). As we will see later in this book, in the chapters that analyze the texts of the 45th President of the USA, that deception is not only still very much present in politics today, but may have reached its height in recent years (Curtis 2018j). However, in Head's paper, what is conspicuous by its absence is any examples of actual language used, in this case, in the American political commentary on which her paper is based.

A study of peace education and peace studies journals showed how these phenomena of 'LiP', 'LisP' and 'Linguistics Lite' can be seen in the research, writing and publications in the fields of Peace Education and Peace Studies (Curtis, 2017a). For example, the first issue of the *Journal of Peace Education* appeared in 2004, and between then and 2017, approximately 30 issues of the *JPE* were published, with an average of around six main papers per issue, totaling nearly 200 published papers on Peace Education published in the *JPE* during that 14-year period. Of those approximately 200 papers, only around half-a-dozen were focused on language—and none appeared to explicitly refer to linguistics, applied or otherwise. Given the importance of language in waging war and making peace, that was an unexpected and unsettling finding. To test that finding further, another 200 or so papers were reviewed in another long-established and well-respected journal in the field, *The International Journal of Peace Studies*, published since 1996 (Curtis, 2017b). This time, of the 200 papers in 42 volumes of the *IJPS* published over 22 years (between 1996 and 2017), only three were found that focused explicitly on language, all of which appeared in the same volume and issue, in a section on *Peace and Language*: 'Racism: A threat to global peace' (van der Valk, 2003); 'The Language Question in Africa in the Light of Globalisation, Social Justice and Democracy' (Brock-Utne, 2003); and 'Language and Ethnic Politics in Taiwan' (Shih, 2003). Although such papers do help to highlight the importance of language studies in peace studies, they are few-and-far between, and finding a grand total of fewer than 10 language-focused papers in approximately 400 publications on peace was one of the reasons that compelled me to found the field of NPL.

Suggestions for Further Reading

Palgrave Studies in Languages at War is a 15-volume series, published between 2012 and 2020, mostly focused on translation and interpretation of languages in different countries during the First and Second World Wars. However, some of the books in the series are somewhat more general, including *Languages at War: Policies and Practices of Language Contacts in Conflict* (2012) edited by Hilary Footitt and Michael Kelly.

The Palgrave Handbook of Languages and Conflict (2019) edited by Michael Kelly, Hilary Footitt and Miriam Salama-Carr is a 500-page, 23-chapter volume. About the wars in Iraq and Afghanistan, the editors note that: "Languages suddenly became visible in war in ways in which they had seldom been before" (p. 4).

Language and Conflict: Selected Issues (2015, Palgrave Macmillan) by Karol Janicki addresses questions about the role of language and communication in conflict, why people engage in arguments, and how our awareness of the social rules of language may help to prevent conflict.

Language: The Cultural Tool by Daniel Everett (Vintage Books, 2012) has chapters on language as a social tool, on how to build a language, and on the relationships between language, culture, and thinking.

http://www.languageinconflict.org/ According to its website: "The Language in Conflict project is looking at the potential contribution of linguistics to conflict studies by examining the use of language in conflict situations and resolution at all levels."

3

Peace Linguistics

What It Is, What It Isn't, and Why It Matters

This chapter begins with a definition of 'Peace Linguistics' and addresses the question: When we describe something as being 'scientific' whose science are we talking about? After responding to that question, a grounded definition of PL is built up, starting with the most basic building block—how language is used to define 'peace'—then deconstructing and reconstructing those meanings to create something new. A brief clarification of what PL is not is also included. 'Warist Discourse' is then discussed, as a concept that has only appeared briefly in the literature, but which is an important aspect of NPL. Two sets of connected relationships are then explored; those between rhetoric, politics and poetry, and those between politics, poetry and the New Peace Linguistics.

Defining Peace Linguistics and Asking 'Whose Science?'

One of the more recent published definitions of Peace Linguistics (Curtis, 2018a) states that PL is:

The New Peace Linguistics and The Role of Language in Conflict, pages 37–60

> an area of Applied Linguistics, based on systematic analyses of the ways in which language is used to communicate and create conflict, and to communicate and create peace. Peace Linguistics is interdisciplinary, drawing on fields such as Peace Studies and Conflict Transformation, bringing those together with fields such as Sociolinguistics and Critical Discourse Analysis. (p. 12)

However, as with any dictionary-type definition, some important details may be obscured by the need for brevity. In this case, both words, 'peace' and 'linguistics', can bring myriad other words, sounds and images to mind. Linguistics, as an academic discipline, has been relatively well-defined, albeit largely defined by linguists for linguists. 'Peace', on the other hand, is understood by everyone, but it can mean very different things to many different people. It is, then, important not to assume a common understanding of PL as being a combination of agreed upon notions of linguistics and of peace. Therefore, to see how I arrived at that definition of PL, we need to engage in some of the philosophical deeper level linguistics we drew on in Chapter 2. However, as I noted in Chapter 2, I will not be taking a classical, philosophical approach to language analysis, firstly, because some philosophers can become so philosophical that they can even argue themselves out of existence, and 'prove' that philosophy does not exist (Pardi, 2012)! Not surprisingly, that claim has been vigorously challenged by other philosophers, who are understandably insistent that they do in fact exist (Pigliucci, 2014).

Secondly, this book is meant to be practical, about what can be *applied* and what can be *done*, rather than what can only be thought about and theorized. As part of that practical focus, the idea and the language of 'doing peace', as an active verb, has been used by some researchers (see, for example, Joyce & Lynch, 2016), and the idea of 'doing linguistics' has been around for some time now (see, for example, Groom and Littlemore's *Doing Applied Linguistics*, 2011). Widdowson (2000) looked at the obverse of applied linguistics, i.e., linguistics applied. Taking that same approach, we could define peace linguistics as the linguistics of peace. But what would that mean? What would that look like? Before getting to those questions, we need to first briefly consider the meaning of 'linguistics', and to distinguish it from 'linguistic'—in which the 's' makes all the difference. The 's-less' adjective can be used to refer broadly and generally to anything "connected with language" (*CALD*, 2021) whereas the noun 'linguistics' refers to "the scientific study of the structure and development of language" (*CALD*, 2021). So far, so good, but there are problems with 'scientific', which has become an integral part of the definition of 'linguistics'. For example, the tagline for the Linguistic Society of America is: "Advancing the scientific study of language" (www.linguisticsociety.org), and on the homepage of its website, the Society explains that: "Linguistics, in a nutshell, is the scientific study of language."

This 'scientification' of linguistics can be traced back more than 50 years to John Lyons' seminal work, *Introduction to Theoretical Linguistics.* Published in 1968, and reprinted a dozen times between then and 1995 (reflecting the long-term influence of that book), the first line of the first page states: "Linguistics may be defined as the scientific study of language" (Lyons, 1968, p. 1). Lyons clarified that, by "the scientific study of language," he meant "investigation by means of empirically verifiable observations and with reference to some general theory of language structure" (p. 1). However, linguists need to be aware of the dangers of 'scientism', described by Tom Sorell as: "the belief that science, especially natural science, is much the most valuable part of human learning... because it is much the most authoritative, or serious, or beneficial" (2013, p. 1). The title of Sorell's book refers to a philosophical "infatuation with science," which he believes is partly because science has been "enormously successful at prediction, explanation and control" (p. 25) and also because "the methods of science confer objectivity on scientific results" (p. 25).

Science and scientific discoveries have been the basis of much of human development for centuries. For example, the current concerns about the destructive and unsustainable global effects of climate change are largely supported by scientific facts and figures, whereas climate change denial rejects the science (Collomb, 2014). However, when we refer to linguistics as "the scientific study of language," it is incumbent upon us ask: Whose Science? In 1986, Nancy Stepan reported on the roles of race and gender in science, and in 1991, Sandra Harding asked *Whose Science? Whose Knowledge?* (1991) in relation to the lives and works of women scientists. Cheryl Fields called the history of Black scientists "a history of exclusion" (1998), and regarding race, Kulis, Chong, and Shaw (1999) reported on "discriminatory organizational contexts and black scientists" (pp. 115–148) in postsecondary settings. According to Londa Schiebinger, who contemplated the question "Has Feminism Changed Science?" (2000, pp. 117–1175), that, White, Western, male-dominated notion of science is had not substantially improved as we entered the new millennium. And from an NPL perspective, Schiebinger reminds us of the popularity of the phrase and the idea of "the science wars," which she referred to as the unfortunate name given to "tussles between scientists and their critics" (p. 1171). Another study of biases of race and gender in science is the 130-page report published by the American Association of University Women (Hill, Corbett & St. Rose, 2010), *Why So Few? Women in Science, Technology, Engineering, and Mathematics.*

More recently, Margot Shetterly, an African-American non-fiction writer, published *Hidden Figures: The story of the African-American women who helped win the space race* (2016), which was adapted as a feature film in the same year. What all of those books and articles illustrate is that when we refer to linguistics as 'the scientific study of language', we are usually referring to—consciously or not, deliberately or not—White, Western, Male, Science. Therefore, rather than adopting the usual definitions and descriptions of Linguistics as the *scientific* study of language, in this book, I will refer to Linguistics as the *systematic* study of language. At the word-level such a distinction may not appear to be all that significant, but at the conceptual level, it may indicate a marked difference, between the scientific and the systemic study of language.

A brief historical note here may explain where this insistence on the 'scientific-ness' of Linguistics comes from, namely, one of the most famous US-based (Prussian-born) linguists of the time, Edward Sapir (1884–1939), who is credited with being one of early founders of modern linguistics. In his 1929 article, The Status of Linguistics as a Science, Sapir claimed that: "In the course of their detailed researches Indo-European linguists have gradually developed a technique which is probably *more nearly perfect* than that of any other science dealing with man's institutions" (p. 207, emphasis added). Even considering the use of hedging terms like 'probably' and 'nearly', we are still left with an extraordinary claim: Sapir's statement is tantamount to saying that, not only is linguistics scientific, but it may even be more scientific than science itself!

Returning to the meaning of PL, the general definition of 'peace' is: "freedom from war and violence, especially when people live and work together happily without disagreements" (*CALD*, 2021). In that case, the linguistics of peace would be: the systematic study of the language related to being free from war and violence; the language that enables people to live and work together happily without disagreements. Peace is also defined as: "the state of not being interrupted or annoyed by worry, problems, noise, or unwanted actions" (*CALD*, 2021). Using that definition, the linguistics of peace would be: the systematic study of the language related to not being interrupted or annoyed by worry, problems, noise or unwanted actions. A third, general, dictionary definition of 'peace' is: "(a period of) freedom from war or violence, [especially] when people live and work together without violent disagreements" (*CALD*, 2021).

At this point, we may find ourselves going in tautological, definitional circles—and that is without considering other peace-related terms such as 'peace dividend', 'peace movement', 'peace of mind', 'peace offering', etc. These days, many of us seem to be thinking, talking or writing about peace, and most of us seem to have some notion of what that word means.

However, each of our own understandings of peace may be profoundly *personal,* anywhere along the continuum from peace within ourselves, i.e., intra-personal peace, to peace between each other, i.e., inter-personal peace, to something more global, such as world peace (Curtis, 2018k). And each one of us may be at different points along that continuum, at different times in our lives. Therefore, we need to take a step back here, and see where we are, in our development of a general definition of Peace Linguistics, as an area within Applied Linguistics.

Creating a Grounded Definition of Peace Linguistics

Taking the three *CALD* definitions above, and adopting a Widdowsonian obverse approach, we could state that:

> Peace Linguistics (PL) is the systematic study of the language related to:
>
> i. being free from war and violence; the language that enables people to live and work together happily without disagreements
> ii. the state of not being interrupted or annoyed by worry, problems, noise, or unwanted actions
> iii. a period of freedom from war or violence, especially when people live and work together without violent disagreements

REACT 3.1: *What do you like or not like about each of the three definitions above and why? How could those definitions be improved upon?*

If we look at each of the three possibilities above in more detail, that can help us understand more deeply what it is that we are doing here:

> Definition 1 (D1). Peace Linguistics is the systematic study of the language related to being free from war and violence; the language that enables people to live and work together happily, without disagreements.

The first thing to notice is that there are multiple levels of embedded meaning, and deconstructing D1 we can see:

> D1. Peace Linguistics is the systematic study of
>
> i. the language related to being free from *war*
> ii. the language related to being free from *violence*
> iii. the language that enables people to *live* together happily without disagreements
> iv. the language that enables people to *work* together happily without disagreements

There is, of course, a lot of overlap among those four statements, but there are also some important differences, for example, 'war' is not the same as 'violence', even though the former entails the latter, i.e., *all war is violent, but not all violence is war*, which relates to the definitional difference between being free from war *and* violence, and being free from war *or* violence. Also, *living* together happily can have little or nothing to do with *working* together happily, as most of us do not live with the people we work with (and vice versa).

The second definition of PL above (D2) proposes that: Peace Linguistics is the systematic study of the language related to the state of not being interrupted or annoyed by worry, problems, noise, or unwanted actions. That is an interesting definition, as there is no indication of what is causing the interruptions or the noise, or who is carrying out the unwanted actions. The mention of 'worry' and 'problems' seems to indicate that this definition would be more at the intra-personal end of the peace continuum, i.e., peace within oneself, which is believed by many to be the foundation of world peace. For example, the World Peace Council states that: "*Only* peace within oneself is that necessary basis towards peace and justice in interpersonal relationships as well as in community, national, and global arena" (Gyatso, 2018, emphasis added). (Tenzin Gyatso has been the 14th Dalai Lama since 1940). However, if the intended meaning of that statement is that *the only way* to achieve world peace is through intra-personal peace, then that is a very different position from claiming that intra-personal peace is an essential starting point or the basis for world peace. Intra-personal peace may well be such a starting point, and while we all have a responsibility to do whatever we can to make the world a more peaceful place, only a tiny fraction of us have the power to bring about peace on an international and on a global scale.

The third possible PL definition above (D3) proposes that: Peace Linguistics is the systematic study of the language related to a period of freedom from war or violence, especially when people live and work together without violent disagreements. We can take the last part of D3 first, as that overlaps with D1, i.e., the language that enables people to live and work together *happily without disagreements*, and the language that helps people live and work together *without violent disagreements*. However, that does raise the question of what constitutes 'non-violent disagreements', which in turn rests on how 'violence' is defined, as discussed in the work of Johan Galtung (see below) and other peace researchers. The first part of D3 is perhaps problematic, as it is not clear what could be meant by 'the language related to a period of freedom from war or violence', which would be clearer if it were to be re-stated as, 'the language that *helps bring about* a period of freedom from war or violence'. Some readers may have spotted what might seem like a linguistic sleight-of-hand here, i.e., the use of 'related to'. In the definitions above, 'related to' might be a good example of a phrase repeated to the point where it becomes 'linguistically invisible', and disappears from view—or, more correctly, which is still there, but which stops being noticed.

With that in mind, we can re-examine the deconstructed and expanded-upon D1:

D1. Peace Linguistics is the systematic study of

i. the language related to being free from *war*
ii. the language related to being free from *violence*
iii. the language that enables people to *live* together happily without disagreements
iv. the language that enables people to *work* together happily without disagreements

If we replace the more neutral 'the language related to' with something more causal and more active, we get:

D1. Peace Linguistics is the systematic study of

i. language that can *help bring about* freedom from war
ii. language that can *help bring about* freedom from violence
iii. language that can *enable* people to live together happily without disagreements
iv. language that can *enable* people to work together happily without disagreements

The reason for dropping 'the' from 'the language that ... ' is the singularity and plurality implied by the definite and indefinite articles in English. Because of how those articles are used in English, 'the' is often processed as meaning 'the one', as in, for example, 'we're looking for *the* right answer', strongly implying that there is *one* right answer. However, 'we're looking for *a* solution to the problem', indicates that there is more than one possible solution (even though they may not all be equally possible or effective). Therefore, by dropping 'the', the definition is opened up.

What happens if we make the same causal/active language change with the other two PL definitions above? Removing 'related to the state of', would create a direct connection and would make the D2 definition: Peace Linguistics is the systematic study of the language of not being interrupted or annoyed by worry, problems, noise, or unwanted actions. But what would the language of not being interrupted look or sound like? Silence? It is possible that the more noisy our worlds become, the more enamored of silence we become. From the American singers Paul Simon and Art Garfunkel's 1964 folksong, The Sound of Silence, to the cover version of that same song by the American heavy metal band, Disturbed, released more than a half-century later, in 2015. From John Cage's (1939) lectures and writings on silence, to Erling Kagge's musing on silence 'in the age of noise' (2017), nearly 80 years later (see also Adam Jaworski's book on the social and pragmatic *Power of Silence*, 1993), we seem to need some silence as part of our peace, both intra- and inter-personal.

A focus on silence would, then, make D2: Peace Linguistics is the systematic study of *the language of silence.* If there are no words, then it is possible that no thoughts or feelings would be expressed. And if there are no thoughts or feelings being expressed, then perhaps interruptions and annoyances, worries and problems would eventually simply fade away... gone in a puff of soundless enlightenment. However, even then, we would still have to deal with the non-language noises all around us. But lest we get too-TM (Transcendental Meditation) about all this, Mark Watney can bring us back down to Earth. Watney is the name of the character played by the American actor, Matt Damon, in the 2015 movie, *The Martian,* which is about an astronaut marooned, alone on the planet Mars, light years from Earth. One of the most quoted lines from *The Martian* movie, as Watney thinks aloud, has become: "So, in the face of overwhelming odds, I'm left with only one option: I'm going to have to science the sh*t out of this" (Zimmer, 2015). Therefore, before we philosophize the sh*t out of PL, let me suggest that the systematic study of the language of silence may be of limited help in making our world more peaceful and less war-torn. However, long periods of silence, sitting quietly, alone, with our own thoughts (which some people consider 'meditation') can help us be more at peace with ourselves. That silent sitting may, in turn, help to make the idea of world peace less of a theory and more of a practice.

REACT 3.2: *How would you define 'world peace', and do you believe such a peace is possible? Why or why not?*

Ironically, one of the areas that may not have helped notions of peace to evolve far enough beyond the individual for there to be world peace is the self-help industry, which was estimated to be worth 11 *billion* US dollars in the USA alone, in 2017 (Gaille, 2017). And as result of the COVID-19 pandemic, that figure may well have grown (Robertson, 2020). There are many self-help books that may have helped many people, such as *Take Your*

Time: How to Find Patience, Peace, and Meaning (1994), written by Eknath Easwaran (1910–1999). Books such as *Negotiating the Inner Peace Treaty: Becoming the Person You Were Born to Be* (2012) by Chelsea Wakefield may also have helped people find that illusive intra-personal, inner peace that so many of us seek, but which so often eludes us. However, the assumption in some circles seems to be that intra-personal peace is enough, *on its own*, to bring about world peace (for example, the World Peace Council statement above). That assumption would be OK, were it not for the fact that having more than seven billion people all be at peace with themselves all the time, or all at the same time—even for one brief, glorious moment—is so problematically unlikely as to be a non-starter. However, that impossibility absolutely does *not* mean that we should give up on world peace being possible—but it does mean that intra-personal peace is *not enough* to bring about world peace. That, in turn, means that we cannot stop at individual, intra-personal peace, in the way that the self-help industry sometimes seems to imply is enough (see, for example, Weyers, 2017).

(D3) proposes that: Peace Linguistics is the systematic study of language related to a period of freedom from war or violence, especially when people live and work together without violent disagreements. Making the same shift from more neutral to more causal/active language, as we did with D1 and D2, would give us something along the lines of: Peace Linguistics is the systematic study of language that can help bring about periods of freedom from war or violence, and enable people to live and work together without violent disagreements. However, for any definition of PL to be more comprehensive, it would also need to include the *opposite* of PL, i.e., the systematic study of language that can help bring about war and/or violence, filling people's lives and work with (violent) disagreements (derived from D1 and D3).

One reason we need to include the *opposite* of PL is that all entities and energies co-exist with their opposites, such as Life-and-Death, Yin-and-Yang, Alpha-and-Omega, etc. When that co-existence is balanced, then peaceful existence becomes more likely. Likewise, when they are unbalanced, conflict becomes more likely. Combining D1 and D3, and including the opposite of 'peace' in PL, we can finally arrive at:

> The New Peace Linguistics is the systematic study of language that can help bring about periods of freedom from war and other kinds of violence, and of language that enables people to live and work together peacefully without violent disagreements. Peace Linguistics is also the systematic study of language that can bring about war and other kinds of violence, and of language that prevents people from living and working together peacefully.

REACT 3.3: *What do you like or not like about these three revised definitions? Please write your own definition of Peace Linguistics, combining elements of D1, D2 and D3. Or you can write a definition of PL that is all your own, and compare it with someone else's.*

Warist Discourse

One kind of discourse that is particularly relevant to NPL is 'warist discourse', as such discourse appears to be more prominent and more powerful now than language being used to communicate and create peace. Like NPL itself, warist discourse is new in the sense of having appeared briefly, some time ago, but then appears to have been largely forgotten about. To begin with, the word 'warist' does not exist in English, which is equally true for 'peace-ist', but the word 'pacifist' does exist, to describe someone who believes that "war is wrong, and, therefore, that to fight in a war is wrong" (*CALD*, 2021). However, the opposite of a 'pacifist' would be someone who believes that war is right, and, therefore, that to fight in a war is the right thing to do. *There is no word in English for such a person.* A warrior is a soldier, who may be fighting because that is what their commanding officers have ordered them to do: Those others, over there, they are the enemy. Maim, kill, capture. Off you go. The soldiers themselves may believe that war is wrong, but they are, in their minds, doing their duty. The closest word in English, to describe the opposite of a pacifist might be 'warmonger', although that is defined as: "a politician or other leader who is often encouraging a country to go to war," or perhaps a 'militarist', but that is someone who "wants more powerful armed forces in their country" (*CALD*, 2021) making them, at best, only partial opposites of 'pacifist'.

Although the word 'warism' is not in any of today's dictionaries of English, 'warism' was used by Duane Cady (see Chapter 1) in the title of his 1989 book, *From Warism to Pacifism: A Moral Continuum* (with a new edition published in 2010). Cady noted that, in spite of the "remarkable changes" (2010, p. ix) that took place in the 21 years between the first and second editions of his book, such as the collapse of the Soviet Union, the end of the Cold War, and the release of Nelson Mandela after 27 years in prison: "the new world order . . . turned out to be much like the old war order." By that, Cady meant, "overt and covert violence remain the predominant means of international conflict resolution" (p. ix). Unfortunately, in the years following Cady's observation, the violence has continued, and in some cases/places escalated. Cady (2010) defines 'warism' as "the frequent presumption of the moral justifiability of war" (p. xvii), which he contrasts with Just War Theory, which he describes as "a more critically adopted set of views on the moral issues related to war" (p. xvii). According to the BBC's *Ethics Guide* (2014): "The Just War theory specifies conditions for judging if it is just to go to war, and conditions for how the war should be fought . . . it was extensively developed by Christian theologians." However, the BBC Guide also warns that: "A war is only a Just War if it is both justified, and carried out in the right way. Some wars fought for noble causes have been rendered unjust because of the way in which they were fought." Therefore, the supposed justness of the war depends not only on the reasons for the war, but also on how the war takes place.

One of the only papers that extensively discussed the concept of warist discourse appears to be the decades-old entry by University of North Carolina professor, William Gay, titled 'The Language of War and Peace', in the *Encyclopedia of Violence, Peace, and Conflict* (1999), which built on his earlier paper, 'Nonsexist Public Discourse and Negative Peace' (Gay, 1997) (see also Gay, 1998). In that paper, Gay wrote: "Words about and attitudes toward gender and war are embedded in language" (1997, p. 45) and: "Linguistic violence is a type of covert violence" (p. 46). Gay (1997) also wrote that: "The language of tolerance and peaceful relations can be negative or positive [because] . . . Merely formally sanctioned nonsexist public discourse and peace as the mere absence of war are negative and superficial forms of transformation" (p. 48). Gay (1999) began his encyclopedia entry by pointing out that language "plays an important role in relation to war and peace" not least because "If knowledge is power, language too is power" (p. 303), and because those in power "exercise an enormous influence on how we perceive . . . and what behaviors we accept" (p. 303). Gay described warist discourse as: "the resulting language which takes for granted that wars are inevitable, justifiable, and winnable" (p. 304). That description relates to: "One of the most elaborate justifications for war [which] arose during the medieval period and continues to this day, namely, the theory of just war" (p. 304), as discussed above.

According to Gay (1999): "warist discourse represents one of the most globally intractable practices of linguistic violence," and "in its multifarious and nefarious manifestations" such discourse results in the large-scale killing of people "by organized groups, such as the state, subnational political organizations, and religious, racial, and ethnic groups" (p. 305). Gay gave many examples of warist discourse, including "nuclear discourse, totalitarian language, and genocidal language" (p. 306). Examples from 'nuclear discourse' include 'collateral damage', which refers to "the thousands or even millions of civilians who would be the victims of nuclear strikes against military targets" (p. 306). Gay also highlighted the Nazi's use of 'special treatment' instead of 'execution', and the use of the phrase 'ethnic cleansing' in Bosnia in the 1990s to refer to "genocidal practices" (p. 306).

The term 'ethnic cleansing' has been used extensively again in more recent years to describe actions being taken by the government and the military of Myanmar against hundreds of thousands of Rohingya Muslims in Myanmar (Albert & Maizland, 2020). According to Gregory Stanton (2017), 'ethnic cleansing' is "a term invented by Slobodan Milosevic" (1941–2006), who served as the President of Serbia from 1989 to 1997 and as President of the Federal Republic of Yugoslavia from 1997 to 2000. Stanton goes on to explain that 'ethnic cleansing' is "a euphemism for forced displacement and genocide" which is "an insidious term because there is no international treaty law against it, whereas there are international laws against forced displacement and genocide." Two troubling examples of the power of language in law and in war are the fact that 'ethnic cleansing' has no legal meaning in international law, and therefore such genocide is not a criminal act under the Rome Statute of the International Criminal Court. That statute came into force in 2002, but it appears to be desperately in need of updating, so that 'ethnic cleansing' is no longer condoned as not being illegal. Gay (1999) described the language of war as "an example of linguistic violence that functions to mask the reality of the violence that is occurring... Such linguistic manipulation is episodic in many areas of social life, but it is constitutive of warist discourse" (p. 307). However, Gay also accepted that: "Some of linguistic manipulation in warist discourse is unintentional and involves self deception on the part of the governmental and military officials" (p. 307), although lack of intention and self-deception do not lessen the damage done by such discourse.

One of the goals of NPL is to bring the very few research papers on warist discourse, from the late 1990s, out of the shadows and into the light, as an important aspect of NPL, in a similar way that PL has been brought to light, after decades in relative obscurity. The second NPL goal related to warist discourse, which emerged as a result of the NPL analyses presented in this book, is that there are different kinds of warist discourse, the most obvious and the most damaging kind of which is discourse that makes armed conflict outcomes more likely than peaceful resolution. For example, when a president says to their followers, "If you don't fight like hell you're not going to have a country anymore," after which people are killed (see Chapter 8), then that would be 'negative warist discourse'. However, it is also possible to refer to wars that have happened in the past as a statement of fact. For example, when a president refers to soldiers who "fought and died in places like Concord and Gettysburg, Normandy and Khe Sanh" (see Chapter 6), which could be called 'neutral warist discourse.' There may even be a notion of 'positive warist discourse', in which war is referred to as a warning, as a deterrent, designed to make more war less likely. For example, Winston Churchill (1874–1965), the UK wartime prime minister, from 1940 to 1945 (and again 1951–1955) famously said: "Jaw, jaw is better than war, war" (Molloy & Graham, 2008), meaning that talking and negotiating is better than going to war. (Unfortunately, Churchill also engaged repeatedly in anti-Indian, race-based hate speech, Oxford, 2021, p. 202–203.)

In another more recent example, at the end of 2020, in his first message to US military forces, acting Pentagon chief Chris Miller described himself as "weary of war" and said that it was "time to end America's wars in the Middle East" (Macias, 2020). In addition to the human costs, there are the socioeconomic costs of war, as it was also reported that: "The wars in Afghanistan, Iraq and Syria have cost US taxpayers more than $1.57 trillion since Sept. 11, 2001, according to a Defense Department report" (Macias, 2020). That kind of discourse may still be considered 'warist' in the broadest sense, but they may constitute instances of 'positive warist discourse', as they are referring to avoiding war or to ending wars. And although 'positive warist discourse' may seem like something of a contradiction in terms, it follows the pattern of, for example, Galtung's (1969, p. 183) idea of "negative peace" (see Chapter 3)—which is, in fact, 'positive' in the general sense of "negative peace" referring to the "absence of personal violence" (Galtung, 1969, p. 183).

REACT 3.4: *Watch, read or listen to five or six international news reports over the next few days, paying particular attention to euphemisms like 'collateral damage'. What kinds of euphemisms are being used to refer to what kinds of conflict and violence?*

Rhetoric, Politics, and Poetry

Another important aspect of NPL is Rhetoric, as there is clearly an overlap between those two areas. However, as stated in the Chapter 1, *while all NPL may be applied linguistics, not all applied linguistics is NPL*, which applies equally here, i.e., *while all NPL may come under the auspices of rhetoric, not all rhetoric is about NPL*, as the field of rhetorical studies, like applied linguistics, cover many areas. Regarding the overlap between politics and rhetoric, in Jonathan Charteris-Black's *Analysing Political Speeches: Rhetoric, Discourse and Metaphor* (2014), he pointed out that: "While a speech is a socially produced text, when it comes to delivery, it is a live performance by a single individual" (p. xviii). One of the focal points in Charteris-Black's (2014) book is how politicians persuade their audiences to trust them, using their speeches as one of the main methods of building trust, along with "fluency, a high level of confidence, sincerity [and] spontaneity" (p. xviii). Going back to definitional basics, we can find at least three quite different dictionary descriptions of 'rhetoric', the first of which is: "speech or writing intended to be effective and influence people" (*CALD*, 2021) The second, specialized meaning is given as: "the study of the ways of using language effectively" and the third: "clever language that sounds good but is *not sincere or has no real meaning*" (emphasis added). In terms of language used negatively by people in power, it is that last meaning that may have most relevance in the world of politics, and therefore in NPL analyses.

The field of rhetorical studies is based on the work of the ancient Greek philosopher, Aristotle, who lived more than 1,600 years ago, between 380 and 320 BCE, but whose influence in rhetorical studies is still being felt today. For example, Ross Winterowd's (1931–2011) book, *Rhetoric: A Synthesis,* published in 1968, focused on the works of Aristotle, who is often described as 'the Father of Western Philosophy' (unfortunately, though rather typically and parthenogenetically, I was unable to find any woman acknowledged as 'the Mother of Western Philosophy'). More than 50 years after Winterowd's publication, books are still being published re-examining the legacy of the philosopher, such as *Aristotle: The Art of Rhetoric* (Waterfield & Yunis, 2018), in which the authors claim that Aristotle's "treatise on the art of rhetoric . . . remains today the most important and incisive works on rhetoric that we possess" (Waterfield & Yunis, 2018, p. ix). The origins of the modern academic discipline of Rhetoric can be seen in the first volume of the first issue of the journal, *Rhetoric Review,* launched in 1982, Jim Corder observed that: "about 1965 . . . there began to emerge a generation of English teachers who had discovered rhetoric" (p. 4). However, Corder did acknowledge that others, including generations of "speech teachers . . . kept rhetoric close by" but who did so "rather quietly" (Corder, 1982, p. 3).

Much has changed in the 40 years since the *Rhetoric Review* was launched, and from an NPL perspective, the increasingly political nature of rhetorical studies is especially relevant. As we will see in Part III of this book, the election of Donald Trump (DJT) as the 45th President of the USA, at the end of 2016—and the four years that followed—were an especially important time in the study of political rhetoric. For example, approximately one year after those presidential elections, in the Fall of 2017, the *Rhetoric Review* published a special issue under the general heading of *Rhetoric, Race, and Resentment: Whiteness and the New Days of Rage* (Carstarphen & Welch, 2017). Carstarphen and Welch begin their introductory overview by looking back: "With the 2008 election of the first African American president of the US, race as both subject and object has infiltrated national conversations in myriad ways" (p. 255)—conversations that reflect the new days of racialized rage, in the USA and elsewhere.

Another paper in that special issue of the *Rhetoric Review* is '(De)coding Whiteness: Rhetorical refinement of coded rhetoric by White Nationalist women appropriated by US politicians' (Anderson, 2017), In that paper, Wendy Anderson reported on the ways in which, although racist rhetoric has existed in the USA for as long as the USA has existed: "Trump's coded rhetoric *validated* racism" (2017, p. 264, emphasis added). After analyzing the language of Trump and language of websites by and for White Nationalist women, Anderson concluded that: "For rhetors [orators] like Trump, white fragility justifies the oppression of others, and his assertions of supremacy are coded within an authoritarian nostalgia that, when ignited, become widespread hateful harassment, intimidation, hate crimes, racist graffiti, and violence" (p. 269). In 2017, 'white fragility' was shortlisted for the *Oxford English Dictionary* (*OED*) 'Word of the Year'. 'White fragility' was first used in 2011 by Robin DiAngelo, who defined it as: "a state in which even a minimum amount of racial stress becomes intolerable, triggering a range of defensive moves [including]... anger, fear, and guilt, and behaviors such as argumentation, silence, and leaving the stress-inducing situation" (DiAngelo, 2011, p. 57). Such language-based, race-based fragility has also been exacerbated in recent years by some world leaders, such as DJT.

One of the other papers in the 2017 *Rhetoric Review* special issue is: *Racing the Trump Card: Rhetorics of whiteness and the politics of adaptive resistance after Obama*, by Mark McPhail and David Frank. McPhail and Frank (2017) refer to their analysis of President Barack Obama's 2004 Democratic National Convention Address (Frank & McPhail, 2005), and they compare and contrast "Obama's rhetoric on race during his eight years as president juxtaposed against the emergence of Donald Trump's rhetoric of white identity politics" (p. 283). They also identify "the rhetorical tactics of Donald Trump and his followers" (p. 284) including their denial that President Obama was born in the USA., and Frank & McPhail remind us that, during his campaign, candidate Trump promised that his presidency would "'promote the values of tolerance, justice, and acceptance" and "steadfastly reject bigotry and hatred and oppression of any form" (McPhail & Frank, 2017, p. 284). (The extent to which such promises have been broken and such statements have proved to be lies will be explored in Part III of this book.) However, one of the aspects of the McPhail & Frank (2017) paper that is conspicuous by its absence is any actual language analysis, which is one important way in which NPL differs from some aspects of Rhetoric, as in-depth, systematic linguistic analysis is at the heart of NPL.

Politics, Poetry, and the New Peace Linguistics

Few of us may think of politics as being poetic, although poetry can certainly be political. For example, in *Voices in Revolution* (2009), John Crespi wrote about 'Poetry and the Auditory Imagination in Modern China'. In an article, 'The Politics of Poetry', Cornell University professor David Orr (2008) described how the head of a machinists' union in Ohio, during the US Democratic party primaries, attempted to criticize Barack Obama and support Hillary Clinton. Said the union leader, of Obama: "This guy won't last a round against the Republican attack machine... He's a poet not a fighter" (Orr, 2008, p. 409). As we will see in the Part II chapters, Obama was/is both. In analyzing that attempted 'put down' or insult, Orr also described what he believed were the two main views of poetry in the USA: "1: That poetry is passive, swoony, and generally not in the business of 'doing things': 2) That politics is active, gritty and comparable to war" (p. 409). And as we will also see in the Part II and Part III chapters, that second statement, about politics being "comparable to war," is exemplified in the political texts analyzed in this book.

In discussing the philological, historical relationships between rhetoric and poetry, Laura Kendrick (1983) wrote that: "Classical rhetoric, the art of oral persuasion, depended on a public forum, a political organization that upheld some degree of free speech and upon an economic system that enabled large numbers of people to live together in cities" (p. 1). According to Kendrick, with the decline of the Roman Empire, around 400 A.D., and the rise of agrarian and feudal societies, "Rhetoric lost its practical purpose and hence much of its value" (1983, p. 1). However, politics in the modern era is filled with sound-bites from politicians, often trying to persuade their electorate, their corporate sponsors and the viewers to vote-for-me! In that sense, rhetoric is back—big time.

Nowadays, it is certainly rare to hear politicians in any country, in any language, reciting poetry to their people. However, it was not always this way, as Albrecht Koschorke and Konstantin Kaminskij point out in their edited book, Tyrants Writing Poetry (2017), and as BBC reporter, Benjamin Ramm (2017) also pointed out: "from classical antiquity to modernity, dictators have been inspired to write verse—seeking solace, intimacy, or glory. Their work informs us about the nature of power, the abiding appeal of poetry, and the perils of artistic interpretation." But given that such poetry-writing politicians are so rare these days, at this point, we can ask: What does politics and poetry have to do with NPL? One of the simplest and most effective ways to create rhythms in English (and similar languages) is to use alliteration, in which the same letter or sound at the beginning of one or more words in the same phrase or sentence is repeated. For example, a lovelorn poetic line could be: 'Like the sands of the Sahara, my heart is dry as dust without you', with repeating s-s and d-d word-initial sounds helping the line flow. However, it would be just as alliterative for one politician to say about one of their opposing counterparts: 'My fine friend fails to grasp the seriousness of the situation', with the alliteration here being carried by the f-f and s-s word-initial sounds. Even William Shakespeare (1564–1616) was fond of alliteration, together with repetition. For example, in one of the most famous soliloquies, delivered by Macbeth, he says: "Tomorrow, and tomorrow, and tomorrow; Creeps in this petty pace from day to day; To the last syllable of recorded time; And all our yesterdays have lighted fools; The way to dusty death. Out, out, brief candle!"

According to the *Los Angeles Times* reporter, Bob Baker (2004): "Americans are awash in alliteration... We are victims of anxious advertising executives and publicity-hungry politicians... That's why [in 1992] a beleaguered Bill Clinton called himself 'The Comeback Kid'... It's why George W. Bush... called himself a 'compassionate conservative'" in 2000 as part of his appeal to moderate Republicans. Citing examples from William Shakespeare to Vladimir Nabokov, Baker shows that: "Alliteration can be graceful... It can be audacious... It can be elegant... It can amplify the emotional power of a great idea" (Baker, 2004). However, Baker also warned that: "Alliteration in American politics can both energize and betray a politician who wants to express disdain," with more examples from US politics in the 1880s to the 1970s. As the spoken and written political texts in this book show, alliteration can be an effective linguistic device for creating rhythm and flow, if it used carefully and consciously. However, these political texts show that there are other ways of using language, directly and indirectly, that can be considered poetic and/or dramatic in the literary sense. That is one of the ways in which the New Peace Linguistics differs from previous iterations of PL, and one of the stylistic aspects of which NPL brings to the analyses of these kinds of texts.

What Peace Linguistics Is Not

Before wrapping-up our exploration of the different possible meanings of 'Peace Linguistics', it may help to clarify what PL is *not*. Firstly, this iteration of PL, the New Peace Linguistics is not about being Politically Correct (PC) or about being some kind of Language Police, dictating who can and cannot write and say what. NPL is about achieving a higher level of awareness of the ways in which we and those around us—especially those more powerful than us – use language in ways that make a more or less peaceful outcome more or less likely. Unfortunately, Political Correctness has been excoriated by so many commentators, both on the political Left and on the political Right. As Norman Fairclough (2003) put it, in his article on the politics and culture of language use and the "dialectics of discourse" (p. 23): "Critics of 'PC' had a plausible target because some (but only some) of the forms of cultural and discursive intervention labelled as 'PC' smacked of the arrogance, self-righteousness and puritanism of an ultra-left politics, and have caused widespread resentment" (p. 25). Fairclough (2001) also wrote about "language and power, more precisely about connections between language use and unequal relations of power" P. 1) in Britain at that time. And like NPL, Fairclough's goal was "to help increase consciousness of how language contributes to the domination of some people by others, because *consciousness is the first step towards emancipation*" (2001, p. 1). In addition, Fairclough and Fairclough's 2012 book, *Political Discourse Analysis*, analyzed the language of UK politics, using a specific theory of argumentation.

To be clear, then, although peace linguists do indeed advocate more self-aware, careful and conscious uses of language, that recognize and respect the dignity of all parties, *NPL is not about being PC.* NPL is not only about using language peacefully, which many (or even most) of us already know that we *should* all do. Instead, NPL is about the systematic, in-depth analysis of how language is *actually* used, rather than how it *should* be used, especially as it used by some of the most powerful people in the world, because it is their words that make war or peace more or less likely.

Following the idea of what NPL is not, this not a book about Social Justice, although that is becoming an increasingly necessary and important area of enquiry and activity. In their book, *Social Justice Isn't What You Think It Is* (2015) Novak, Adams and Shaw defined social justice as: "a decisive rejection of individualism and liberalism" (p. 7), and they "denounce the ideology of the atomistic, autonomous, unencumbered self, the freely choosing individual detached from culture, family, church and community" (p. 7). Instead, they subscribe to the view of "man as a social animal, reciprocally indebted from before birth and at every stage of their life" (p. 7). Novak and Adam's conceptualization of social justice is based largely on religious texts, specifically those of Catholicism, including an extensive discussion of sixteen principles of 'Catholic Social Thought' (pp. 55–88). In more recent years, the focus of social justice has shifted from religion to politics and economics (although the three often overlap in many countries and contexts), and grown to encompass an ever-expanding circle of societal concerns. For example, in *Contemporary Inequalities and Social Justice in Crisis Times* (2018), Janine Brodie stated that: "Contemporary grammars of social justice typically dissect pressing social issues such as income inequality and precariousness at the intersections of race, indigeneity, sexuality, gender, and ecology" (p. 9). Linguistically, Brodie's use of grammatical metaphors such as, "the emerging grammar of social justice" (p. 9), but the primary focus of NPL is not on social justice, although NPL may include analyses of the language used to discuss "race, indigeneity, sexuality, gender, and ecology."

Why Does Peace Linguistics Matter?

To put it simply, as stated previously: *PL Matters Because Peace Matters.* In Chapter 1, I made the claim that: *Language is an essential prerequisite for conflict,* which is one of the reasons why PL matters. However, looking at the more general claim, *PL Matters Because Peace Matters,* words like 'peace' can mean different things to different people, as discussed above. In 1969, Johan Galtung published a seminal paper, 'Violence, Peace, and Peace Research', which began with his observation that, when it comes to the word 'peace': "Few words are so often used and abused—perhaps, it seems, because 'peace' serves as a means of obtaining verbal consensus—it is hard to be all-out against peace" (p. 167). Sadly, although it may be "hard to be all-out against peace," it is clearly not impossible, as the many, long wars in the 50-plus years since the publication of Galtung's 1969 paper have shown. Regarding the potential power of the word 'peace', Galtung explained that it gives us "a one-word language in which to express values of concern and togetherness *because peace is on everybody's agenda*" (p. 167, emphasis added). Unfortunately, the last part of that statement is also not as true as Galtung might have hoped, again, as shown by the number of wars over the past 60 years, including, to mention just a few, the Ethiopian Civil War (1974–1991), the Angolan Civil War (1975–2002), the Lebanese Civil War (1975–1990), the Cambodian-Vietnamese War (1975–1989), the Sri Lankan Civil War (1983–2009), and the Second Sudanese Civil War (1983–2005). Those six wars alone add up to a total of more than 120 years of armed conflict and killing over a 30-year period, and that list does not include the current, on-going wars.

If peace really had been on *everybody's* agenda, then those wars would not have taken place, or if they did, then each of them would not have lasted for decades. And from an NPL perspective, it is ironic that most of the longest-lasting wars over the last 60 years have been called 'civil', as that word means, in its most general sense, "polite and formal" (*CALD*, 2021)—adjectives which do not describe any armed conflict ever fought on any battlefield. However, the more specific meaning of 'civil' is "*not* military or religious" (*CALD*, 2021, emphasis added), and its military meaning, as in 'civil war', is "a war fought by different groups of people living in the same country" (*CALD*, 2021). Those definitions make such wars, in fact, about geography, not civility.

In his seminal 1969 paper, Galtung proposed what he called, "three simple principles":

1. The term "peace" shall be used for social goals at least verbally agreed to by many, if not necessarily by most.
2. These social goals may be complex and difficult, but not impossible, to attain.
3. The statement peace is absence of violence shall be retained as valid. (p. 167)

Galtung defined violence as: "the cause of the difference between the potential and the actual, between what could have been and what is" (p. 168). To illustrate what he meant by that potential-actual difference, Galtung gave the following example, showing the importance of context in relation to time and place: "if a person died from tuberculosis in the eighteenth century it would be hard to conceive of this as violence since it might have been quite unavoidable, but if he dies from it today... then violence is present" (p. 168). Galtung (1969) made many other important distinctions, for example, between physical and psychological violence (p. 169), "*whether or not there is an object that is hurt*" (p. 170, original emphasis) and "*whether or not there is a subject (person) who acts*" (p. 170, original emphasis).

One of the key distinctions Galtung made is between what he called 'personal or direct violence' and 'structural or indirect violence', with the former referring to: "the type of violence where there is an actor that commits the violence," and the latter to violence "where there is no such actor" (p. 170). In cases of 'personal or direct violence' it is possible to point to a specific individual or group of individuals as being those who carried out one or more acts of violence. In cases of 'structural or indirect' violence, "The violence is built into the [societal] structure and shows up as unequal power and consequently as unequal life chances" (p. 171). To illustrate the concept of 'structural violence', Galtung gave the following marital example: "when one husband beats his wife there is a clear case of personal violence, but when one million husbands keep one million wives in ignorance there is structural violence" (p. 171). Building on that distinction, Galtung (1969) created another critical distinction, between the "absence of personal violence," which he referred to as "negative peace," and the "absence of structural violence," which he referred to as "positive peace" (p. 183).

To return to the idea that *PL Matters Because Peace Matters*, it is tempting to assume that the importance of creating and having more peace and less war is a 'no-brainer', i.e., does not require any explication. It should not be necessary to make a case for more peace and less war, as the benefits of that situation—and the dangers of the reverse, i.e., more war and less peace—should be self-evident. However, as the wars listed above (and all those not listed) show, the benefits of a more peaceful, less conflict-ridden world do not appear to be as obvious to everyone as we might assume, hope or believe. In 2018, the US diplomat, educator and author, Rick Barton, who served as the Assistant Secretary of State for the Bureau of Conflict and Stabilization Operations at the US Department of State, asked, as the title of his opening book chapter: "Is the World Going to Hell?" According to Barton, the answer appears to be (for now at least) 'No', although he did sum up some of the major sources of conflict in the world today, including: "Religion, tribal feuds, economic distress, income and wealth divides, traditional alliances, historic divisions, colonial patterns, social pressures, ideology and separatism" (Barton, 2018, p. 3). However, in spite of such a daunting list of barriers to peace, Barton remained upbeat about 'America's unifying role in a turbulent world', which he chose as the subtitle for his book, *Peace Works* (2018).

Leaving aside the fact that the USA may be one of the major contributors to the current global 'turbulence' (McGrath, 2014), Barton asked, about the conflicts in the 1990s in Bosnia, Rwanda and Haiti, as well as the conflicts in Iraq, Afghanistan and Syria: "Why do these places and conflicts matter?" (p. 5). Barton gave the following answer to his question: "Instability threatens our allies, entire regions, and our homeland. It has a way of becoming personal, whether we are there or not" (p. 5), thereby highlighting the impact of such conflicts internationally, nationally and individually. Barton also made the economic case for less conflict: "If we reach out, these countries are potential or actual trading partners, home to markets of more than two billion people" (p. 5). And in making the political case for more peace, Barton stated that: "Global power vacuums have a way of attracting terrorists or incubating longer-term problems" (p. 5). No one would disagree that the cost of wars—the human, social, economic, political and other costs—is high. But what is the cost of war? Can such costs even be estimated? As it turns out, perhaps they can be.

The Watson Institute for International and Public Affairs is housed within Brown University, in Rhode Island, USA. According to its website, the Institute: "seeks to promote a just and peaceful world through research, teaching, and public engagement" (watson.brown.edu). The Institute estimates that more than 5.9 *billion* US dollars has been spent by the US Government on waging war, between 2001 and 2019. Approximately 1.9 billion USD of that 5.9 billion USD has been spent by the Department of Defense, and from an NPL perspective is worth noting that such departments are called 'defense departments' not 'war departments.' One of the initiatives of the Institute is the 'Costs of War Project', which was started in 2011, and which is made up of a team of scholars, legal experts, human rights practitioners, and physicians. The Project's goal is to: "use research and a public website to facilitate debate about the costs of the post-9/11 wars in Iraq and Afghanistan, and the related violence in Pakistan and Syria," acknowledging that: "There are many hidden or unacknowledged costs of the United States' decision to respond to the 9/11 attacks with military force" (watson.brown.edu/costsofwar). Based on the data gathered, the Project estimates that, since the 9/11 attacks in the USA, approximately half-a-million people: "have died due to direct war violence, and several times as many indirectly," and that the number of war refugees and displaced persons is more than 20 million. To reiterate, that is only in the last 20 years, since 2001, which does not include, for example, the 45 million civilian deaths, the 15 million battle deaths, or the 25 million battle wounded during World War II (1939–1945; nationalww2museum.org).

Drawing on interviews with researchers working on the Costs of War Project, Rami Khouri, an American University of Beirut professor and a Harvard Kennedy School senior fellow, reported that, by 2016: "The financial cost of the wars to the US alone (not counting spending by Iraq, Pakistan and Afghanistan) is at least $4.8 *trillion* [USD] to date" (Khouri, 2016). Khouri added that that 4.8 trillion USD did not include "the costs incurred by state and local governments, the costs to the economy of families caring for injured veterans, or lost productivity due to men and women who leave work to care for injured family members." These costs continue to mount, every day, week, month and year. For example, in 2019, BBC reporter, Safa Al Ahmad, reported on 'The human cost of a US strike on al-Qaeda' in Yemen, which has been "devastated" by a war that began in 2014. If language is an essential prerequisite for conflict, then NPL, as defined above, has the potential to help reduce such unimaginable costs, no matter how small a reduction, which makes NPL an important area of enquiry.

At this point, one obvious, relevant question arises: Given the horrific costs of war, why are there still so many wars being fought? One of the main answers to this question appears in the 2005 movie, *The Lord of War.* The lead character is called Yuri Orlov (played by Nicolas Cage), who is an arms dealer. At one point during the movie, Orlov explains: "There's nothing more expensive for an arms dealer than peace" (*Lord of War,* 2005, imdb.com). A deep sense of sadness and irony runs throughout the movie, including a scene in which Orlov meets one of the biggest buyers of weaponry, Andre Baptiste Jr. (played by Sammi Rotibi)—during peace talks at the

United Nations, presumably to maximize the bitter irony. In another scene, Orlov explains to an Interpol agent pursuing him: "And while the biggest arms dealer in the world is your boss—the President of the United States, who ships more merchandise in a day than I do in a year—sometimes it's embarrassing to have his fingerprints on the guns." Unfortunately, the Lord of War was not exaggerating: "The United States was the largest exporter of major arms from 2015–2019, delivering 76 percent more materiel than runner-up Russia, according to a new study by the Stockholm International Peace Research Institute think tank" (Vercellone, 2020).

The Man Booker Prize-winning Indian author Arundhati Roy, in her non-fiction book *War Talk* (2003), wrote about "the British arms dealers and the American weapons manufacturers [who] grow fat on our spilled blood" (p. 30). Roy also referred to President George W. Bush's September 20, 2001 address, during which he offered up the either-or 'false dichotomy' or 'informal fallacy': "Every nation, in every region, now has a decision to make. Either you are with us, or you are with the terrorists" (See Chapter 5). In her commentary on those lines, Roy wrote: "Those words hang frozen in time like icicles. For years to come, butchers and genocidists will fit their grisly mouths around them... in order to justify their butchery" (2003, p. 30). There are, then, those for whom peace is bad for business; for whom more war = more dollars; for those people, the never-ending forever wars translate into an endless source of monetary gain, paid for by the blood of others.

One of the many books to research and report on the profits being made from waging war is Stuart Brandes' *Warhogs: A History of War Profits in America* (1997). The investigative reporter, Pratap Chatterjee, has also been documenting such profiteering in a number of books, including *Iraq, Inc.: A Profitable Occupation* (2004) and *Halliburton's Army: How a Well-Connected Texas Oil Company Revolutionized the Way America Makes War* (2010). Others, such as *The Telegraph* reporter, Anthony Holden, have written about 'How War is Big Business' (2009), and George Washington University professor Jonathan Turley (2014) reported that, in the USA, military budgets "now support millions of people in an otherwise declining economy. Hundreds of billions of dollars flow each year from the public coffers to agencies and contractors who have an incentive to keep the country on a war-footing." Turley also pointed out that the human costs of war are not spread equally, but are socio-economically distributed disproportionally, as "roughly 75 percent of the fallen in these wars come from working class families" in the United States. Turley concluded that: "War may be hell for some but it is heaven for others in a war-dependent economy."

More recently, the historian, Michael Beschloss, who is the author of no fewer than nine books about the presidency of the USA, published his (750-page) magnum opus, *Presidents of War* (2018), starting with the War of 1812, fought between the USA, the UK and their respective allies, between 1812 and 1815, covering wars up to 2018. He concluded his book by referring to the so-called 'Founding Fathers' of the USA (again, no 'Founding Mothers', so more parthenogenesis). Beschloss believed that those Fathers would be: "thunderstruck to discover that the option to start a war of a magnitude they would find inconceivable—killing hundreds of millions of human beings in less than hour—*may now rest on the whim of a President*" (p. 583, emphasis added). Although there are, of course, other world leaders, in other countries, who start such wars and resist peace for personal, financial and political gain, the vast majority of the books on this topic, written over the last 20 years, appear to have been about presidents of the USA.

Suggestions for Further Reading

The *TESL Reporter* is one of the only publications in the field of English language teaching and learning that has been published continuously for more than 50 years. In the Fall of 2018, the *TESL Reporter* published a special issue on Peace Linguistics (Volume 51, Issue 2), making that the first issue of an academic journal ever to be published on PL. In 2019, all of the seven articles, and a book review, in that PL special issue were made freely available online at: http://ojs-dev.byuh.edu/index.php/Issue1/issue/view/129

The special issue contains articles on The Interplay of Language and Peace Education (Oxford, Gregersen, & Olivero, 2018), on Peace-Making-Languaging (Johnson & Murphey, 2018), on Peace Linguistics in the Classroom (Curtis & Tarawhiti, 2018h), and on Using Global Issues in the English Language Classroom to Create a More Sustainable Dialogue (Rothman & Sanderson, 2018), as well as my interview with Francisco Gomes de Matos (Curtis, 2018i).

4

The "New" Peace Linguistics

How New or New How?

The question How New? can be read in a number of different ways. For example, in terms of quantity and quality, scale and scope: In what ways and to what extent is the 'new' Peace Linguistics different from the 'old'? It is also important to acknowledge that terms such as 'new' and 'old' are entirely relative and highly contextual, and so it is with the New Peace Linguistics (NPL), as the term 'Peace Linguistics' has been around for decades. For example, Francisco Gomes de Matos, a Professor Emeritus of Linguistics in Brazil, dates the first formal mention of Peace Linguistics (PL) back to the late 1970s (Gomes de Matos, 2014). However, in the 40 years since then, very few applied linguists appear to have come across the term, or to have read about it, and until recently very little PL research appears to have been carried out, presented, or published (Curtis, 2018f).

REACT 4.1: *Before picking up this book, had you heard about Peace Linguistics before? If so, where did you hear about PL before? And what did you think of—what words and/or images came to mind—when you first heard the phrase 'Peace Linguistics'?*

The New Peace Linguistics and The Role of Language in Conflict, pages 61–79

Francisco Gomes de Matos, David Crystal, Rebecca Oxford, and Other PL Pioneers

Gomes de Matos' published work includes the book *Dignity: A Multidimensional View* (2013), and he is a member of the Human Dignity and Humiliation Studies group (www.humiliationstudies.org), which was nominated for the Nobel Peace Prize for three consecutive years (2015–2017). He is also a founding member of the World Dignity University initiative, which describes itself, on its website, as a "human-to-human network of networks" (www.worlddignityuniversity.org). Since the early 1980s (Gomes de Matos, 1982), Gomes de Matos has been writing about the potential contribution of peace linguists to the "harmonizing and humanizing of political discourse" (2000, pp. 339–344), as well as many articles on the peaceful use of language. Some of his more recent work in the area of PL includes a chapter, '16 Planning Uses of Peace Linguistics in Second Language Education', in the book *Un(Intended) Language Planning in a Globalising World: Multiple levels of players at work* (Chua, 2018). Gomes de Matos distinguished between communicating about peace and communicating peacefully, and in his version of what he has called 'Peace Linguistics', communicating peacefully is the goal and the focus (Chua, 2018, p. 290).

In his 2018 chapter, Gomes de Matos cited a note from Dell Hymes (1927–2009), known for his work on the comparative, ethnographic study of languages, and Communicative Competence:

> If we are not able to share the world, we will surely live in unending violence. Perhaps attention to the conditions of communicative peace may help achieve the social and personal requisites for such sharing. Dell Hymes, personal communication to Francisco Gomes de Matos, August 20, 1993. (Gomes de Matos, 2018, p. 290)

While the view that sharing the world as a way to end violence is relatively easy to agree with, communicating peacefully makes little or no mention of linguistics, or of the scientific, systematic study of language, which is how linguistics has been defined for more than a century now (Lyons, 1968).

Gomes de Matos (2018) quoted an entry by David Crystal in the *Penguin Dictionary of Language* (1999): "Peace Linguistics emphasizes attitudes which respect the dignity of language users and communities, David Crystal, 1999" (p. 291 in Gomes de Matos, 2018). Later, in the fifth edition of his *Dictionary of Linguistics and Phonetics* (2003), Crystal's entry described 'Peace Linguistics' as a term: "reflecting the climate of opinion which emerged during the 1990s among many linguists and language teachers, in which linguistic principles, methods, findings and applications were seen as a means of promoting peace and human rights at the global level" (p. 341). In 2004, Crystal described 'Peacelinguistics' (which he wrote as one word) as "a new notion" (p. 23), and he explained to his audience that, if you typed the term 'Peacelinguistics' into the Google search engine "you get zero hits" and a query "Did you mean paralinguistics?" (p. 23). That situation has improved a little over the many intervening years—but not much. If you use the search terms 'Peace Linguistics' or 'peacelinguistics' with Google today, there are a few 'direct matches', though still not many. Crystal went on to note that, in spite of such unsuccessful Internet searches, the term had "been in linguistics dictionaries—*well, in mine, at least*—for a few years" (2004, p. 23, emphasis added). That conversational aside—"well, in mine, at least"—may be more important than such throw away lines might seem, as Crystal went on to explain that, 'peacelinguistics' was "not in the first edition of [his] *Penguin Dictionary of Language*, 1992, but it was certainly in the second, 1999" (p. 23). Crystal added that PL was also in the fifth edition of his *Dictionary of Linguistics and Phonetics* (2003).

Two important points emerge from Crystal's definitions of PL. First is that it was repeated over a number of years, in 1999, in 2003, and in 2004, without revision, which is noteworthy because during the years between 1999 and 2004, PL remained largely unknown and unheard of, and the reference to "many linguists and language teachers" appears to have been considerably overstating the case—not only back then, but still today. Secondly, although "the climate of opinion" about PL may have "emerged during the 1990s," the first academic paper on PL does not appear to have been published until decades later (Curtis, 2017b). Connecting PL with Gomes de Matos' work on language and dignity, Crystal's Dictionary entries described PL as an approach that "emphasizes the value of language diversity and multilingualism . . . and asserts the need to foster language attitudes which respect the dignity of individual speakers and speech communities" (2003, p. 341). Crystal's use of the simple present tense indicates that those actions—the emphasizing and the asserting—were assumed to have been happening *at that time*. However, that does not appear to have been the case. On the contrary, PL appeared to have fallen by the wayside, and has been largely been absent from discussions in language education and applied linguistics over the last two decades since Crystal first claimed that PL had arrived.

According to Gomes de Matos (2018), the key concept of his version of PL was to help "create conditions for language users to communicate peacefully in varied settings" (p. 291). That focus on using language peacefully has been called 'Peace Languaging' (Johnson & Murphey, 2018), incorporating the notion of 'languaging', which has "become quite popular and applied in many disciplines" (Lankiewicz & Wąsikiewicz-Firlej, 2014, p. vii). According to Lankiewicz and Wąsikiewicz-Firlej, the foundations of the concept of 'languaging', "rest on the assumption that language is a way of knowing, making personal sense of the world, becoming conscious of oneself and a means of creating an identity" (2014, p. vii). However, the peaceful, respectful use of dignified and dignifying language—or 'Peace Languaging'—is different from NPL, as 'Peace Languaging' does not entail the systematic, in-depth analysis of language as it is being used, as opposed to how language should or could be used peacefully.

The work of Patricia Friedrich is discussed below, but in a published interview with Gomes de Matos, Friedrich described him as: "one of the international scholars whose work inspired the Universal Declaration of Linguistic Rights (Barcelona, 1996) to be ratified by UNESCO and then by the United Nations" (2012a, p. 157). The interview also includes some of the 'rhyming reflections' that characterize much of Gomes de Matos' writing, for example, as an activity that could be done with students, "to challenge them linguistically and also in their ability to think in Nonkilling ways" (p. 159), he offered the following stanza:

> When non and killing are juxtaposed
> [a] specific view of nonviolence is proposed
> When as an adverb nonkilling is used,
> by peace, nonkillingly is wisely infused (Friedrich, 2012a, p. 159)

Although such rhymed reflections may be somewhat difficult to unravel and make complete sense of without multiple readings, they can also serve as helpful reminders of the power of language to hurt and to harm, or to heal and to cure (see below for more on using language 'nonkillingly').

REACT 4.2: *Create your own short rhymed reflection which relates to what you have read in this book so far. If others are also reading this book, compare your rhymed reflection with theirs.*

Another pioneer in the PL field is Rebecca Oxford, a professor emerita at the University of Maryland, who was originally widely known for her extensive early work on language learning strategies (see, for example, Oxford & Crookall, 1988; Oxford, 1990; Oxford 1992; Oxford 1996). After some years, Oxford turned her attention to "transformative eco-education" (Oxford & Jin, 2011), and the relationships between language and peace, in books such as *The Language of Peace: Communicating to Create Harmony* (2013), which was used as the course textbook for the first PL course, taught at Brigham Young University-Hawaii (BYU-H) in 2017 and in 2018 (Curtis & Tarawhiti, 2018h). In her *Language of Peace* book, Oxford (2013) begins with six principles describing the languages of peace, including six dimensions of peace language: inner (or intrapersonal), interpersonal, intergroup, international, intercultural, and ecological (pp. 12–22). She also includes details of six principles related to the language of peace, including: "The language of peace is not always simple" (p. 23), which we adapted, during the BYU-H PL course, as: The language of peace is never simple—though it may sometimes seem so.

Oxford's (2013) book includes chapters on 'The Language of Peace in Action' (pp. 35–66) and on 'Naming and Transforming Violence' (pp. 105–142), as well as a critical discourse analysis of Dr. Martin Luther King Jr.'s 'I Have a Dream' speech (pp. 145–165), and multiple chapters on 'Peace through Words and Images' (pp. 145–248), and on 'Using Peace Language with Other Cultures' (pp. 251–325). Regarding peace-making, peace-keeping, and peace-building, Oxford (2013) highlighted the problems of "contradictions among theorists about phases of the peace process" (p. 65), and the "contradictions in concepts and vocabulary [that] concern the peace process" (p. 66), thereby reiterating the importance of linguistics and language analysis as the basis of NPL.

One of Oxford's more recent papers in this area is The Interplay of Language and Peace Education: The Language of Peace Approach for Peace Communication and Linguistic Analysis in Language Teaching and Teacher Education (Oxford, Gregersen & Olivero, 2018). In their paper, Oxford et al. present a framework that they refer to as a "language of peace approach," the main purpose of which is to "foster peace in multiple dimensions . . . and peaceful communication through (a) peace language activities that are smoothly interwoven into language teaching and language teacher education and (b) expert research, including multimethod research designs and linguistic analysis" (p. 16). Oxford et al. (2018) also presented an extensive review of published research in different areas related to their language of peace approach, which expanded on some of Oxford's earlier work in this area (Oxford, 2013), and which drew on the important early work of Claudia Schäffner and Anita Wenden in the mid-1990s (Schäffner & Wenden, 1995), which is discussed below. Oxford et al. (2018) also included helpful discussions on the role of applied linguistics and peace linguistics in their language of peace approach, as well as research on the use of that approach in teacher education and language teaching. To briefly recap, on the one hand, PL is not new, in the sense that the idea of PL has been around for decades. However, statements about the widespread use of PL are at best over-optimistic over-estimations, and at worst are simply incorrect and unfounded. Furthermore, in most cases in the past, when reference was made to Peace Linguistics, the focus appears to have been largely on the 'Peace' part of PL, with little in the way of 'L', i.e., the systematic, in-depth analysis of language used.

The First Peace Linguistics Course

In the Fall of 2016, I was invited to develop a new course, for Brigham Young University-Hawai'i (BYU-H), titled 'Peace Linguistics', details of which have been reported elsewhere (Curtis, 2017a), but I will briefly report on the course here, as it still appears to be the only PL course of its kind, as far as we know. BYU-H and I carried out extensive searches, looking to see if anyone, anywhere had taught a university, credit-bearing, degree-level PL course before, but found nothing. The location is important as a key part of the BYU-H's vision is to: "assist individuals... in their efforts to influence the establishment of peace internationally," and to prepare "men and women with the intercultural and leadership skills necessary to promote world peace" (www.byuh.edu). The course was offered by the English Language Teaching and Learning Department at BYU-H, rather than as part of the University's Intercultural Peacebuilding program, because of the intended focus on language and linguistics, rather than peace studies or peace education (Curtis, 2018f). Despite the desire to focus on language and linguistics, finding suitable materials around which to build the course proved formidable, as there are myriad materials on applied linguistics, but none designed for a PL course (see Gkonou, Olivero & Oxford, 2021, for recent research on helping language teachers to take more active roles in peacebuilding).

The course was first offered at BYU-Hawai'i in January and February 2017, over eight weeks, with a total of 36 hours of in-class, face-to-face teaching, plus two weeks of online learning.

As stated in the original course syllabus, the course objectives were:

By the end of this course, successful participants will be able to:

1. demonstrate an in-depth understanding of the linguistics of language used to communicate for peaceful purposes
2. explore, examine and articulate the cultural and linguistic aspects of the languages of conflict and of peace
3. present and explain the use of poetic language, drawings, photographs, music, and other forms of text to illustrate different aspects of communicating for peaceful purposes
4. gather, analyze and present data on people's perceptions of peace, in relation to language and culture

5. carry out a critical discourse analysis of a text which shows how language can be used to create peace or to create conflict. (Curtis, 2017a)

After careful consideration of a number of possible course texts, we chose *The Language of Peace: Communicating to Create Harmony*, by Rebecca Oxford (2013), which was available to the course participants through BYUH's library, as a downloadable e-book, free to the course participants. In 2018, I was invited to teach the course for a second time, working closely with a BYU-H English Language Teaching and Learning Department professor. That arrangement was chosen so that, in future, the course could be taught by a full-time, BYU-H teacher who was a member of the Church of Jesus Christ of Latter-day Saints (sometimes referred to as 'LDS' or 'Mormons') who understood the teachings of the Church in ways that non-members, such as myself, may not be able to understand as fully or as deeply. Although the same core text was used in 2018 (Oxford, 2013), a number of changes were made when the PL course was taught the second time, including a greater balance between the linguistics content and the peace studies content. The students' assignments and assessments were also revised, with less of an emphasis in 2018 than in 2017 on the remembering of facts and figures, names and dates, definitions and descriptions.

From 2019 onwards, the PL course has been taught on a regular semester schedule, rather than being taught intensively, which gives the course participants more time to explore the large volumes of material, and to connect their PL course to their majors. In both of the first years of the PL course at BYU-H (2017 and 2018), the class size was approximately 20, and as a result of BYU-H's highly multilingual, multicultural, all-undergraduate student population, the course participants were from Australia, Canada, Fiji, Hong Kong, Japan, Mainland China, Mongolia, the Philippines, Samoa, Tahiti, the USA, and elsewhere. The two main majors of the students were TESOL and Peacebuilding, as well as a number of other departments, such as Communication Studies, Cultural Anthropology, Elementary Education, Political Science, and Social Work.

Other Contributors to the Development of Peace Linguistics

One of the earliest papers—and one of the few to appear in a journal of applied linguistics—that recognized the importance of linguistics in PL was published in 1987 in the *Australian Review of Applied Linguistics*, 'The role of Linguistics in Peace and Conflict Studies'. The paper was written by the Australian linguist, Michael Clyne (1939–2010), known for his work in a variety of applied linguistics fields, including sociolinguistics, pragmatics, bilingualism and multilingualism. In his paper, Clyne discussed the different meanings of the words 'peace' and 'war' in a variety of languages, in terms of the notion of 'markedness', an applied linguistics term used to distinguish between the dominant or 'unmarked' and the secondary or 'marked' uses of a word. Clyne (1987) argued that 'peace' had "developed as the marked alternative to 'war'" (p. 76), and encouraged linguists to "reduce the markedness of 'peace' at the international, national and interpersonal levels" (p. 76), to make peace the norm, rather than the exception, instead of the other way around.

Oxford, Olivero and Gregersen (2018) highlighted the important book, *Language and Peace,* edited by Schäffner and Wenden (1995), who described language as "a factor that must be considered, together with political and economic factors in seeking to understand the structural causes of conflict" (p. xiv). Schäffner and Wenden (1995) also stated that: "Social change, politics, and language (i.e., discourse) are inextricably intertwined" (p. xiv), which is one reason why NPL pays particular attention to the written and spoken texts of political leaders. However, I would add a fourth item to their list, i.e., social change, politics, *power,* and language are inextricably intertwined, because knowledge = power and all knowledge is stored and communicated via language. Without language, knowledge is not possible. Without knowledge, language is not possible. Therefore [knowledge = power] + [knowledge = language] means that [language = power] which is why NPL focuses on the language of people in power. Schäffner and Wenden's *Language and Peace* (1995), which includes a chapter on "discourse analysis as ideology analysis" (van Dijk, 1995, pp. 17–33), is an important collection of writings in the development of the field of NPL. There are also two chapters on metaphors: 'foreign policy by metaphor' (Chilton & Lakoff, 1995, pp. 37–60); and 'the balance metaphor in relation to peace' (Schäffner, 1995, pp. 75–92), as well as chapters on language and war, language and social discrimination, and language, education and peace. There are no chapters on Peace Linguistics.

Some years after their *Language and Peace* (1995) book, Anita Wenden (1933–2020), President and co-founder of the organization Earth and Peace Education International (www.globalepe.org), published a paper in the journal *Peace and Change,* 'Achieving a Comprehensive Peace: The Linguistic Factor' (2003). In that paper, Wenden argued that the linguistic factor should be "taken into account in the analysis of and prescription for problems deriving from social and ecological violence that challenge contemporary societies" (2003, p. 169). Wenden (2003) presented "the components of a linguistic framework that can be used to uncover the ideology in discourse" (p. 170), and defined 'ideology' as "an organized set of fundamental and often normative ideas and attitudes about some aspect of social reality shared by members of a group, society, or culture" (p. 170). Wenden's linguistic framework was based on three main areas: thematic context, i.e., "the themes of a text or talk that are central to its meaning" (p. 171); linguistic macro-structures; and linguistic micro-structures. Linguistic macro-structures are made up of: discourse schemata; text schema categories; and scope of identification, the latter of which, "initially referred to the group with whom the author identified when discussing the use of nuclear weapons, but by extension it can be applied to the analysis of discourse on any topic related to social or ecological peace" (p. 174). In Wenden's framework, linguistic micro-structures are made up of argumentation, metaphors, and lexical choices.

Wenden (2003) applied her framework to three documents: two reports written for the 1992 United Nations Conference on Environment and Development; and President George W. Bush's September 20, 2001 address on terrorism to a joint meeting of Congress, nine days after the 9/11 (September 11) terrorist attacks in the USA, in which nearly 3,000 people were killed and more than 6,000 others injured, making it the deadliest attack in the USA in history (see Chapter 5). Decades after that attack, scholars are still poring over the world-changing events of that day (see, for example, Keskin, 2018). After analyzing Bush's September 20, 2001 speech, Wenden (2003) found what she referred to as three "propositions about the war on terrorism," namely: "(1) Terrorism threatens to overthrow the freedom and way of life of all civilized states; (2) The American war on terrorism will be unlike previous wars; and (3) Our enemy in this war is a radical network of terrorists and governments that support it" (p. 183). Those three propositions "reveal[ed] the militarist ideology that [would] justify the war on terrorism" (p. 183).

Wenden (2003) sampled a 'thin slice' (approx. 250 words) of the approx. 3,000 words of the September 2001 speech by Bush, focused on his use of wh-questions, such as: "How will we fight and win this war?" (Wenden, 2003, p. 183), and highlighted "the adversarial stance that pits 'us' against 'them'," which she classified as a "pro-war... scope of identification" (p. 184). Also, in her analysis of metaphors, Wenden found that: "Dehumanizing the enemy is also part of a militarist strategy" (p. 185) (see Chapter 1, on the Rwandan Genocide). Wenden (2003) concluded that: "While active readers and listeners may be engaged deliberately in comprehending... They remain *unaware of the manner in which language is being used* to shape their understanding and to communicate beliefs and values, such as an ideology" (p. 186, emphasis added). Chapter 5 presents a more in-depth analysis of the same speech given by George W. Bush, on September 20, 2001, which includes a discussion of 'othering', and which also relates to Wenden's comment about "the adversarial stance that pits 'us' against 'them'" (Wenden, 2003, p. 185).

Wenden (2003) pointed out that: "Despite the fact that language can contribute indirectly to practices that lead to social and ecological violence... *it has remained a neglected variable* in the analysis of and prescription for problems that present an obstacle to a comprehensive peace" (p. 187, emphasis added). And she concluded that: "For the greater part it [language] is conspicuously absent from the peace research literature" (p. 187). To a large extent, the conspicuous absence of that neglected variable, language, has continued until recently. Some aspects of Wenden's (2003) framework could be challenged, for example, it could be argued that argumentation is different from metaphors and lexical choices, as argumentation may refer to more of a macro- than a micro-structure. Also, it could be claimed that, rather than "indirectly," language can contribute *directly* to practices that lead to violence, for example, in the case of verbal abuse. However, what matters more than how Wenden's (2003) framework could be critiqued is the fact that she appears to have been one of the very few researchers to apply linguistic analyses to these kinds of texts, that are said or written by world leaders, and which can have greater potential to start or escalate wars, rather than to make peace.

As we will see in the following chapter, the terrorist attacks on the USA in September 2001 sparked a series of responses that are still shaping the wars and the war talk of today. As the University of Washington professor, Sandra Silberstein, put it, in the beginning of her book, *War of Words: Language, Politics and 9/11*: "language has consequences... through the use of language, we create and recreate particular worlds of understanding" (2004, p. 1). And regarding the power of language, and how it can be used, Silberstein opened her first chapter with a quote from the political scientist, Richard Nuestadt (1919–2003), who served as an adviser to a number of presidents of the USA: "Presidential power is the power to persuade" (Silberstein, 2004, p. 1). That comment on the power of presidential persuasion can be re-stated to highlight the crucial importance of language: Presidential power is the power *to use language* to persuade, or the ability to use persuasive language powerfully—for good or for bad, for better or for worse. From an NPL perspective, who is being persuaded by world leaders to do what and to whom, rest on the language being used by those leaders, which can make the difference between waging war and making peace.

Drawing on Roderick Hart's *Verbal Style and the Presidency: Computer-Based Analysis* (1984), Silberstein pointed out the ways in which, "the media age has transformed the very office of the US presidency" (2004, p. 2). Evidence of that transformation can be seen in the nearly 500% increase in public speeches given by US presidents in the decades between 1945 and 1975, as a result of the beginning of the Golden Age of Television, from 1948 to 1960. Before 1945, US presidents "rarely spoke at all" in public (Hart, 1984, cited by Silberstein, 2004, p. 2). However, since 1945, "presidential speech and action increasingly reflect the opinion that speaking *is* governing" (Hart, 1984, cited by Silberstein, 2004, p. 2, original emphasis). In the 35-plus years since Hart's computer analyses of the verbal style of presidents of the USA, much more presidential spoken text is being uttered, and due to (anti)social media, more of the presidential writing is in the form of a few lines, communicated instantly, to very large numbers of readers all over the world. In analyzing the language of the media after the 9/11 attacks, Silberstein asked: "How did a response to terror become the War on Terrorism?" (p. xv). To answer that question, she looked at how "the construction of a nation at war" was "aided through the strategic deployment of language" (p. xv)—perhaps more than language-aided/assisted, and maybe even language-driven.

George Herbert Walker Bush (1924—2018) served as the 41st President of the USA from 1989 to 1993. As his son, George Walker Bush (b. 1946), served as the 43rd President of the USA from 2001 to 2009, the elder Bush was referred to as, for example, 'Bush 41', to avoid confusion caused by such patriarchal naming conventions (some of which may indicate the passing-on-of-privilege). Carol Eastman was a Professor of Anthropology at the University of Hawai'i from 1994 until her death in 1997. Two of those timelines, Bush 41's and Eastman's, came together in a collection of essays, *Language, Linguistics, and Leadership: Essays in Honour of Carol M. K. Eastman* (O'Mealy & Lyons, 1998). In that collection, Silberstein, along with her co-authors, Doyle, Eastman and Watkins, published an important chapter, 'Talking Peace, Waging War: Mining the Language of Leadership'. That chapter is based on the texts that followed the Iraq invasion of Kuwait, in 1990, referred to as the Persian Gulf Crisis, which culminated in the First Gulf War, fought between August 1990 and February 1991.

In relation to the interdisciplinarity of NPL, Silberstein et al. (1998) stressed that: "applied linguists need to consider *other disciplinary insights if* we seek to become effective peacemakers in a world where distinctions between peace and war have been lost" (p. 2, emphasis added). More than two decades later, we are still searching for those distinctions, and NPL may be able to help in the search, as seen in Silberstein et al.'s rhetorical question-answer exchange: "Where are linguistic categories useful in this enterprise? They help us understand the extraordinary rhetorical challenges facing *speakers* who are talking peace and ultimately waging war" (1998, p. 2, emphasis added). However, NPL also pays careful attention to the challenges facing the *recipients* of such messages; the people listening to the spoken texts, and reading those that are written, and the effects that such texts may have on the message-recipients. Silberstein et al. (1988) were realistic about the limitations of such approaches, accepting that: "The methods of applied linguistics can examine the things people do with language...Yet tools to uncover the underlying context-sensitive impacts of language use cannot alter the course of world events" (1998, p. 15). Fortunately, in spite of the limitations of academic enquiry, the last line of the Silberstein et al. chapter shows how an area of enquiry such as NPL may be able to help, as the authors state that: "the peace activist must not only work for new leaders, but for a different representational system" (p. 15). The system they were referring to could include a different way of using language to transmit and to decode messages, which may make the difference between going to war and negotiating peace.

In 2003, an important collection of chapters, edited by Mirjana Dedaić and Daniel Nelson, was published in *At War with Words.* In the book's introduction, 'A peace of word' (pp. 1–23), Dedaić observed that: "Political power cannot be divorced from the power of words" (p. 1), and continued: "Apart from the technical difficulties of defining the linguistic concept of word, we understand that 'words are loaded pistols' as Jean-Paul Sartre avowed" (p. 1). Sartre's observation relates to the notion of 'weaponizing language' (see Chapter 2), and in terms of what texts can tell us about the sender and the receiver, Dedaić also stated that: "The linguistic profile of political power reveals the message and messenger, as well as the reception and the response" (p. 1). That relates to the points made earlier about the messages sent by those in power, and the effects of such messages on those who receive them.

Following her 2003 paper in *Peace and Change,* Wenden (2007) published a paper in the *Journal of Peace Education,* 'Educating for a Critically Literate Civil Society: Incorporating the Linguistic Perspective into Peace Education'. Wenden (2007) began her paper with a quote from a book chapter by the Russian scientist and anthropologist, Valery Tishkov, which echoes those of Sartre above:

> Conflicts start with words and *words can kill no less than bullets.* In order to fight effectively, one should not only be trained on how to master Kalashnikovs and grenade launchers but also be able to explain why it is necessary to fight, who is the enemy and why it is the warrior's honor to die for a nation. Without these arguments people are poor fighters. (Tishkov, 2004, p. 80; cited in Wenden, 2007, p. 163, emphasis added)

Commenting on those words from Tishkov, and employing her own military metaphors, Wenden (2007) wrote that: "the use of spoken and written language in all aspects of social life is both an essential and effective weapon in the arsenal of war-makers" (p. 163).

After discussing discourse and peace education (pp. 165), Wenden (2007) presented a framework for critical language education, based on critical discourse analysis, made up of six main concepts: narrative; scope of identification; mode of reasoning; attribution of agency; characterization; exclusion/inclusion (p. 166). Wenden explained that: "Each concept points to either a linguistic or rhetorical cue of which citizen learners should be made aware if they are to understand how meaning is assigned and biases communicated" (2007, p. 166). Wenden concluded her paper by urging peace educators: "to contribute to the education of critical literate citizens, who are aware of the power of discourse, bias-resistant in its comprehension and mindful in the reproduction of what they have comprehended" (p. 177). Anita Wenden may, therefore, have been more important in the development of the New Peace Linguistics than was realized at the time.

Some other scholars have also been important in the development of Peace Linguistics, including Arizona State University professor, Patricia Friedrich. In her paper, English for Peace: Toward a Framework of Peace Sociolinguistics (2007), she wrote that: "As of the 1990s, the world witnessed a growing concern for issues of peace and an emerging awareness of the relationship between communication and peace... Peace Linguistics has branched out of Linguistics as a specialized field in Peace Studies" (p. 72). However, PL does not in fact appear to have emerged as a field within Peace Studies—nor within any other areas of study. Some of the main academic and scholarly criteria marking the emergence and establishment of a new field are books, book chapters, journals, journal articles and courses, and as far as PL is concerned, most of those have only appeared recently, and certainly long after the 1990s. That long delay between the 1990s and now may be because the "emerging awareness of the relationship between communication and peace" did not in fact emerge to the extent of reaching the world of applied linguistics.

If Friedrich's comment about PL emerging within Peace Studies had been correct, then we would have seen a number of articles on PL in journals in Peace Studies, Peace Research or Peace Education. However, that does not appear to have been the case (Curtis, 2017b). On the contrary, during the years I have been working in the field of PL and NPL, I have regularly encountered what might considered some form of academic snobbery from within applied linguistics community. On more than one occasion, I have heard at applied linguistics conferences, the incredulous replies: You're a what? What's a peace linguist? Peace linguistics, is that really a thing? You mean Peace and Love, like some kind of Hippie Linguistics? Some skepticism may be healthy, but those kinds of questions and comments show that we still have a long way to go before NPL is recognized as being as important as any other area of applied linguistics.

As Friedrich referred to 'Peace Sociolinguistics', perhaps PL emerged along that route, but that also does not appear to have been the case either, apart from Friedrich's own chapter, 'World Englishes and Peace Sociolinguistics: Towards a common goal of linguistic understanding' (2009), in which she described 'Peace Sociolinguistics' as a "budding field" (p. 407). However, the journal *Sociolinguistics*, which began in 1997, does not appear to have published any articles on PL or NPL, and apart from Friedrich's work, there appear to have been very few (if any) books, book chapters, journals, journal articles or courses on Peace Sociolinguistics. Friedrich (2007) stated that: "the viability of Peace Sociolinguistics as a subfield of Peace Linguistics has not been addressed at all" (p. 72). That unrealized potential viability may have been because PL as a sub-field of applied linguistics was not addressed. Friedrich (2007) also described PL as "the youngest descendant of Peace Studies" (p. 74); a description based on the work of Gomes de Matos (e.g., 1986, 1992, 2012), in which, as noted previously, there is little actual language analysis. Drawing on Gomes de Matos' (2000) work, Friedrich (2007) reiterated his point that "communicating peacefully [is] an important focus for Peace Linguistics" (p. 75). While that may be true, as also noted above, communicating peacefully is not at all the same as carrying out linguistic analyses, as it is perfectly possible for people to communicate peacefully without engaging in any linguistics. Friedrich (2007) described the relationship between language and peace as "intuitive" (p. 75), which some may agree with. However, perhaps it is that assumed intuitiveness that may also have delayed the development of NPL as an area of enquiry, as the growth and establishment of such areas requires movement beyond intuition.

Another possible reason for (N)PL not emerging as a recognized field even after all these years may have been identified by Friedrich (2007), when she explained that: "Crystal (1999 and 2003) has defined Peacelinguistics as *more of a concept* than a discipline" (p.76, emphasis added). It appears that PL remained in the conceptual realm, not making the transition from theory to practice. For example, as far as we can tell, PL did not appear as a university-level, credit-bearing course until 2017 (Curtis, 2017a), with journal articles on PL, which include in-depth language analyses, only starting to appear even more recently. Another reason for the decades-long delay in the emergence of PL—from Crystal first describing PL, in 1999, as having "emerged during the 1990s," to it actually emerging, closer to the 2020s than to the

1990s—may also have been given by Friedrich (2007), when she noted that PL had "not been systematized into a theoretical model" (p. 72). Such a conclusion appears to be premised on the idea that theoretical models come first, followed by the practical application of those models. However, (N)PL may be a case of linguistic analyses being carried out first, out of which models may grow, depending on what is meant by a 'model'.

Drawing on Crystal's (2004) work, Friedrich (2007) referred to an area called 'Linguistic Peace Education' (p. 79), which she described as: "a specialized form of Peace Education (and Peace Linguistics), one that focuses primarily on conflict resolution through language, the dissemination of linguistic rights, sensitivity to linguistic cross-cultural differences, and the teaching of awareness-raising practices to help individuals use language responsibly" (p. 79). That list may also help to explain why PL (like Peace Sociolinguistics) has not developed as it could have done (or as it was claimed to have developed). The reason is that it may be difficult to "focus primarily" on anything in particular when so many large areas are grouped together, each of which is large enough to constitute a separate disciplinary domain.

Conflict resolution is an area of study going back more than 60 years, as seen in the journal *Conflict Resolution*, first published in 1957. Also, "conflict resolution through language" may be somewhat tautological (or even redundant) as conflict resolution may be impossible without language, in the same way that conflict may be impossible without language, as discussed earlier (see Chapter 2). Similarly, the study of language rights is also a sizeable area of research, going back decades (May, 2005), as is the study of cross-cultural differences (Pirani & Smith, 2016). Although those areas of enquiry and fields of study do overlap with each other, one of the reasons for (N)PL having taken until now to be more widely recognized may be that it got lost, misplaced or simply overshadowed in amongst all the other fields with which it has been lumped together. And apart from the two articles by Wenden (2003, 2007) on Linguistic Peace Education, and one by Friedman on Linguistics Peace Activism (Friedrich, 2007, p. 80), those two areas also never became established in the ways that were hoped for, thought or assumed to have been.

From 'Not Killing' to 'Nonkilling'

The Center for Global Nonkilling, based in Hawaii, aims to "promote change towards the measurable goal of a killing-free world" (www.nonkilling.org). According to the Center's mission statement, it aims to achieve that goal by: "globally advancing nonkilling knowledge and skills, incorporating them into education and training, and applying them in individual and social decisions for the well-being of all." The Center for Global Nonkilling grew out of the Center for Global Nonviolence Planning Project, the origins of which began in 1986, with the establishment of the University of Hawai'i Institute for Peace. The Center was initially led by Glenn D. Paige (1929–2017), who was an American political scientist, known for developing the concept of 'nonkilling', as well as for his studies of political leadership and decision-making. His early works include a case study of the 33rd President of the USA (from 1945 to 1953), Harry S. Truman (1884–1972), specifically Truman's decision to involve the United States in the Korean War (Paige, 1970). Paige's later works include the book, *Nonkilling Political Science*, first published in 2002 (with a 2009 version published by the Center for Global Nonkilling).

In the same way that this NPL book appears to be the first to use the term 'Peace Linguistics' in its title, Paige (2009) explained his controversial coining of 'nonkilling' as follows: "This may be the first book in the English language to contain the word 'nonkilling' in its title . . . It seeks to direct attention beyond 'peace' and even 'nonviolence' to focus sharply upon the taking of human life" (p. 9). Paige accepted that the term might be perceived as being "too negative" and/or "too narrow" (p. 9), but his hope was that the reader: "on reflection, might be persuaded that concentration upon liberation from killing as source and sustainer of other forms of violence could be a significant step forward in the political science of nonkilling" (p. 9). After proposing the notion of 'nonkilling', Paige described a 'nonkilling society' as being characterized by: "no killing of humans and no threats to kill, neither technologies nor justifications for killing, and no social conditions that depend upon threat or use of lethal force" (p. 22). Neither the Vision statement nor the 10-point Mission statement of the Center for Global Nonkilling mention language, which may be one reason why Paige is recognized as a pioneer in Peace Studies, but he is relatively unknown in Language Studies. Likewise, the nine main goals of the Center do not mention language either. However, the Center does acknowledge the importance of linguistics, for example, as seen in their book, *Nonkilling Linguistics: Practical Applications* (Friedrich, 2012b).

In *Nonkilling Linguistics* (2012a), Friedrich and Gomes de Matos (2012) pointed out that: "Surprisingly enough, given the ubiquitous nature of language, it took linguistics quite a long time to be more formally recognized as an important element of peace" (p. 20). Syntactically and semantically, the use of 'it took . . . quite a long time' signals to the reader that that time has passed, and therefore, by now, linguistics is "more formally recognized as an important element of peace." However, one of the recurring themes in this NPL book is that the formal recognition of the importance of the in-depth study of language in peace and conflict research has not happened yet (apart from on a small scale) and is still very much a work-in-progress. Friedrich and Gomes de Matos' comment about the "ubiquitous nature of language," relative to the recognition of the importance of linguistics, echoes Nunan's observation made in *What Is This Thing Called Language?* (2013) (see Chapter 2). In that book, Nunan concluded that: "most of us remain largely ignorant [at the conscious level] of this phenomenon [language] that defines us as humans" (p. 200), in spite of the fact that most of us spend much of our lives speaking, listening, reading or writing. In *Nonkilling Linguistics* Friedrich and Gomes de Matos (2012a) put it this way: "Language is so intricately connected to human experience that it...permeate[s] all aspects of our lives...Yet, we often take language for granted and *fail to recognize its power* and reach, and we often trivialize its use" (p. 20, emphasis added). Friedrich and Gomes de Matos (2012a) put forward a case for not only seeing language as important, but also that: "In a nonkilling society, *language must play a pivotal role as a tool for peace*" (p. 20, emphasis added).

In *Nonkilling Linguistics* (2012a) Friedrich and Gomes de Matos (2012) proposed two principles and made two pleas. The two principles are: "Language is a system for communicating in nonkilling ways," and "Language users should have the right to learn to communicate nonkillingly for the good of humankind" (p. 21). The two pleas are: "Let us be communicative Humanizers, treating all language users with compassion and dignity," and "Let us opt for communicatively nonkilling uses of language" (p. 21). Although those are indeed laudable principles and heartfelt pleas, an important question is: Where is the linguistics in those principles and pleas? Of Friedrich and Gomes de Matos' (2012a) 13 educational practices, two explicitly refer to linguistics (pp. 25–26). The first practice is phrased as a response to the question "When do we kill a person linguistically?" (p. 25), the answer to which is: "When we antagonize, coerce, desecrate, frighten with threats of harm, intimidate violently, oppress, provoke in a violent way, exclude from our network" (p. 25). The second practice is also presented as a question-and-answer sequence, but in an equal and opposite direction, posing the question "How can we humanize a person linguistically?" (p. 25), and answering it: "When we refer to him or her in admiring respectful ways" (p. 25). Those ways including calling him/her, for example, "a creative genius, a luminary, a mentor, a patriot, a prodigy, a role model...a virtuoso, a visionary, a prophet" (p. 25). While all of those ways of referring to someone are certainly admiring, respectful and dignifying, the term 'peace linguist' should really only apply to those who engage in the in-depth, systematic analysis of language.

REACT 4.3: *If you are an educator, you might set 'deadlines' for your students, by which time they have to have completed assigned work. However, 'deadline' might be an example of 'killing' language (according to Gomes de Matos). Instead, you could use, for example, 'due dates.' What are some of the pros and cons of using phrases like 'due dates' instead of words like 'deadlines'?*

The most telling example of the difference between language and linguistics is the fact that Friedrich and Gomes de Matos' (2012a) chapter, while offering much useful advice on how language should and could be used, no texts are presented (written or spoken) and no language is analyzed in their chapter, even though it is titled *Nonkilling Linguistics* (2012). There is some creative use of language, and readers of their chapter are encouraged to come up with "constructive alliterations" (Principle 4, p. 25), for example, "AAA = Activate life-Affirming assertions; MMM = Monitor manipulative messages (in the media); TTT = Transform tension into tranquility; VVV = Value a vital vocabulary" (p. 26). But creative language play is not linguistics, unless the language is analyzed, rather than just given, in this case, as a useful mnemonic or aide memoire. Some confusion may be due to the fact that the word 'linguistics', in its most general sense, can be used to mean something—maybe anything—to do with language, but in its academic, scholarly and technical sense, it refers to the systematic study of language. A key point here is: *Language is not Linguistics.* Language is the stuff we make and use to communicate with each other and with ourselves. Linguistics is the systematic study and analysis of that stuff (see Nunan 2013).

In this chapter we have addressed the question: How is the 'new' Peace Linguistics different from the 'old' Peace Linguistics? We have also considered some of the features and characteristics of NPL that show how it can help to bridge the gap between the bodies of work that have come before, and the work that we are doing now. On the one hand, there is the work that has been referred to as 'Peace Linguistics' although there was little or no evidence of linguistic analysis. On the other is the work that has employed some kinds of peace/war-oriented linguistic analyses, but which have not used the term 'Peace Linguistics'. For the remainder of this book, we will be referring to and focusing on the New Peace Linguistics (NPL).

REACT 4.4: *If you are a language educator, what are some of the ways in which you could modify your use of written and spoken language to make it more peaceful, keeping in mind the languages of peace-building, peace-keeping and peace-making.*

Suggestions for Further Reading

The (170-page) online book *Nonkilling Linguistics: Practical Applications* (Friedrich, 2012b) referred to above is freely available at the link below. As well as Friedrich and Gomes de Matos's chapter, 'Toward a Nonkilling Linguistics', there are also chapters on 'Teaching Peace Peacefully' by Lauren Chamberlain, 'Comparative Linguistic Law and Nonkilling Linguistics' by Joseph-Giuseppe Turi, and 'Applied Nonkilling Linguistics in the Developmental Composition Classroom' by James Whitton. http://w.nonkilling.org/pdf/nklinguistics.pdf

In the book *English for Diplomatic Purposes* (2016, Multilingual Matters), edited by Patricia Friedrich, there is a chapter, 'World Englishes and Peace Linguistics: Their Contribution to English for Diplomatic Purposes' (pp. 94–108), written by Friedrich. Although there is little language analysis, there are some helpful suggestions for how English might be used diplomatically, for example, when introducing yourself and others, and when exchanging pleasantries.

Details of the organization, Earth and Peace Education International, of which Anita Wenden was the co-founder and president, can be found at http://www.globalepe.org/. According the organization's website: "EPE's educational activities aim to contribute to the achievement of a culture of social and ecological peace, i.e., a society whose norms are based on ecological sustainability, nonviolence, social justice, intergenerational equity and participatory decision-making."

PART II

New Peace Linguistics Analyses of the Language of George W. Bush, Colin L. Powell, and Barack H. Obama

5

Othering, Justifying, and Denying

In this chapter, we begin with an NPL analysis of what may be, in terms of war and peace, one of the most important speeches given by a world leader in the last 20 years—the declaration by the USA of the War on Terror, following the attacks in and on the USA on September 11, 2001, in which nearly 3,000 people were killed, and 6,000 more injured. That declaration exemplified one of the most effective ways of using language to justify conflict, which is to engage in 'othering'. We will, then, present a detailed account of the language of othering, including the identification of 'in-group' and 'out-group' status and membership, as reflected in the use of inclusive or exclusive language, including pronouns and other parts of speech. We then carry out an NPL analysis of the speech given by the President of the USA on September 20, 2001—nine days after the 9/11 terrorist attacks.

In the second part of this chapter, we take a longitudinal view of the language of an individual in a position of great power, Secretary of State Colin Powell, who took the USA into a war—at best unnecessarily, and at worst under false pretenses—largely as a result of the language he used when

The New Peace Linguistics and The Role of Language in Conflict, pages 83–104

addressing the U.N. Security Council, during a historic speech he gave in 2003. That address is analyzed here, partly because it is an example of how a single speech can lead to the loss of up to 200,000 lives, showing how powerful and how destructive this kind of language can be. In addition, the language used by Powell over 14 years, between 2003 and 2016—the same person describing the same event—also shows how language can be used to engage in shielding oneself from the consequences of one's actions. That kind of language is of interest in NPL analyses, as such language can be used by powerful people to justify their actions, to others and to themselves, no matter how catastrophic the consequences.

A Brief Introduction to the Language of Othering

Regarding perspective and distance, there are times when being far away can help us see things more clearly than being up-close. That may be the case with the speech that George W. Bush (GWB), the 43rd President of the USA (2001–2009) gave to a joint session of Congress 20 years ago, on September 20, 2001—nine long days and nights after the 9/11 terrorist attack, and less than eight months into what would be an eight-year presidential term. In some ways, it is as if time stopped during the moments of the 9/11 attack, with the weeks, months and years being counted as Before 9/11 or After 9/11. For example, in *Muslims in a Post-9/11 America: A Survey of Attitudes and Beliefs and Their Implications for US National Security Policy* (2018), Rachel Gillum explained that: "The ratcheting up of security measures following the 9/11 attacks changed the way of life for all Americans, restricting some civil liberties in exchange for security" (2018, p. 3). The 9/11 attacks also became one of the main recurring talking points during the 2016 presidential elections in the USA, when DJT, "on his campaign website and in several media appearances, called for a total and complete shutdown of Muslims entering the United States" (Gillum, 2018, p. 3).

The permanent after-effects of the 9/11 attack are discussed in Tugrul Keskin's 2018 book, *Middle East Studies after September 11: Neo Orientalism, American Hegemony and Academia*—and it is worth noting that it is not necessary to specify which year is being referred to by *September 11*, as though there were only one. On the 18th Anniversary of the attacks, John Barron, writing for *The New York Times*, likened the date to "personal memories as powerful as those associated with Nov. 22, 1963, the Friday on which President John F. Kennedy was assassinated, or perhaps Jan. 28, 1986, the Tuesday on which the space shuttle Challenger exploded . . . a minute after takeoff" (Barron, 2019). For many millions of people, the world as we (thought we) knew it changed on September 11, 2001, in fundamental ways that we are still living with today—and as with all such fundamental changes, the language changed too.

The State of the Union Address (SOTU) is an annual event, in which the President of the USA addresses a joint session of the US Congress, usually given at the beginning of the calendar year. However, as a result of the 9/11 attacks, a second such session was held on September, 20, 2001, as the culmination of a number of live, televised speeches given by GWB to the people of the USA, and the world, immediately following the September 11 attacks. In his opening remarks GWB said: "Mr. Speaker, Mr. President Pro Tempore, members of Congress, and fellow Americans, in the normal course of events, presidents come to this chamber to report on the state of the union. Tonight, no such report is needed; it has already been delivered by the American people." Looking at that speech event through an NPL lens, we can see that what followed is an exemplar of linguistic othering.

A relatively recent entry into mainstream dictionaries, 'othering' is defined as: "to treat or consider (a person or a group of people) as alien to oneself or one's group (because of different racial, sexual, or cultural characteristics)" (*Merriam-Webster*, 2021). That dictionary entry also gives a powerful example of the messages that can be communicated by such othering, from the Black American Pulitzer Prize-winning and Nobel Prize-winning author, Toni Morrison (1931–2019): "I am a black writer struggling with and through a language that can powerfully evoke and enforce hidden signs of racial superiority, cultural hegemony, and dismissive 'othering' of people" (*Merriam-Webster*, 2021).

Before the term 'othering' caught on, pioneering Dutch text linguist, Teun van Dijk (b. 1943) published his extensive study of *Elite Discourse and Racism* (1993), in which he discussed how language is used to include or exclude individuals and groups in political discourse. In his work, van Dijk drew on that of William Du Bois (1868–1963), the first African-American to earn a doctorate from Harvard University, and one of the founders of the National Association for the Advancement of Colored People (NAACP, www.naacp.org) in 1909. van Dijk stated that: "As predicted by W.E.B. Du Bois in 1903, race and ethnic affairs have been and continue to be a major political issue throughout the twentieth century (Du Bois, 1969)" (van Dijk, 1993, p. 49). van Dijk also advocated for "a closer analysis of the discourse of political elites on these issues" (p. 49), which is one of the goals of NPL. In a later work, van Dijk (2006) reported that: "The ideological polarization between ingroups and outgroups . . . may also be systematically studied at all levels of text and talk" (p. 115), for example, "by analysing how members of ingroups typically emphasize their own good deeds and properties and the bad ones of the outgroup, and mitigate or deny their own bad ones and the good ones of the outgroup" (p. 115). As we will see, in GWB's September 20, 2001 speech, extensive use was made of the extremely simplistic but nonetheless equally effective formulae: in-group = good people, out-group = bad people. In that kind of language formulation, 'differentness is synonymous with 'dangerous', while at the same time 'differentness' can also be seen as an essential aspect of diversity. (See Prado, Uguralp-Cannon, Green, Harrison, & Smith, 2021, on seeking connection through difference.)

Following the work of van Dijk (1993), an important early collection of works on othering was published in 1997 and edited by Stephen Riggins, *The Language and Politics of Exclusion: Others in Discourse.* That book is based on 10 case studies of language, politics and exclusion from Canada, the Netherlands, Austria and Mexico. Related to the inherent interdisciplinarity of NPL, the contributors to the collection came from anthropology, communications, discourse studies, linguistics, and law. Based on those case studies, Riggins found that: "expressions that are most revealing of the boundaries separating Self and Other are inclusive and exclusive pronouns and possessives such as we and they, us and them, and ours and theirs" (1997, p. 8). And referring to the relationships between language analysis and politics, Riggins stated that: "Most critical discourse analysts take an explicit political stance, identifying with those who lack the institutional levers to produce counter-discourses, and their ultimate motivation appears to be the hope that their work will contribute to social emancipation" (1997, pp. 2–3). "Most [CD] analysts" may have been an optimistic over-estimation on the part of Riggins, and also about the hope that critical discourse analysis could "contribute to social emancipation." But it is possible that a greater understanding of how language is used by those in power to communicate with and/or to manipulate those with less/little power may lead to a more critically aware populace. We might then not be as easily persuaded to adopt a Them-vs.-Us mindset, in which 'They' are 'The Enemy', against whom 'We' must 'fight the good fight with all thy might' (as the title of the 1860s Christian hymn by John Monsell (1811–1875) put it).

The essential role that language plays in othering should be self-evident, as we can state that: *language may exist without othering, but othering cannot exist without language.* An example of this language-dependent aspect of othering is studies of 'multiethnolects'; a three-part portmanteau made up of: multiple + ethnicity + dialect. The term 'multiethnolects' was coined by Professor Michael Clyne (1939–2010, see Chapter 4), working in Australia (2000), and by Professor Pia Quist (2008), working in Denmark. Building on that work, and based on a linguistic analysis of "the politics of representation and exclusion" (Pandey, 2004, p. 153) among approximately

100 freshman compositions at a US university, Professor Anjali Pandey put forward a framework for "constructing otherness" (p. 153) based on five lexico-syntactic strategies:

> a) Lexical strategies: overt denigration; b) Distance markers: voice and speaking space; c) Declaratives: constructing semantic overgeneralizations in and through syntax: stereotypes; d) Linguistic contrasts and qualifications: positive self-representation vs. negative other presentation; e) The use of passive voice and other syntactic strategies: mitigated and disguised othering. (Pandey, 2004, p. 161)

Of those five strategies, the one that is most relevant in the analysis of GWB's 2001 speech is "positive self-representation vs. negative other presentation", which relates to the in-group = good, out-group = bad formula mentioned above. Drawing on Pandey's (2004) work, Nilsen, Fylkesnes and Mausethagen (2017) looked at how Norwegian teacher educators talked about cultural diversity, in relation to "the linguistics in othering." Nilsen *et al.* (2017) define 'othering' as, "the manner in which social group dichotomies are represented in language via binary oppositions of 'us' and 'them'" (p. 40). In their analysis of what they referred to as "the discourse practice of othering" (p. 44), Nilsen *et al.* found seven such practices: "cultural, social, cognitive, multilingual, migrational, visible and religious" (p. 45), based on the pronouns: they, this, these, those, and your.

One of the multiethnolects that has been researched in recent years (Kircher & Fox, 2019) was called, by Professor Heike Wiese, at the University of Potsdam in Germany, 'Kiezdeutsch'. Wiese describes 'Kiezdeutsch' as "a new way of speaking in multilingual urban neighbourhoods" (2015, p. 341) in Germany, which she contrasts with "an idealised standard language 'High German'", in contrast to the "Othering of Kiezdeutsch and its speakers" (p. 341). Wiese concluded that: "Language seems to be one of the final hide-outs where openly racist remarks are still socially acceptable in modern society", making language "a very powerful domain for the construction of social out-groups" (p. 363). Drawing on William Labov's early work on Black English (1982), Wiese states that: "as linguists we should contribute to exposing such [in-group/out-group] projections... in public discourse" (p. 363), which is one of goals of NPL, especially the public discourse of those in positions of power, such as presidents and other world leaders.

In 'Othering Obama: Racial Attitudes and Dubious Beliefs about the Nation's First Black President', Daniel Tope and his co-researchers (Tope, Pickett, Cobb & Dirlam, 2014) found that, from a sociological perspective: "An important theme in the race literature has been that... racial language has become more subtle and opaque" (p. 451). However, one of the changes that appears to have taken place since the publication of their paper, and since the 2016 Presidential Election in the USA, is that race-related and racialized language has become (much) less subtle and (much) more obvious. Nevertheless, the research by Tope *et al.* (2014) shed some light on how othering is not always done *by those* in power *to those* without power. For example, in the case of the 44th President of the USA (2009–2017), Barack Obama, the othering was being done to one of the most powerful people in the world, by those who wished to be in power and/or those who wished Obama was not the President.

Another important change since 2014 has been Tope *et al.*'s finding that: "Changes in acceptable language have *diminished* conduits for the political expression of traditional overt racism" (2014, p. 453, emphasis added). As we will see in Part III, "political expressions of... overt racism" may have, in fact, *grown significantly*. For example, in 2018, the United Nations Special Rapporteur on Contemporary Forms of Racism, Racial Discrimination, Xenophobia and Related Intolerance, Professor Tendayi Achiume, found that racism in Britain had become significantly more prominent and more acceptable since the UK voted, in 2016, to leave the European Union in 2019 (Dearden, 2018). And in 2019, a study published by the American Educational Research Association reported that: "For every 10 percentage point increase in voter support for Trump, the researchers found an 8 percent rise in reported bullying and a 5 percent increase in bullying because of a student's race or ethnicity" compared with the researchers' findings that there were "no meaningful differences in school bullying rates between Democratic and Republican localities prior to the 2016 presidential election" (Busby, 2019). Tope *et al.* (2014) concluded that: "racial sentiments—both overt and symbolic—continue to play a major role in politics and in evaluations of prominent political figures" (p. 463). That conclusion reiterates the importance of linguistic analyses in helping to understand the messages being communicated, as those "racial sentiments", especially when overt, cannot be expressed without language—language that has been carefully designed to target specific groups, and even particular individuals, such as the first Black President of the USA, and his supporters of color.

An important concluding point in this discussion of the language of othering is that, in the same way there are different kinds of warist discourse (See Chapter 3), some potentially more negative or more positive, not all collective pronouns are used to exclude in a them-vs-us way. An example of 'negative othering' would be, for example, when a president says: "Why do they hate us?... They hate what they see right here... a democratically elected government... They hate our freedoms: our freedom of religion, our freedom of speech, our freedom to vote and assemble and disagree with each other" (see below). Hate may indeed have been in the hearts of the terrorists who carried out the 9/11 attacks on the USA in 2001. But posing the question in the form of "Why do they hate us?" may appear to strongly imply that *all of them* hate *all of us*, which could constitute a potentially dangerous over-generalization of approximately two billion Muslims around the world, and millions of people across the USA.

Although it is unlikely that anything like 'positive othering' exists, an opposite intent can also be expressed using the same language, i.e., using the same collectivizing pronouns, but in a way that promotes the idea that, 'we are all in this difficult situation together, so we must work together to make it better'. For example, when a president says to their inaugural audience (see Chapter 12): "With unity we can do great things. Important things . . . We can teach our children in safe schools. We can overcome this deadly virus . . . We can . . . make health care secure for all. We can deliver racial justice." Whether or not such lofty goals can actually be achieved is open to question, but the use of collective pronoun phases such as 'we can' and 'our children' reminds the audience of their shared goals and common struggles, as opposed to stressing the differences, to sow the seeds of division, for personal and political gain. Therefore, the opposite of 'othering' could be 'ouring'. (See Wei & Zhou, 2021, for recent research on othering in universities, involving international faculty and international students.)

REACT 5.1: *What are some of the groups that you belong to and identify with—personally and professionally? Are there words and phrases that have special meaning within those groups? Can you give any examples of how some groups can use language to exclude outsiders or to include insiders?*

An NPL Analysis of the Address Given by President George Bush on September 20, 2001

We can now return to the speech given by GWB to a joint session of Congress on September 20, 2001, nine days after the 9/11 terrorist attacks (referred to in this chapter as the War on Terror Address, abbreviated to 'WoTA'). As discussed above, GWB started by stating that the report on the state of the union was not needed as it had "already been delivered by the American people." The next four opening statements all begin with 'We have seen/We've seen', thereby creating images of a shared vision:

> *We have seen* it [the SOTU] in the courage of passengers who rushed terrorists to save others on the ground . . . *We have seen* the state of our union

in the endurance of rescuers working past exhaustion... *We've seen* the unfurling of flags, the lighting of candles, the giving of blood, the saying of prayers in English, Hebrew and Arabic... *We have seen* the decency of a loving and giving people who have made the grief of strangers their own" (emphases added).

'The' is the most commonly occurring word in English (Schumacher, 2020). However, even taking that frequency into account, 'the' occurs ten times in those few opening lines: "the courage... the ground... the state... the endurance... the unfurling... the lighting... the giving... the saying... the decency... the grief." The use of 'the' so many times in a relatively short stretch of text not only adds emphasis but also gives a rhythm, especially when repeated with 'of', in this case, eight times: "the state of... the endurance of... the unfurling of... the lighting of... the giving of... the saying of... the decency of... the grief of." Of the eight instances of [the + of] four employ the present participle '-ing' form of the verbs: "unfurling... lighting... giving... saying", emphasizing the active and immediate nature—the 'nowness'—of those actions. The idea that language is layered, in the sense of 'layers of meaning', is commonly accepted (Kellett, 2007), and research has been carried out on 'linguistic layering' in, for example, language development and digital technologies (Domingo, 2012). And in our NPL analyses of the 'We have seen' passage above, we also employed a kind of layered approach, starting with identifying the sentence-initial 'We have seen', followed by the repetition of the definite article, then the use 'of', and lastly the present participle of some of the verbs.

GWB concluded his opening remarks, composed of six main statements, made up of a total of approximately 170 words, by saying: "My fellow citizens, for the last nine days, the entire world has seen for itself the state of our union, and it is strong"—not referring to '*the* union', as is unusual, but to '*our* union'. Those opening lines from the President that day did what they needed to do, which was to reassure a traumatized nation of people, some of whom had perhaps grown used to thinking of their country as 'invincible', that the USA was still strong, in spite of such a strike at the heart of their nation. Those opening lines also recognized the sacrifices made by those up in the air and those on the ground, as well as "the saying of prayers" in three of the world's most widely used languages, English, Hebrew and Arabic, thereby including a large part of the world's population. Also, by including Arabic, the first language of the 9/11 terrorists, GWB was distinguishing between the terrorists and the rest of the Arabic-using world. Therefore, from an NPL perspective, what we can see in these opening lines is the use of language, in this case, by a world leader during a time of crisis, to comfort as well as to condemn. And one of the goals of NPL is to be able to more clearly identify when and where, how and why such language is being used.

Professor Leeat Granek, a specialist in studying grief and loss, at the Ben-Gurion University of the Negev, in Israel, included the above opening lines of GWB's speech in her study of what she refers to as "mourning sickness" in "the politicizations of grief" (Granek, 2014, p. 61). In her analysis of GWB's September 20, 2001 speech, Granek found that he: "liberally used the words 'grief, 'mourning,' and 'losses' throughout his talk as a strong justification for revenge, 'justice,' and what later became extremely violent action in the war against Iraq" (Granek, 2014, p. 65). Granek points out that such language can not only be used to justify war, but it can also be used by those who oppose war: "in the years following 9/11 when the rhetoric of the nation's grief as a justification for war increased by the American government, the political uses of the affect were also taken up by antiwar activists opposing the war" (p. 65). Although Granek takes a medical approach to such uses of language, identifying three types of "mourning sickness," and she does not mention othering, it is clear that the repeated use of "we," in "we have seen" is designed to emphasize what might be called the "Us-ness" of the in-group, which can then be set in opposition to the "Them-ness" of the out-group.

Following the opening four 'We' statements, GWB added two more, combining 'we' with 'our': "Tonight, *we* are a country awakened to danger and called to defend freedom. *Our* grief has turned to anger and anger to resolution. Whether *we* bring *our* enemies to justice or bring justice to *our* enemies, justice will be done." In addition, the use of 'justice' three times—twice to be brought and once to be done—presents a desire for revenge, although understandable under the circumstances, as a need for justice, which is a clever conflation, as justice and revenge are not the same thing at all. Indeed, as the clinical psychologist, Dr. Leon Seltzer, warned: "Revenge can masquerade as justice, but it frequently ends up perverting it" (2014). In Seltzer's analysis, revenge is emotional, personal, vindictive, cyclical, and retaliatory, whereas, in contrast, justice is rational, impersonal/impartial, about vindication, about closure, and about restoring balance.

REACT 5.2: *Think of a time when someone wronged or offended you. How did you respond? What kind of language did you use, to talk to the person who wronged you, or to process the experience with an intra-personal dialog? Now, think of a time when you wronged or offended someone. What did you say? What kind of language did you use that time?*

The collectivization of GWB's audience continued, this time through the repeated use of 'we will not', starting with: "We will not forget South

Korean children gathering to pray outside our embassy in Seoul, or the prayers of sympathy offered at a mosque in Cairo." Here, GWB consciously and carefully included an indirect reference to Muslims and Islam, by talking about "a mosque in Cairo", which helps to balance some of the othering, by being seen/heard to acknowledge an essential aspect of the 9/11 terrorists, i.e., their religion. Continuing the 'we will not' sequence, while including three continents, GWB went on to say: "We will not forget moments of silence and days of mourning in Australia and Africa and Latin America." Expanding on the idea that the 9/11 attacks were not an attack on the USA but an attack on the entire world, GWB went on to give some facts and figures which recognized the loss of non-US lives, using a variation of the 'we will not' formula: "Nor will we forget the citizens of 80 other nations who died...Dozens of Pakistanis, more than 130 Israelis, more than 250 citizens of India, [people] from El Salvador, Iran, Mexico and Japan, and hundreds of British citizens." In terms of rhythm, the three-part monosyllabic beat of 'we will not' is preserved in the 'nor will we' formulation. The collectivization pronouns then shift from 'we' to 'our', to which is added 'country': "On September the 11th, enemies of freedom committed an act of war against *our country*...Americans have many questions tonight. Americans are asking, 'Who attacked *our country*?'" (emphases added).

Some countries and organizations are then identified as being targets for retaliation, including "the Egyptian Islamic Jihad" "the Islamic Movement of Uzbekistan" and Afghanistan, which was believed to be the base of Al-Qaeda, a militant, international Sunni Islamist organization founded in 1988 by Osama bin Laden, who was identified as the person who planned the 9/11 attacks. (Ten years later, in 2011, bin Laden was reportedly shot and killed in Pakistan by US soldiers.) GWB also referred to the Taliban, aligned with Al-Qaeda and based in Afghanistan, and issued a dire warning: "The Taliban must act and act immediately. They will hand over the terrorists or they will share in their fate." However, again, GWB did appear to be distinguishing between the terrorists who were Muslims, who claimed to be acting in the name of their god, and the rest of the Islamic world: "The enemy of America is not our many Muslim friends. It is not our many Arab friends. Our enemy is a radical network of terrorists and every government that supports them." And again, we see the thrice-repeated use of 'our', in "our many Muslim friends" and "our many Arab friends" contrasted with "Our enemy." There is also a tripartite use of 'they' (and one 'their') to refer to "thousands of these terrorists in more than 60 countries": "*They are* recruited from *their* own nations and neighborhoods and brought to camps...where *they are* trained in the tactics of terror. *They are* sent...to hide in countries around the world to plot evil and destruction" (emphases added). The use of the present simple tense, 'they are', reiterates the 'nowness' of the recruiting, training, hiding and plotting, happening as the speaker is delivering his message.

At approximately two-fifths of the way into his WoTA (at approx. 1,200 of 3,000 words), GWB went into them-vs.-us 'othering overdrive', with more than a dozen uses of 'they' and 'their' in close succession, beginning with a repetition of his earlier "Americans are asking", followed this time, instead of, "Who attacked our country?", by "Why do *they* hate *us*?" (emphases added). GWB answered his rhetorical question with a three-part [they + their + they] contrasted with four 'ours': "They hate what they see right here... a democratically elected government. Their leaders are self-appointed. They hate *our* freedoms: *our* freedom of religion, *our* freedom of speech, *our* freedom to vote and assemble and disagree with each other." That results in the concentration of seven other-our pronouns (three 'others', four 'ours') in just 40 or so words, which was followed by another threesome of 'they-ing': "They want to overthrow existing governments in many Muslim countries such as Egypt, Saudi Arabia and Jordan. They want to drive Israel out of the Middle East. They want to drive Christians and Jews out of... Asia and Africa." While such statements may well have been true at the time, the language of othering is nonetheless one of the most prominent linguistic aspects of GWB's WoTA.

The multiple uses of 'they' and 'their' continued: "These terrorists kill not merely to end lives, but to disrupt and end a way of life... they hope that America grows fearful, retreating... and forsaking *our* friends. They stand against us because *we* stand in their way." Breaking that down, we can see the following pattern: [these + they vs. *our*] + [they vs. *we* vs. their]. The next line adds some alliteration to the we-their division: "We're not deceived by their pretenses to piety", using the contracted form of 'we're' instead of the more formal full-form 'we are', perhaps to sound more natural, although probably deliberately not conversational. The last one-third of this 220-word chunk of textual othering builds to a high-point, which began with: "*We* have seen their kind before. They're the heirs of all the murderous ideologies of the 20th century." That was followed by: "By sacrificing human life to serve their radical visions, by abandoning every value except the will to power, they follow in the path of fascism, Nazism and totalitarianism"—invoking the unholy trinity of evil ideologies that may have been feared most by many Americans, as well as the homophonic use of 'their' and 'they're'. The climax of this part of the text is: "And they will follow that path all the way to where it ends in history's unmarked grave of discarded lies", wrapped-up with the third rhetorical question after "Who attacked *our* country?" and "Why do *they* hate *us*?": "Americans are asking, 'How will *we* fight and win this war?'"

After asking the third Wh-question above, GWB employed an inverted version of his 'we will not', in a series of statements designed to show strength, starting with: "*We will* direct every resource at our command... to the destruction and to the defeat of the global terror network", with 'every' repeated five more times between "command" and network", for emphasis. Some key 'we will' statements followed, including: "We will starve terrorists of funding, turn them one against another, drive them from place to place until there is no refuge or no rest", identifying three actions (starve, turn, drive), and ending the sentence with a two-part negative alliteration (no refuge/rest) for rhythmic momentum.

As noted earlier, one of the single most important statements in this speech is: "And we will pursue nations that provide aid or safe haven to terrorism. Every nation in every region now has a decision to make: *Either you are with us or you are with the terrorists*" (emphasis added). That statement effectively presented all of the countries of the world with a dichotomous, mutually exclusive and polarized good-bad, right-wrong, black-white world, ignoring the fact that a country could condemn the 9/11 terrorist attacks but not condone starting a war, leading to the loss of yet more lives. The origins of these kinds of false dichotomies have a long history, usually in the context of an armed conflict of one kind of another. For example, in the Old Testament of the *Bible*, it is written: "And it came to pass, when Joshua was by Jericho, that he lifted up his eyes and looked, and, behold, there stood a man over against him with his sword drawn in his hand: and Joshua went unto him, and said unto him, *Art thou for us, or for our adversaries*?" (Book of Joshua, Chapter 5, Verse 13, emphasis added). These kinds of false you're-either-with-us-or-against-us dichotomies may be especially dangerous, as they rule out any possibility of finding a middle ground or common ground on which mutual understanding can be built, and which can lead to less armed conflict rather than more.

The point was made above that one of the goals of this speech by GWB was to 'rally the troops', in both the literal as well as the metaphorical sense, and to highlight the global nature of the 9/11 attacks. To that end, GWB used a series of alternating 'is-is not' constructions, made up of [is-not + is + is-not + is + is + is], saying: "This is not... just America's fight. And what is at stake is not just America's freedom. This is the world's fight. This is civilization's fight. This is the fight of all who believe in progress and pluralism, tolerance and freedom." Such a construction, assisted by the double-p alliteration of "progress and pluralism", drives the sentence forward, while including all those "who believe" in those four espoused values of the USA. The culminating line, following "freedom", starts: "We ask every nation to join us", which may have been seen by many nations as less of an invitation and more of a command. GWB then expanded on his theme of a 'global fight', saying: "Perhaps the NATO charter reflects best the attitude of the world: *An attack on one is an attack on all.* The civilized world is rallying to America's side" (emphasis added), strongly implying that any part of the world that is not rallying to the side of the USA is, by definition, 'not civilized'.

As the conclusion of GWB's WoTA approached (at around the 2,400-word mark), he employed a particular five-word phrase five times in little more than 100 words:

> *We will come together to* improve air safety... *We will come together to* promote stability and keep our airlines flying... *We will come together to* give law enforcement the additional tools it needs to track down terror here at home... *We will come together to* strengthen our intelligence capabilities to know the plans of terrorists before they act... *We will come together to* take active steps that strengthen America's economy and put *our people* back to work (emphases added).

After the five-time use of the five-word phrase, "We will come together to...," the climax continued to build, within a piece of text fewer than 100 words, but with nine 'our' phrases run together: "our grief... our mission... our moment... our time... our nation... our people... our future... our efforts... our courage." In addition to those nine-fold instances of 'ours', the same short stretch of text also includes five uses of the we/us formula, culminating with a three-part 'we will not' and a double-f alliteration: "We will not tire, we will not falter and we will not fail." It is important to see how these phrases work in concert and in context:

> Great harm has been done <u>to us</u>. <u>We have</u> suffered great loss. And in *our grief* and anger <u>we have</u> found *our mission* and *our moment*... the great achievement of *our time* and the great hope of every time, now depends <u>on us</u>... *Our nation*, this generation, will lift the dark threat of violence from *our people* and *our future*. <u>We will</u> rally the world to this cause by *our efforts*, by *our courage.*

The first person singular, 'I', was used carefully and sparingly throughout GWB's WoTA, far less than the collective we/us/our or the othering they/them/their(s) pronouns. The first I-cluster was made up of three phrases in the introduction, expressing gratitude (between the first 200 and 300 words of the speech). The first instance was: "*I* thank the Congress for its leadership at such an important time", then, referring to four of his deputies (Speaker Hastert, Minority Leader Gephardt, Majority Leader Daschle, and Senator Lott): "*I* thank *you* for your friendship, for *your* leadership and for *your* service to *our* country", which can be shown as: [1 'I' + 1 'you' + 2 'your' + 1 'our'). That sequence built up to: "And on behalf of the American people, I thank the world for its outpouring of support." More thanks were also given by GWB, in a later part of the speech (at approx. 2,300 words into the WoTA), emphasizing actions taken and to be taken, past and future, individually and collectively: "*I thank my fellow Americans* for what *you have already done* and for *what you will do*... [members of] the Congress, *I thank you*, their representatives, *for what you have already done* and for *what we will do together*."

Giving thanks while announcing war can certainly seem at least somewhat contradictory, but expressing gratitude may also be an important aspect of this kind of political speech-giving, especially during times of large-scale loss and tragedy. The origins of phrase, 'my fellow Americans', which would be recognized by the audience as an historical, presidential honorific, dates back to Lyndon B. Johnson (Fraga, 2018) (1908–1973), the 36th president of the USA, from 1963 to 1969. In relation to language and gender inclusivity, it is worth noting that for a long time 'fellow' referred to males only, with the expansion to include everyone coming later. The next I-cluster does not occur until approx. 1,700 words into the speech, with two announcements plus two 'I have' actions, to emphasize the taking of action by the person in charge, as well as asking others to carry out their commands:

> So tonight, *I announce* the creation of a Cabinet-level position *reporting directly to me,* the Office of Homeland Security. And tonight, *I also announce* a distinguished American to lead this effort, to strengthen American security...And tonight a few miles from the damaged Pentagon, *I have* a message for our military: Be ready. *I have* called the armed forces to alert, and there is a reason (emphases added)

There is also an emphasis here on strength ("to strengthen American security"), on preparedness ("Be ready"), and on danger ("called...to alert"), together with a reminder of some of the physical, structural damage done during the 9/11 attacks ("the damaged Pentagon").

The third I-cluster occurs approx. two-thirds into the speech (at around 2,100 words), in reply to GWB's rhetorical question: "Americans are asking, 'What is expected of us?'" to which he replied with seven 'asks', using language which is personalized, in the sense of one person asking another for help, using 'I ask you to': "*I ask you to* live your lives and hug your children...and *I ask you to* be calm and resolute, even in the face of a continuing threat. *I ask you to* uphold the values of America and remember why so many have come here." The reference to 'American family values' implies a coherent set of such values across a vast and diverse population, which may not apply to everyone, but which are also not unique to the USA. Those first three 'action asks', in which the audience or listener is being asked to do something, were followed by two more: "*I ask you to* continue to support the victims of this tragedy with your contributions... The thousands of FBI agents who are now at work in this investigation may need your cooperation, and *I ask you to* give it."

Those five 'action asks' were followed by what can be called 'for asks' or 'asks for', as the speaker is asking the listener *for* something, rather than asking the listeners *to do* something: "*I ask for your* patience with the delays and inconveniences that may accompany tighter security and *for your* patience in what will be a long struggle. *I ask for your* continued participation and confidence in the American economy." Here, GWB, was in effect asking his listeners to act by doing nothing, i.e., by being patient, which is balanced by his request for action, i.e., participation, making this a balanced equal-opposite set of requests, i.e., requests to his audience to do and not-do, to be and not-be.

The fourth and final set of I-clusters comes at the end of the speech, in the form of four sets of 'I will not' plus four verbs: 'forget' and 'yield', as well as the alliterative 'rest' and 'relent': "*I will not* forget the wound to *our* country and those who inflicted it. *I will not* yield, *I will not* rest, *I will not* relent in waging this struggle for freedom and security for the American people." Those phrases emphasize the personal commitment being made by GWB to take actions himself, as well as giving presidential commands that others act too. It is also important to note that, rather than 'waging war', GWB instead referred to the coming War on Terror as "waging this struggle." The last two lines of the speech returned to the now-familiar pattern of [We + Our + Us]: "Fellow citizens, *we'll* meet violence with patient justice, assured of the rightness of *our* cause and confident of the victories to come. In all that lies before *us*, may God grant *us* wisdom and may He watch over the United States of America. Thank you." Those last words, rallying and comforting though they may have been, also recall Granek's (2014) observation, discussed above, about equating justice and rightness with revenge and retribution.

REACT 5.3: *Video recordings of the speech given by GWB, on September 20, 2001 can be found online, for example, on the C-Span network and on YouTube. Listen to a few minutes of the recording and make notes on where the speaker pauses, when the audience applauds, and other moments of interaction between the speaker and the audience. What additional understandings can you gain from watching and hearing those moments, in addition to reading the transcript?*

An NPL Analysis of the Address Given by Colin Powell on September 5, 2003

It is not only the speeches of presidents that can have global repercussions. A case in point is the 90-minute presentation given by the 65th Secretary of State of the USA, Colin Luther Powell (CLP; sworn-in in January 2001) to the United Nations Security Council, in New York City, on February 5, 2003 (referred to in this chapter as the Weapons of Mass Destruction Address, abbreviated to 'WoMDA'). Not only was that speech one of the most important ever given by a US Secretary of State, but it also shows how the language of the same person talking about the same event can change dramatically over time. In this case, CLP initially accepted some responsibility and expressed regret for having started a large-scale, long-term war, but eventually denied any responsibility, and blamed everyone else, even those who lost their lives in the war. In his WoMDA, Powell urged the Council to declare war on Iraq, based on their possession of and refusal to give up Weapons of Mass Destruction. Powell's arguments were accepted by the Council, and the 2003 Iraq Invasion began the following month. However, after the invasion, no such weapons were found.

The impact of CLP's 2003 speech can be seen in the publication of an entire 350-page book about that one, single presentation. The book, by John Oddo, is titled *Intertextuality and the 24-Hour News Cycle: A Day in the Rhetorical Life of Colin Powell's U.N. Address.* (2014), which, though somewhat ungainly as a 17-word title, makes it clear that CLP's speech took on a life of its own, from the moment the words were uttered. Such is the power of the language of those in power. Oddo's book is meticulously researched, and includes more than 500 references, 80 pages of appendices, and 30 pages of explanatory notes. In his book, Oddo explained that he chose CLP's 2003 U.N. address because it represented "a monumentally important rhetorical event, a 'critical discourse moment'." Indeed, the historical significance of CLP's speech can hardly be overstated as it was "unlike any other call-to-arms in American history" (p. 4). Never before had a sitting US Secretary of State addressed the UN Security Council directly, to make a case for war, and for the first time in history such a presentation was broadcast live worldwide. "Thus, it is not an exaggeration to say that war and peace hung in the balance. Billions of dollars and hundreds of thousands of lives were at stake" (Oddo, 2014, p. 5)—making every word, every pause, and every inflection count.

Oddo's (2014) book focuses more on the role of the media, as: "Within ten seconds of Powell's concluding remarks, his speech was being reanimated and re-presented by reporters and political pundits" (p. 2). Therefore, it was not so much CLP's language during his speech that was examined by Oddo as much as it was what the media did with CLP's words, so that "not only was Powell's speech *kept alive* by journalists, but, in a sense, it was *brought to life* by journalists... Like mad Dr. Frankenstein" (p. 3, original emphases). That is an especially interesting analogy for Oddo to draw, conjuring up as it does images of a crazed and dangerous madman, bringing the dead to life, as opposed to war, which brings death to the living.

Oddo's book was published more than ten years after CLP's now-infamous presentation to the U.N. Security Council, but in 2007, David Zarefsky's article, 'Making the Case for War: Colin Powell at the United Nations', was published in the journal *Rhetoric & Public Affairs*, as part of a special issue on 'Rhetoric and the War in Iraq'. Zarefsky pointed out how often Powell drew on his own credibility "to vouch for the quality of his evidence" (2007, p. 293). For example, a critical phrase in CLP's WoMDA was when he said: "My colleagues, every statement I make today is backed up by sources. Solid sources. These are not assertions. What we are giving you are facts and conclusions based on solid intelligence", and when he said: "These are not assertions. These are facts, corroborated by many sources" as well as, "This is evidence, not conjecture" (Zarefsky, 2007, p. 293). Zarefsky concluded that a detailed analysis of CLP's speech yielded, "some unsettling conclusions" (p. 298), including the following: "Audiences do not probe evidence very deeply. The appearance of evidence often counts as evidence" (p. 298), and "The credibility of the source will outweigh internal deficiencies in the evidence" (p. 298). From a philosophical perspective, Zarefsky's conclusions relate to the fallacious *argumentum ad verecundiam*, also known as an 'argument from authority' or an 'appeal to authority'. And from an NPL perspective, we the message-recipients need to be able to identify when language is being used to make such arguments, in which the perceived truth of statements is based not on evidence but on personality.

The importance of the source of the news reports was highlighted by Seth Ashley's (2015) study comparing the coverage of CLP's 2003 presentation to the United Nations Security Council by the BBC and by CNN. Ashley's comparison confirmed my own finding that more reliable news reports can often be read and heard from *outside* the country that is being reported on (Curtis, 2018c). For example, if someone is interested in learning about what is happening in the USA today, as reported in the news, then it can be more informative to read and hear reports from, for example, the BBC or European news agencies, such as those in France or Germany.

Likewise, if someone wants know more about what is happening in the UK today, as reported in the news, then it can be more informative to read and hear reports from, for example, American news agencies such as CNN, or Middle Eastern news agencies such as Al Jazeera. There may be some sort of in-country/home-country bias with news reporting, but whatever the reason, Ashley found that, when it came to reporting on Powell's presentation: "The BBC was far more likely to reflect views critical of the war effort and to publish statements challenging the case for war" (p. 134). Ashley's detailed text analysis revealed "a more international and critical orientation by the BBC and a more ethnocentric and pro-state orientation by CNN" (p. 134). In terms of the similarities and differences between societal systems within the USA and the UK, Ashley concluded that: "even though the political, legal, and economic systems within which American and British media exist are quite similar, cultural and institutional forces seem to be somewhat different" (p. 136), with "somewhat different" perhaps being something of an understatement.

REACT 5.4: *Find a recent in-country news report of a national conflict of some kind, such as an armed battle between opposing forces. Now, find two or three other reports of the same conflict as it is reported by new agencies in two or three other countries. What are some of the similarities and some of the differences you see and hear?*

Having considered how some others researched and reported on CLP's 2003 WoMDA, we can now examine CLP's own words, which he used to describe his presentation to the UN Security Council. Two years after his speech, during a televised interview, in 2005, Powell said that his speech, "in which he gave a detailed description of Iraqi weapons programs that turned out not to exist, was 'painful' for him personally and would be a permanent 'blot' on his record" (Weisman, 2005). However, CLP's understanding of 'a permanent blot' appears to have changed considerably over time, and by 2012, while he was promoting his book *It Worked for Me: In Life and Leadership* (2012), his position had moved dramatically, as all of the regret and remorse that he expressed in 2005 appeared to have evaporated.

By 2012, CLP was claiming that, "Frankly, a lot of the stuff [about] the supposed weapons of mass destruction, WMDs] will stand the test of time", and saying that he thought, in 2003, that "we should see if there was a way to get rid of this problem of WMDs [Weapons of Mass Destruction] through diplomatic and peaceful means" (Farndale, 2012). According to the 2012-CLP, it was Saddam Hussein's fault for "giving us worthless documents when we said 'show us what you got'. When he didn't show us, and the [US] president and Mr. Blair [the UK Prime Minister] decided we should take military action, *I fully supported it*" (Farndale, 2012, emphasis added). In fact, not only did CLP appear to have conveniently and completely forgotten how he said he felt in 2005, but by 2012 he was empathically insisting that: "you will find nothing in the record from the UN speech and onwards that I spoke against it [declaring war on Iraq]", appearing by then to be proud of his role in starting that particular war (Farndale, 2012).

A reporter for *The Telegraph* newspaper in the UK tried to press CLP about what he said and did in 2003, but he was cut off: "He stops me. 'Look, if this [interview] is going to be all about this [his WoMDA presentation], we might as well stop' [but] ... It was an extraordinary time. 'Well it is an extraordinary episode, but it is what it is", CLP reportedly said (Farndale, 2012). At that point, the reporter accepted the shutdown, changed the subject, and talked instead about Powell's much-praised military career. Although the 'Multi-National Force' that invaded Iraq in 2003, referred to as 'MNF–I' and/or as the 'Coalition Forces', was led by the USA, it also involved the United Kingdom, Australia, Spain and Poland, making the responsibility for starting that war shared between many countries, not just the USA. However, to refer to the death of an estimated 150,000 Iraqis and 30,000 American soldiers (BBC, 2011) as "it is what it is" sounds like a callous disregard for human life. Such an expression might be said by someone who is either desperate to absolve themselves of all blame, or someone who simply cannot live with the truth anymore, even though they were able to acknowledge it earlier, shortly after the event, when memories of what they had done were still fresh in their mind. Coincidentally—or perhaps not—that same phrase, "it is what it is", was used by the President Trump, in September 2020, when asked why 1,000 Americans were dying from the COVID-19 virus every day; said the President: "They are dying. That's true... it is what it is" (Cole & Subramaniam, 2020).

The after-effects of powerful words from people in power can be felt for a very long time after an event has ended. For example, in 2016—more than 13 years later—CLP's WoMDA continued "to haunt the administration [of the government of the USA]—not just for what it got wrong, but for the unintended consequences it may have set in motion" (Breslow, 2016). The 2016-CLP appeared to have more-or-less completely exonerated himself, saying: "at the time I gave the speech... the president had already made this decision for military action... The Congress had passed a resolution three months before that speech that essentially gave the president the authorization to do it" (Breslow, 2016). In addition to the decision to go to war being the fault of President George W. Bush and Congress, it was, Powell claimed, also the fault of the National Intelligence Estimates. Those

Estimates are classified, federal government documents, produced by the National Intelligence Council, which is a collection of several information-gathering bodies within the government of the USA. The 2016-CLP said: "I think that it was a great intelligence failure on our part, because the problems that existed in that NIE should have been recognized and caught earlier by the intelligence community" (Breslow, 2016). Such claims bring to mind the phrase, 'Don't shoot the messenger': "said to warn someone not to be angry with the person who tells them something bad" (*CALD*, 2021).

By 2016, Powell appeared to be presenting himself as merely an innocent bringer of bad news, rather than someone whose words were instrumental in starting a war, that was waged based on what turned out to be a disastrously false premise. CLP may have *appeared* to have been shouldering some of the responsibility for a war that should not have happened with his use of "it was a great intelligence failure *on our part*" (emphasis added). However, that phrase was immediately followed by a blame-shifting, scapegoating move, in which CLP claimed it was the fault of the National Intelligence Council, not CLP, that resulted in the massive loss-of-life that could have been avoided.

The on-going, long-term after-effects of CLP's 2003 speech continue to be examined, for example, in a 15th anniversary report in 2018, tellingly titled, 'Lie after Lie: What Colin Powell knew about Iraq 15 years ago and what he told the U.N.' (Schwarz, 2018). Schwarz started by stating that: "While the corporate media has never taken a close look at this record, we can go through Powell's presentation line by line to demonstrate the chasm between what he knew and what he told the world." Schwarz (2018) analyzed CLP's 2003 speech under five main categories: Public Certainty, Private Doubt; Unambiguous Lies; Fabricated Evidence; Deception by Omission; Ignored Warnings. One of the limitations of NPL, and of any linguistic analysis, is that although many of the behaviors identified by Schwarz in those five categories are expressed through language, without complete access to everything said and written, it can be difficult to clearly distinguish between, for example, 'Public Certainty' and 'Private Doubt'. However, an NPL approach can sensitize us to some of the kinds of key phrases used by CLP to persuade the USA to declare war on Iraq—a war that would last nearly nine years (2003–2011), leading to the loss of up to 200,000 lives. For example, when CLP said, "regarding whether Iraq had reconstituted a nuclear weapons program…'There is no doubt in my mind" (Schwarz, 2018), what that phrase indicates is certainty on the part of the individual speaking, which may or may not be shared by others.

As message-recipients, we should also be wary in such situations of 'translation errors', either deliberate or accidental, that fundamentally alter the language being used. For example, according to Schwarz (2018), CLP added his own words to those translated from Iraqi intelligence to not just *change* the meaning, but to completely *reverse* it: "Powell took evidence of the Iraqis doing what they were supposed to... searching... to make sure they weren't accidentally holding onto banned chemical weapons—and doctored it to make it look as it Iraq were hiding banned weapons" (Schwartz, 2018). Another important language marker that should have set off alarm bells was CLP's repeated use of "we know that", for example: "We know from sources that a missile brigade outside Baghdad was disbursing [*sic*] rocket launchers and warheads containing biological warfare agents to various locations, distributing them to various locations in western Iraq" (Schwarz, 2018). Questions that should have been asked of that phrase include: Who is 'we'? What does 'know' mean here? Which 'sources'? Where are these 'various locations'? Some of those details may have been withheld for reasons of national security, but not all of them. There is little anyone can do when a very powerful and trusted person says to a group of even more powerful people, as CLP did in his WoMDA to the U.N. Security Council: "These are facts, corroborated by many sources, some of them sources of the intelligence services of other countries." However, careful and close NPL analyses of the kind of language CLP used may help in future conflicts to reduce the likelihood that such speeches result in such devastating loss-of-life.

Suggestions for Further Reading

In relation to using language to include, to exclude and to 'other', in *The Secret Life of Pronouns* (2011), James Pennebaker wrote: "Your brain is not wired to notice... pronouns, articles, prepositions... but if you pay close attention, you will start to see their subtle power" (p. ix). I would go one step further, and suggest that our brains may, in fact, be wired to *not* notice pronouns, articles and prepositions, as they make up only one tenth of one percent (0.1%) of our vocabulary in English (Pennebaker, 2011, p. ix), which is what gives them their subtle but considerable linguistic power. Professor Pennebaker's book is one of the most in-depth and engaging studies of how pronouns in English shape our understanding.

https://www.ineteconomics.org/perspectives/blog/obamas-people-and-the-african-americans-the-language-of-othering

The Director of the Haas Institute for a Fair and Inclusive Society at UC Berkeley, Professor John A. Powell, has written and talked extensively about othering. In 'Obama's People and The African Americans: The Language of Othering' (2016), Powell wrote:

> When Donald Trump refers to 'the African Americans,' his use of the word 'the' attempts to put Black Americans into one subordinate monolithic category. The 'the' becomes a code, a signal that he distances himself from an entire group. He is reassuring his supporters that 'the' group he is referring to is the Other.

https://www.theguardian.com/inequality/2017/nov/08/us-vs-them-the-sinister-techniques-of-othering-and-how-to-avoid-them

Professor Powell also wrote a piece for the UK newspaper, *The Guardian*, 'Us vs Them: The sinister techniques of 'Othering'—and how to avoid them' (2017). In that piece, Powell pointed out that 'Othering', "is based on the conscious or unconscious assumption that a certain identified group poses a threat to the favoured group. It is largely driven by politicians and the media, as opposed to personal contact."

A number of short talks (four-to-five minutes) given by Professor Powell, in 2016 and 2017, can be found on YouTube, under 'Talks about the language of Othering during the 2016 election'.

6

Compacting Meaning, Audience Relations, Using Narrative and Strategic Substitution

In Chapter 5, we saw how language can be used to mark, accentuate and highlight differences between in-group and out-group members, using the language of 'othering'. We then applied those ideas to analyze what may have been one of the most important speeches given by a political leader in the USA in the last 20 years, President George W. Bush, marking the start of a seemingly never-ending so-called 'War on Terror', sometimes called 'America's Forever Wars' (Engelhardt, 2020). The speech that started that war was given by GWB in 2001, followed by Secretary of State Colin Powell's speech in 2003, and in this chapter, we come to 2009, and the (first) inaugural address of the 44th President of the USA (2009–2017), Barack Hussein Obama (BHO). (BHO also stands for Butane Hash Oil, a cannabis concentrate, but as this book is being written in Canada, which in 2018 became only the second country in the world to legalize recreational cannabis, the use of 'BHO' seems appropriate here.)

The New Peace Linguistics and The Role of Language in Conflict, pages 105–119

As we saw in some of the earlier chapters in this book, an important question for NPL practitioners is: How do powerful people use language to communicate with those less powerful? And following on from that question we can derive: What kinds of messages are communicated to the audience, about war, other kinds of conflict, and/or peace? Although we cannot know the responses of readers or the reactions of listeners, by analyzing the language of those in power, we can develop a better understanding of how such language can help make ours a more peaceful planet, or a more war-torn world. In this chapter, we will look at how BHO used a number of recurring techniques during his 2009 inaugural address, including Compacting Meaning, i.e., condensing a great deal of meaning, and multiple messages, into relatively little language. We will also consider the pros and cons of language that may connect with some audience members but which may distance others, as well as the use of narrative story-telling structures, rhythmic linguistic devices, and strategic omissions or 'language substitutions.'

An NPL Analysis of President Barack Obama's (first) Inaugural Speech in January 2009

Since 2009 (except for 2017, 2019 and 2020) *Forbes* financial magazine has published its list of the most powerful people in the world, based on selecting one person for every 100 million people on the planet. In the ten years between 2009 and 2018, the President of the USA occupied the first, second or third position nine times. BHO was ranked, by *Forbes* magazine, as the most powerful person in the world for three years: 2009, 2011 and 2012, and he was ranked the second most powerful person in the world for three other years: 2010, 2013 and 2014. The one-term 45th President of the USA (2016–2020), DJT, was ranked second in 2016 and first in 2018. The other world leaders who have occupied the top spot are: Chinese President Hu Jintao (2009), Russian President Vladimir Putin (2013–2016), and General Secretary of the Communist Party of China, Xi Jinping, in 2018. The only female world leader to be in Forbes' top three since 2009 has been the Chancellor of Germany, Angela Merkel, who became Chancellor in 2005, and who was ranked second in 2012, and third in 2016. The *Forbes* ranking considers, "hundreds of candidates from various walks of life all around the globe" and estimates their power "along four dimensions" (Ewalt, 2018). The first parameter is the candidate's power over people, and the second is the financial resources under the control of each candidate. The third set of *Forbes'* criteria is how powerful the candidate is "in multiple spheres", and the fourth and final *Forbes'* parameter is how actively the candidates use their power (Ewalt, 2018).

There are, of course, other ways to measure power, for example, a world leader's capacity to end the world with nuclear weapons. But however 'power' is measured, for now, for better and for worse, whoever is the President of the USA is one of the most powerful people in the world—many would say *the* most powerful (although supporters of other world leaders, such as Xi Jinping and Vladimir Putin, might beg to differ). Therefore, in these two chapters, we will present NPL analyses of two texts, separated by eight years, from one of the most recent Presidents of the USA. That is not to say that the specific language features identified in this chapter and those that follow are only used by world leaders, as that is clearly not the case. However, when these features are used by world leaders, their effects—direct and indirect, immediate and long-term—are amplified because of the global attention such written and spoken texts receive.

Through in-depth, systematic linguistic analyses of these kinds of texts, we can see more clearly potential underlying meanings, which enable us to understand more of what is being said (or written), as well as the how, where and why of the word, phrases and sentences. However, there is a cost to doing this kind of deconstructing, which is that, because analyzing every word of such long speeches would result in book-length accounts, rather than chapters in books, these analyses have to be selective. And in the case of NPL that selectivity is decided based on the relevance of those parts of the text that refer to war, peace, conflict, violence, etc. However, for completeness and for context, it is necessary to see and hear full texts. The complete 19-minute, version of BHO's 2009 (first) inaugural address can be seen and heard on such sites as C-Span and YouTube, and the full 2,420-word version of his speech is available on the website archive of the US Government (see Appendix B).

Opening Lines

On January 20, 2009 BHO delivered his first Inaugural Address (referred to in this chapter as the Obama Inaugural Address, abbreviated to 'OIA'). (A second address was given in 2013, at the start of his second four-year term.) After the formal introduction and initial applause, here are the first four paragraphs (P = paragraph) spoken by BHO, totaling approximately 140 words, which took approximately 90 second to say.

P1: "My fellow citizens: I stand here today humbled by the task before us, grateful for the trust you've bestowed, mindful of the sacrifices borne by our ancestors.

P2: I thank President Bush for his service to our nation, as well as the generosity and cooperation he has shown throughout this transition.

P3: Forty-four Americans have now taken the presidential oath. The words have been spoken during rising tides of prosperity and the still waters of peace. Yet, every so often, the oath is taken amidst gathering clouds and raging storms. At these moments, America has carried on not simply because of the skill or vision of those in high office, but because we, the people, have remained faithful to the ideals of our forebears and true to our founding documents.

P4: So it has been; so it must be with this generation of Americans."

REACT 6.1: *The first mention of peace occurs early on in this speech, in the third paragraph, with the reference to "the still waters of peace." What does that phrase mean to you? How would you explain the meaning of that phrase to someone for whom English is a new language, and who is encountering that phrase for the first time?*

The first few words of any text, spoken or written, can be some of the most important, as they set the stage for what is to come, and shape the expectations of the listeners/readers, which can greatly influence the way the central message, and the supporting messages, are received and decoded. As we can see, the speaker, BHO, chose to start with "My fellow citizens", rather than "My fellow Americans", perhaps to highlight the importance of being citizens first and foremost. In a piece titled, 'Thomas Jefferson, Steve Jobs, and the Rule of 3', Carmine Gallo (2012) claimed that giving information in threes is "The most persuasive number in communications", citing the US Declaration of Independence to support his claim, describing "life, liberty, and the pursuit of happiness" as being perhaps "the three most important words in American history" (even though "the pursuit of happiness" is a four-word phrase).

Gallo's claim may be a stretch, but the second sentence of the OIA opening paragraph made use of that kind of three-part presentation, in this case, with three, positive self-descriptors, i.e., [humbled + grateful + mindful], together with clear, concise indicators of what it was that humbled BHO (the task), what he was grateful for (the trust), and what he was mindful of (ancestral sacrifices). The mention of such sacrifices may also have been an allusion to the slave-trading history of the USA, and of BHO himself. The word-choice of "bestowed" and "borne" rather than 'given' and 'made', respectively, reflect a preference for using lower frequency, less commonly occurring vocabulary items. Whatever the reasons for using such items, those kinds of vocabulary items risk creating some distance between a speaker and a listener (or between a writer and a reader) especially if the recipient of the message has a more limited vocabulary than the sender.

At approximately 80 words in length, P3 is longer than P1, P2 and P4 combined, which illustrates the value of varying not only sentence length but also paragraph length, as length can reflect units of thought in spoken and written texts, in which shorter, simpler sentences may be taken as the articulation of shorter, simpler thoughts, and vice versa. There are clear echoes from the preamble to the United States Constitution, which begins: "We the People of the United States..." which appears in this OIA text as: "because *we, the people,* have remained faithful to the ideals of our forebears and true to our founding documents" (emphasis added). We can also see and hear a three-part f-alliteration with [faithful + forbears + founding], employing the historical but also gender-neutral 'forbears', rather than, for example, forefathers/foremothers (see Chapter 3 for a discussion of the relationships between rhetoric, politics, poetry and NPL).

REACT 6.2: *In these opening lines, we can see examples of low-frequency words and phrases, rather than high-frequency words and phrases. When you are speaking and trying to connect with your listeners, what kinds of words and phrases do you use? How do you decide which words and phrases to use?*

The next paragraph, P5, at fewer than 100 words, illustrates the concept of 'lexical density', which is defined as: "the proportion of content words to function words in a text. The higher the proportion of content words, the greater the lexical density. Lexical density measures how much information there is in a text" (*Macmillan Dictionary,* 2021). In the Science Fiction world, the equivalent of 'lexical density' is 'dimensional transcendentalism', which originated in the 1960s UK BBC television series *Dr. Who.* The device used by the good doctor to travel across time and space was called the TARDIS, which stands for Time and Relative Dimension in Space. That explained how the TARDIS (which even made it into the *Oxford English Dictionary,* where it is defined as "a time machine") could be extremely large on the inside, while looking like an ordinary old-time British police box on the outside (approx. nine feet tall, 3½ feet wide, and 3½ feet deep, or approx. 3 × 1 × 1 in meters). Both concepts, lexical density and the TARDIS, capture the idea that it possible to squeeze a great deal of substance into a relatively small space, in this case, to convey a great deal of meaning with relatively few words, which may also recall the poetic conciseness of Japanese Haiku verses. This 96-word, fifth paragraph of this BHO text is where we see the first explicit reference to war.

As stated in previous chapters, one of the features of NPL that distinguishes it from earlier versions of PL is the way NPL deconstructs the language of specific texts, going into greater depth, with the aim of applying linguistic analyses to language related to conflict, and/or related to peace. Unpacking P5 gives us the following layout, which bears more than a passing resemblance to a blank verse, non-rhyming poem:

P5.1: That we are in the midst of crisis is now well understood.
P5.2: Our nation is at war
P5.3: against a far-reaching network of violence and hatred.
P5.4: Our economy is badly weakened,
P5.5: a consequence of greed and irresponsibility on the part of some,
P5.6: but also our collective failure to make hard choices
P5.7: and prepare the nation for a new age.
P5.8: Homes have been lost,
P5.9: jobs shed,
P5.10: businesses shuttered.
P5.11: Our health care is too costly,
P5.12: our schools fail too many—
P5.13: and each day brings further evidence that the ways we use energy
P5.14: strengthen our adversaries
P5.15: and threaten our planet.

These lines were said approximately two minutes into the inaugural address, and took around 40 seconds to deliver. The relatively simple act of unpacking those 96 words, with even minimal linguistic analysis, shows that a great deal of meaning has been packed into relatively few words, with a clear focus on war—not the threat of war, but a war that was happening at the time the text was created and presented, as seen at P5.2: "Our nation is at war", using the present simple tense to mean: we are at war *now*, at this moment, as I am speaking and as you are listening, we are at war. And not just a war between nations, but at war with "a far-reaching network of *violence* and *hatred*" (emphases added). However, as noted in Chapter 3, there are different kinds of 'warist discourse'; one of which makes war-like reactions, responses and outcomes more likely, i.e., 'negative warist discourse', another of which describes a current situation, i.e., 'neutral warist discourse', which may be the more likely case here.

The four phrases from P5.4 to P5.7 can be analyzed as a group, partly because they are all part of the same sentence, and also because they are connected thematically. When BHO gave this speech, in January 2009, the 2008 Financial Crisis was still in full swing, as a result of which: "Homes have been lost, jobs shed, businesses shuttered." Those three consequences refer to three of the perennial concerns of many audiences: home-life, work-life, and businesses, thereby linking the personal with the professional and the business world. P5.11 to P5.15 can also be analyzed as a group, as the collective pronoun 'our' is used four times—to refer to healthcare, education, adversaries and the planet. In addition, the immediacy and urgency of the situation was expressed at the beginning of P5, starting with "We *are in the midst of* crisis" (P5.1, emphasis added), which continued: "health care *is* too costly" and "schools *fail* too many" (two x 'too'), followed by "each day brings."

The use of the word and concept of 'enemy' appears to have been carefully avoided here, with 'adversary' used instead. These are the kinds of vocabulary choices that may not seem so significant to the majority of listeners and readers, but for NPL practitioners, these are uses of language that need to be noticed more often, noted more consciously, and studied more deeply. For example, an 'enemy' is defined as: "a person who hates or opposes another person and tries to harm them or stop them from doing something" and as: "a country, or the armed forces of a country, that is at war with another country" (*CALD*, 2021). However, an 'adversary' is defined as: "one that contends with, opposes, or resists: an enemy or opponent" (*Merriam-Webster*, 2021). Therefore, in spite of the overlap between the meanings of the two words, the use of 'adversary' may have been part of a conscious decision to avoid explicitly referring to an enemy, as the former has fewer militaristic connotations than the latter.

Explicit References to Peace and to Conflict

The first explicit reference to conflict, rather than war, appeared at the beginning of P8: "On this day, we gather because we have chosen hope over fear, unity of purpose over conflict and discord" (P8.1), employing another way to emphasize immediacy, using "On this day" together with the simple present tense again: "we gather", rather than 'we have gathered', which is saved for the next phrase, "we have chosen", repeating the pattern of choosing-A-over-B, for emphasis, and repetition for rhythm. "On this day", rather than 'today', was also used for a third time at the start the following sentence: "On this day, we come to proclaim an end to the petty grievances and false promises, the recriminations and worn-out dogmas that for far too long have strangled our politics" (P8.2). Here the use of 'proclaiming' rather than 'announcing' or even just 'saying' gives some gravitas to the line, as well as a three-part string of negative adjectives: 'petty', 'false', and 'worn-out', building up to murderous metaphor of strangulation, for sentencing-ending dramatic effect.

P10 can be analyzed as an object lesson in allusion, indirectly referring to multiple major historical events—without naming a single one—and again compacting a considerable amount of meaning, this time into fewer than 60 words:

> "For us, they packed up their few worldly possessions and traveled across oceans in search of a new life. For us, they toiled in sweatshops, and settled the West, endured the lash of the whip, and plowed the hard earth. For us, they fought and died in places like Concord and Gettysburg, Normandy and Khe Sanh" (P10)

These three, short sentences (averaging approximately 19 words each) appear to have been carefully calibrated to create an almost poetic effect, using ['for us' + 'they'] three times, at the beginning of each sentence, followed by 16, 18, and 13 words, respectively. As with the use of 'adversary' instead of 'enemy', the vocabulary employed here is not coincidental. People work in shops, which is normal and natural, but in sweatshops they do not work—they toil, giving a markedly different sense of more exploitative work, in which the work is too hard and the workers are not properly paid—if they are paid at all. If the two phrases are juxtaposed, we can see the difference more clearly: working in a shop = not great but OK vs. toiling in sweatshop = bad, definitely not OK. The ultimate example of exploiting labor is slavery, and "the lash of the whip" is highly likely to have been an allusion to slave-owners beating their slaves. P10 concludes with: "For us, they fought and died in places like Concord and Gettysburg, Normandy and Khe Sahn", referring to the site of four famous battles, two in the USA, one in Europe, and one in Asia, thereby covering all the geographic bases. The sacrifices of the forebears were also emphasized by, "For us, they fought", paralleling the pattern of, "they fought and died."

The next reference to conflict occurred at P18, which began: "As for our common defense, we reject as false the choice between our safety and our ideals." That line signaled that defending safety and ideals should not be seen as a mutually exclusive, either-or, zero-sum game, but instead that both are possible, at the same time, i.e., being safe *and* acting according to values and beliefs. Returning to historical themes, BHO then explained that the "Founding Fathers, faced with perils that we can scarcely imagine, drafted a charter to assure the rule of law and the rights of man—a charter expanded by *the blood of generations*" (P18, emphasis added). The second explicit reference to peace (after "the still waters of peace" at P3) occurs in the following paragraph, P19:

> And so, to all the other peoples and governments who are watching today, from the grandest capitals to *the small village where my father was born*, know that America is a friend of each nation, and every man, woman and child who seeks *a future of peace and dignity*" (P19, emphases added).

That was the only explicit mention of BHO's origins in the OIA, and even then, the "small village" (Nyang'oma Kogelo, in Siaya County, Kenya, with a population of fewer than 4,000, as of 2021) was not named. That may have been a good example of the less-is-more approach, in which details that could easily be included are deliberately omitted, for political, social, economic and/or other reasons. As mentioned in Chapter 3, in relation to language and gender, the countless references in American literature to the Founding Fathers completely and pseudo-parthenogenetically ignores the role of the Founding Mothers. However, as a US women's history professor has pointed out: "women were involved in almost every aspect of the Revolutionary War... They played a significant role in the political discourse of the era at a time when women were expected to stay home and take care of the family" (Graves, 2020).

The whole of the following paragraph, P20, can be read as a miniature treatise on war and peace, while invoking the specter of two of the most-feared ideologies in the USA, Fascism and Communism, while also comparing and contrasting bullets and bombs with values and beliefs: "missiles and tanks" vs. "alliances and convictions." And again, there is a high lexical density, with a great deal of meaning packed into relatively few words and sentences (in this case, approximately 70 words and three sentences; with one semi-colon):

P20.1: Recall that earlier generations faced down fascism and communism not just with missiles and tanks, but with the sturdy alliances and enduring convictions.

P20.2: They understood that our power alone cannot protect us, nor does it entitle us to do as we please.

P20.3: Instead they knew that our power grows through its prudent use; our security emanates from the justness of our cause, the force of our example, the tempering qualities of humility and restraint.

The phrase "the justness of our cause" recalls Just War theory (see Chapter 3), and for those familiar with some of the best-known works of

Shakespeare, references to "the justness of our cause" and "the tempering qualities of humility and restraint" may recall *The Merchant of Venice* (first performed in 1605). Specifically, the climactic courtroom scene, in which the heroine Portia is defending the nobleman Antonio, against the demonized, Jewish moneylender, Shylock. In Act 4, scene 1, Portia's famous soliloquy begins:

"The quality of mercy is not strained.

It droppeth as the gentle rain from heaven ..." and ends with:

"... And earthly power doth then show likest God's

When mercy seasons justice."

That Shakespearean sound and feel is helped by the use of phrases such as "sturdy alliances" and "enduring convictions" (both at P20.1). However, adopting such a Shakespearean tone could have at least two effects; one positive, one negative. One effect could be to impress the audience with the apparent literary awareness of the speaker, tapping into the rhythms of iambic pentameter. But it is also possible that some listeners could either be put off by such literary allusions, or simply not notice them at all. Therefore, these kinds of language and communication strategies are risky, and can either work to the benefit of the speaker, in helping them identify and bond with their listeners, or they can work against the speaker, and prevent them from establishing rapport with their listeners. Some rhythmic momentum is also provided by the repetition of 'power' (at P20.2 and P20.3), as well as one triple-P and one double-P alliteration: [power + protect + please] + [power + prudent].

The next five paragraphs, P21 through to P25, which are a total of approximately 260 words, take place approximately 11 minutes into the speech, and take about two minutes to deliver, include direct and indirect references to war and peace, bombs and terrorists, death and destruction. Therefore, if P20 can be read as a mini-treatise on war and peace, then these five paragraphs may constitute a short essay on the same subject:

P21: We are the keepers of this legacy... We will begin to responsibly leave Iraq to its people and forge a hard-earned peace in Afghanistan. With old friends and former foes, we'll work tirelessly to lessen the nuclear threat, and roll back the specter of a warming planet.

P22: We will not apologize for our way of life, nor will we waver in its defense. And for those who seek to advance their aims by inducing terror and slaughtering innocents, we say to you now that our spirit is stronger and cannot be broken—you cannot outlast us, and we will defeat you.

P23: For we know that our patchwork heritage is a strength, not a weakness... We are shaped by every language and culture... and because we have tasted the bitter swill of civil war and segregation... we cannot help but believe... that as the world grows smaller, our common humanity shall reveal itself; and that America must play its role in ushering in a new era of peace.

P24: To the Muslim world, we seek a new way forward, based on mutual interest and mutual respect. To those leaders around the globe who seek to sow conflict, or blame their society's ills on the West, know that your people will judge you on what you can build, not what you destroy.

P25: To those who cling to power through corruption and deceit and the silencing of dissent, know that you are on the wrong side of history, but that we will extend a hand if you are willing to unclench your fist.

At P21, BHO said to his audience that: "We will begin to responsibly leave Iraq to its people and forge a hard-earned peace in Afghanistan", which is immediately followed by: "With old friends and former foes, we'll work tirelessly to lessen the nuclear threat", incorporating a trio of alliterative f-words: [friends + former + foes], building on the first f-word, in the previous sentence, "forge." Again, we can see another ingenious way of avoiding the e-word, 'enemy', this time using the low-frequency, high-register, and again somewhat Shakespearean 'foe', as in, for example: Halt! Who goes there? Friend or foe? From an NPL perspective, it is also important to notice that the commitment made was to "to *lessen* the nuclear threat, and *roll back* the specter of a warming planet" (emphases added), but not to *end* the nuclear threat, or to *end* global warming, which could have been perceived as an over-optimistic, over-commitment.

The next paragraph, P22, is one of the shorter ones, (two sentences and a total of approximately 50 words) but regarding the imagery conjured up, it is also the bloodiest and most violent. BHO's un-apology at P22, including an attack-defend clause—"We will not apologize for our way of life, nor will we waver in its defense"—is followed by a reference to terrorists who "slaughter... innocents", potentially evoking extremely violent images in the minds of the listeners, which may have been an allusion to the 9/11 attacks, discussed in previous chapters. Regardless of the possible 9/11 attack reference, 'slaughter' may be one of the few words in the English language that expresses a more violent loss of/taking of life than even 'murder'.

However, perhaps to balance the shock of the "slaughter", P22 concluded with the alliterative and uplifting "our spirit is stronger and cannot be broken", ending on the war-winning note of "we will defeat you." Having issued the dire warning in P22, in the paragraphs that follow, BHO's tone changed to include references to "a new era of peace", "mutual interest... mutual respect" and a willingness on the part of the USA to "extend a hand."

At P23, BHO began by stating that: "We are shaped by every language and culture", that "we have tasted the bitter swill of civil war and segregation", and "that America must play its role in ushering in *a new era of peace*" (emphasis added). Although "*every* language and culture" is an exaggeration, P23 does highlight the linguistic and cultural diversity of the USA, and the idea of less war and more peace in the future. P24 was an explicit appeal to "the Muslim world", with whom BHO said he wanted to find some common ground: "a new way forward, based on mutual interest and mutual respect." But that olive branch was followed by a warning from BHO, "To those leaders around the globe who seek to sow conflict, or blame their society's ills on the West", concluding with a comparing/contrasting of what can be built vs. what can be destroyed. P25 contains another clear, concise warning: "To those who cling to power through corruption and deceit and the silencing of dissent, know that you are on the wrong side of history, but that we will extend a hand if you are willing to unclench your fist." The vivid imagery of the open hand, symbolizing a willingness to communicate, is contrasted with the clenched fist, signaling a desire for battle, war, or some other form of hand-to-hand combat.

P27: As we consider the role that unfolds before us, we remember with humble gratitude those brave Americans who at this very hour patrol far-off deserts and distant mountains. They have something to tell us, just as the fallen heroes who lie in Arlington whisper through the ages.

P28: We honor them not only because they are the guardians of our liberty, but because they embody the spirit of service—a willingness to find meaning in something greater than themselves.

At P27, we hear/see another eloquent exercise in euphemistic avoidance, in this case, there are three references to soldiers—"brave Americans... fallen heroes... guardians of our liberty", without a single use of the word 'soldier'. A solider is defined as "a person who is in an army and wears its uniform, especially someone who fights when there is a war" (*CALD*, 2021). Therefore, although there may be no clearly negative connotations with the word 'soldier', there may not be any positive ones either. However, "brave Americans... fallen heroes... guardians of our liberty" are not just positively connoted, but they almost sing of the soldiers' sacrifices, in the style of, for example, Rupert Brooke's poem 'The Soldier' (1914) or Robert Frost's sonnet 'A Soldier' (1928). In the same way that the word 'soldier' is avoided, so too is 'warring', instead of which 'patrolling' is used, as that has a much more positive, preventative, peace-keeping ring to it. P28 continued in the same vein, emphasizing the importance of honoring the sacrifices made by soldiers of the USA, in "the spirit of service" for "something greater than themselves", with no mention of the shooting, bombing and killing that soldiers are generally required to do when fighting on the battle field. P27 and P28 show how effective word-choice can be—choosing words with positive or neutral connotations, while being careful to avoid those with negative associations.

Concluding Comments and Closing Statements

At P34, there is more poetic imagery and heroic glorification:

P34.2: "In the year of America's birth, in the coldest of months, a small band of patriots huddled by dying campfires on the shores of an icy river.

P34.3: The capital was abandoned.

P34.4: The enemy was advancing.

P34.5: The snow was stained with blood."

Deliberately omitting important details, such as which battle, which year and which month, i.e., who, where and when, shows that the listeners share—or are assumed to share—with the speaker in-group knowledge of the details of the specific battle being referred to, but without being named. In the same vein, there is no mention of whose blood it was that stained the snow that fateful night. Such omissions may also help to create a sense of dramatic story-telling, in which the narrative tension is heightened. Presumably, BHO was referring to the American Revolutionary War, also known as the American War of Independence, fought against Britain, between 1775 and 1783, and the "icy river" was the Delaware River, which George Washington's "small band of patriots" is said to have crossed on Christmas night (December 25), 1776. A key question that emerges here is: How to honor the dead for having made the ultimate sacrifice without glorifying killing? It is possible that the limits of language make it difficult to do one without the other.

P34.3 through to P34.5 continue to build the dramatic tension, using a three-part repeating definite article + noun pattern: "The capital... The enemy... The snow ..." incorporating two a-descriptors—one adjective, one verb—combined with one bloody image: "abandoned... advancing... stained with blood." According to the fairytale telling of that night, the forces of the British Empire were defeated and everyone lived happily ever after (expect the servants, the slaves, the women, the poor, etc.). As Francesca Polletta (2015) wrote, in her article on characters in political storytelling: "Many of the stories that are most effective in politics are not told. Instead, they are *alluded to*" (p. 34, emphasis added), which is well-illustrated, as noted above, by BHO omitting far more details of the battle than were given.

No matter how exaggerated, how non-factual and even how nonsensical such mythic and fabulous story-telling may be, there is a deep human need for narrative, which cannot exist without language. As a species, we are hard-wired for narrative, possibly even at some genetic level, as one of the few things that can be said of all human civilizations at all times is that they have all told stories (Curtis, 2006). According to Jag Bhalla (2013), writing in *Scientific American*: "It is in our nature to need stories. They are our earliest sciences, a kind of people-physics. Their logic is how we naturally think. They configure our biology, and how we feel, in ways long essential for our survival." Bhalla went on to explain that: "Like our language instinct, a story drive—an inborn hunger for story hearing and story making—emerges untutored universally in healthy children. Every culture bathes their children in stories to explain how the world works... to engage and educate."

The last two paragraphs of this OIA text ends with a call to action, and perhaps a call to arms, based on the historical drama presented in the immediately preceding paragraphs: "America: In the face of our common dangers, in this winter of our hardship, let us remember... With hope and virtue, let us brave once more the icy currents, and endure what storms may come" (P36). That is followed by the final paragraph, and the standard closing of: [thanks given + godly blessings given + call for such blessings to be bestowed upon the USA]: "Thank you. God bless you. And God bless the United States of America" (P37).

REACT 6.3: *Video and audio recordings of this speech/spoken text are freely available online, for example, on YouTube and C-Span. Look closely and carefully at the first few minutes of this OIA text. What do you notice about BHO's body language, and do you see any connections (or disconnects) between his verbal and non-verbal language in those first few minutes?*

Suggestions for Further Reading

Tom Engelhardt's book, *The American Way of War: How Bush's Wars Became Obama's* (2010, Haymarket Books), includes a chapter on 'The Language of War: American Style'. Another book by Engelhardt that is relevant to this chapter is *The United States of Fear* (2011, Haymarket Books), which contains chapters on 'American Warscapes', 'Obama's Flailing Wars' and 'Living with War'. Engelhardt's more recent book is *A Nation Unmade by War* (2018, Haymarket Books).

We Are the Change We Seek: The Speeches of Barack Obama by E.J. Dionne Jr. and Joy-Ann Reid (2017, Bloomsbury) contains transcripts of more than 20 of BHO's speeches, which are not analyzed, but which could be used as the basis for NPL analyses. Another book that provides texts that could be used for NPL analyses is the collection of quotations compiled by Lisa Rogak (2008, Perseus Books), *Barack Obama: In His Own Words,* which contains approximately 100 quotes, alphabetically arranged, by subject.

7

Uses of Echoing, Medical and Military Metaphors, Warist Discourse, and Re-Presentations of History

In Chapter 6, we looked at how US President Obama used a number of recurring techniques during his first inaugural address, given in 2009, in relation to two key recurring questions in NPL: How do powerful people use language to communicate with their audience? and: What kinds of messages are communicated to the audience, about War and/or Peace? Those techniques included Compacting Meaning, i.e., squeezing a lot of meaning into relatively little language, using language that may distance some audience members but draw others in, as well as BHO's use of narrative structures, rhythmic structures, and strategic omissions or 'language substitutions.'

In this chapter, we fast-forward eight years, from 2009 to 2017, and carry out an NPL analysis of President Barack Obama's Farewell Address (in this chapter, referred to as the Obama Farewell Address, abbreviated to 'OFA'). In analyzing the OFA, we will explore a number of ways in which BHO used

The New Peace Linguistics and The Role of Language in Conflict, pages 121–138

language, including the recurring themes of connecting (or not) with the audience, 'othering', and the strategic use of some specific words and phrases while appearing to deliberately avoiding others. We will also look at re-presentations of history, and the presentation of key concepts such as Democracy, Rights and Values, and the relationships between them. And we will look in more detail at the technique of 'echoing' or using 'callbacks' to refer backwards/forwards to previous/upcoming points, as well as the use of medical and military metaphors, if-then warnings, and explicit references to armed conflicts and other forms of warist discourse (as discussed in Chapter 3).

An NPL Analysis of President Barack Obama's January 2017 Farewell Address

The Opening Paragraphs

On January 11 2017, President Barack Obama (BHO) began his farewell address by saying: "It's good to be home. My fellow Americans, Michelle and I have been so touched by all the well-wishes we've received over the past few weeks." The opening paragraph continued:

P1.3: But tonight, it's my turn to say thanks.

P1.4: Whether we've seen eye-to-eye or rarely agreed at all, my conversations with you, the American people—in living rooms and schools; at farms and on factory floors; at diners and on distant outposts—are what have kept me honest, kept me inspired, and kept me going.

P1.5: Every day, I learned from you.

P1.6: You made me a better president, and you made me a better man.

The OFA was given in the city of Chicago, where BHO spent some years in his 20s (in the 1980s), and where he first worked on community development projects. Therefore, "my fellow Americans" was preceded by a phrase that may have been an equally powerful—though seemingly ordinary: "It's good to be home." According to evolutionary social psychologist, Frank McAndrew (2015), writing in *Psychology Today*, the concept of 'home' is: "the primary connection between you and the rest of the world... home is the center of the world and a place of order that contrasts with the chaos elsewhere." McAndrew also quoted a line from the American poet Robert Frost's (1874–1963) 'The Death of the Hired Man', published in 1914: "Home is the place that, when you have to go there, they have to take you in." The deep resonance of sayings such as 'Home is where the heart is' make a short, simple-sounding, unassuming opening like "It's good to be home" more powerful that the listeners may consciously realize.

At P1.4, BHO acknowledged those who had disagreed with him, over his eight years in office, but focused on the breadth and depth of discussions in which he had engaged during those years, summarizing thousands of interactions, with tens of thousands of people in a single phrase of fewer than 20 words: "in living rooms and schools; at farms and on factory floors; at diners and on distant outposts." The prepositions are varied but within a repeating pattern [in + at + on + at + on] to create an almost iambic pentametric rhythm, while referring, directly and indirectly, to five major contexts [home + school + work place + eating place + military base]. Within that structure, there is also a three-part f-alliteration [farms + factory + floors] as well as a two-part d-alliteration [diners + distant], with "distant outposts" being used as way of euphemistically referring to far-flung military bases, without having to say the word 'military'. An 'outpost' is defined as: "a small town or group of buildings in a place that is far away, usually established as a center for military or trade operations" (*CALD*, 2021) with the military-base meaning being more common than the trade-related meaning today. P1.4 concluded with another three-part structure, based on ['kept me' + adjective/verb]: "kept me honest, kept me inspired, and kept me going," followed by an expression of humility: "Every day, I learned from you" (P1.5), and concluding the opening paragraph with: "You made me a better president, and you made me a better man" (P1.6), placing his position before his sex, i.e., president first, man second.

The first example of what may count as 'neutral warist discourse', regarding explicit references to specific, past wars, can be seen/heard in P5, which begins with a historical note, starting with US citizenship and leading to the naming of specific battle sites and protest sites:

P5.1: "For 240 years, our nation's call to citizenship has given work and purpose to each new generation . . .

P5.4: It's why GIs gave their lives at Omaha Beach and Iwo Jima; Iraq and Afghanistan—and why men and women from Selma to Stonewall were prepared to give theirs as well."

'G.I' stands for 'Government Issue' or 'General Issue', which are the initials used to refer to soldiers in the armies of the USA. 'Omaha Beach' was the codename given to World War II Allied invasion of German-occupied Normandy, France in June 1944, and the Battle of Iwo Jima took place between the Marine Corps of the USA and the Imperial Japanese Army, on the island of Iwo Jima, in February and March of 1945. Those two WWII references are followed by references to two more recent wars, one of which was the Iraq War, which began in 2003, with invasion of Iraq by the USA, and continued for much of the following decade, with the USA becoming more actively re-involved in the war in 2014, while the US war in Afghanistan lasted 23 years, from 1999 to 2021. BHO's inclusion of a reference to Selma was an acknowledgment of the three marches, to allow African-Americans to exercise their right to vote, between Selma, Alabama and the state capital of Montgomery. 'Stonewall' referred to the police raids, and the resulting violent clashes, that took place in June 1969, on lesbian and gay bars in Greenwich Village, New York City.

REACT 7.1: *Do you know of some other key events in the history of the USA? Why do you think BHO chose the events that he did? How might the speech have been differently received if he had chosen other events from other histories?*

The following paragraph, P6, includes the line: "The work of democracy has always been hard, contentious and sometimes bloody." Again, we see the giving of information in threes, starting with "hard," as in 'difficult', building up to "contentious," involving disagreements and even arguments, and culminating with the graphic descriptor, "bloody." In British Englishes 'bloody' can be "used to express anger or to emphasize what you are saying in a slightly rude way" (*CALD*, 2021), as in 'Don't be such a bloody fool!' However, in American Englishes, 'bloody' usually means "with much loss of life and many serious injuries" (*CALD*, 2021), which appears to be the meaning BHO was alluding to, with the modifying, lessening "sometimes," which was chronologically contrasted with "always." In describing "the work of democracy" as having always been "hard, contentious and sometimes bloody," BHO was recalling the words of Dr. Martin Luther King Jr., who said that "overcoming racism was the USA's unfinished "work of democracy"" (Keppel, 1995, p. 1). The bloody reference also recalls some of the closing lines from BHO's (first) inaugural address, given eight years earlier, in 2009, when he described the snow as being "stained with blood" (see Chapter 6).

From P7 of the OFA text:

> if I had told you, eight years ago, that we would... shut down Iran's nuclear weapons program without firing a shot, and *take out* the mastermind of 9/11... you might have said our sights were set a little too high. But that's what we did. That's what you did. (emphasis added)

These lines at P7 are of particular interest to NPL practitioners, partly because of the contrast between "without firing a shot," which highlights the effectiveness of non-military, diplomatic approaches, which is in sharp contrast to "take out the mastermind of 9/11," as the transitive verb 'take out' here means "to eliminate, kill, or destroy" (*Merriam-Webster*, 2021). Therefore, by using 'take out', which can have more than a dozen non-lethal meanings, instead of 'kill', which has far fewer meanings, and all of them deadly, BHO was able to use euphemisms to avoid explicitly referring to the deliberate, planned killing of 'enemy targets' associated with the 9/11 attacks on the USA. Sometime later in the OFA, at P28, 'taken out' is used two more times, this time to refer to killing on a much larger scale: "We've *taken out* tens of thousands of terrorists—including Osama bin Laden. The global coalition we're leading against ISIL has *taken out* their leaders, and taken away about half their territory." BHO then concluded that part of his speech with dire and definite future-tense warnings: "ISIL *will be* destroyed, and no one who threatens America *will ever be* safe" (P28, emphases added). Coming back to P7, chronological markers are employed again, as the [conditional + specific-past-time] construction, "if I had told you, eight years ago," occurs three times in that paragraph.

Speaking of Peace

The first explicit mention of 'peace' appeared at P8: "In 10 days, the world will witness a hallmark of our democracy: *the peaceful transfer of power* from one freely elected president to the next" (emphasis added). P8 began with another time-marker, 'ten days', which started the clock, and emphasized the upcoming immediacy of a change in political and governmental leadership at the highest level, which would be closely watched by the world. In addition to the rhythm created by the alliteration of [world + will + witness], there may have been an implied warning: the world will be (everyone, definitely) watching, so let us (shared responsibility) not make any mistakes (not embarrass ourselves) while we are on the world stage. The use of the possessive pronoun 'our', in "our democracy" is interesting, as it could have been "the world will witness a hallmark of democracy." But the use of "our" here may indicate a number of different possible meanings, from 'this kind of democracy belongs to us', all the way to 'this version of democracy is not for everyone'. Either way, the focus on a peaceful transfer of power, in BHO's 2017 speech, turned out to be much more than some sort of platitude that could be taken for granted, as the 2021 transfer of power from the 45th to the 46th President of the USA was deliberately made to be "anything but a peaceful transfer of power" (Godula, Cheval, Cockerll, Baritello, 2020). The culmination of this violently non-peaceful transfer of power manifested itself as deadly attack on the US Capitol Building in Washington

DC on January 6, 2021, just two weeks before the inauguration of the 46th President of the USA, Joseph R. Biden (see Chapter 12), when the USA:

> finally witnessed the price of its five-year experiment turning its election process into a reality show that produced an unhinged megalomanic [*sic*] as commander-in-chief who amassed so much power through his lies and fear-mongering that he was able to engineer an insurrection as a final act that left democracy dangling by a thread. (Reveston & Liptak, 2021)

To return to the OFA, at the approximate halfway point, there is a clear echoing between BHO's first speech as President of the USA, given in January 2009, and his last, given eight years later, in January 2017 (after completing the maximum-allowed two four-year terms in office). The echoing relates to the notion of diversity, which BHO, in 2017, said should be seen as a strength not a weakness, and perhaps even as a force for peace, rather than a cause for race-based conflict. Connecting the inaugural and the farewell addresses, in his 2009 inaugural address BHO said: "For we know that our patchwork heritage is a strength, not a weakness... We are shaped by every language and culture" (P23, see Chapter 6). Eight years later, in his 2017 farewell speech, BHO said: "For native-born Americans, it means reminding ourselves that the stereotypes about immigrants today were said, almost word for word, about the Irish, Italians, and Poles. America wasn't weakened by the presence of these newcomers... it was strengthened" (P20). Very few of the audience members in 2017 may have been aware of the connection to the speech given eight years earlier. But connecting to the idea of diversity being a strength not a weakness (Curtis, 2017c) is one way in which BHO highlighted the importance of such beliefs in shaping policy and planning for the country, based on diversity rather than dichotomy, such as 'American' vs 'Non-America'.

At P20, BHO's use of the phrase "word for word" highlights the power of language in shaping our thoughts and feelings, influencing our reactions and responses, in this case, about three of the largest groups of immigrants to the USA, from Ireland, Italy and Poland. BHO then went on to state his position that, "America wasn't weakened by the presence of these newcomers... it was strengthened," with the weak-strong pairing contrasting the views of those who believe that immigrants have weakened America, with those who believe the opposite.

Military and Medical Metaphors

At P23 a military metaphor is made use of: "Politics is *a battle* of ideas; in the course of a healthy debate, we'll prioritize different goals, and the different means of reaching them" (emphasis added). According to Coxall, Robins and Leach (2003), in their chapter, 'Political Ideologies: The Battle of Ideas': "politicians and parties compete for the middle ground and abandon controversial ideas" (p. 50), thus employing their own topographical and militaristic metaphor, based on land being fought over. However, in its non-literal sense, 'middle ground' refers to: "a position between two opposite opinions in an argument" (*CALD*, 2021) which relates to BHO's mention of "a healthy debate." That comment may have been an allusion to the opposite, i.e., the unhealthy or toxic debates that characterized much of the 2016 presidential campaign in the USA (see, for example, Lopez, 2017)—which set the tone for most of the US presidential discourse of the following four years (see Part III).

The notion of a "healthy debate" recalls Galtung's fondness for medical metaphors when discussing notions of peace (1969, 1985 and see Chapter 3), and relates to the publication of a seminal book on the subject, *Metaphors We Live By*, by George Lakoff and Mark Johnson, in 1980. Those authors began their book by discussing the metaphor, "Argument is War" (p. 2), and explained that: "This metaphor is reflected in our everyday language by a variety of expressions" (p. 2). Their examples included: "Your claims are *indefensible*; He *attacked every weak point* in my argument; His criticisms were *right on target*; I *demolished* his argument; I never *won* an argument with him" (p. 3, original emphases). Although the male-only, he-his-him language dates the first edition of the Lakoff and Johnson book, the use of the 'argument is war' metaphor is still 'alive and kicking' in today's English. The linguistic relationship can be represented as: [politics = battle] + [debate = argument = war].

At the end of P25, BHO referred to "the essential spirit of innovation and practical problem-solving that guided our Founders," which is immediately followed, at the start of P26, by:

> It's that spirit, born of the Enlightenment, that made us an economic powerhouse... It's that spirit—a faith in reason, and enterprise, and *the primacy of right over might*, that allowed us to resist the lure of fascism and tyranny during the Great Depression. (emphasis added)

The description of the USA as "an economic powerhouse" connects to an earlier reference to how powerful the USA is, at P9.1, when BHO said: "we remain the wealthiest, most powerful, and most respected nation on Earth." Whether or not any of those claims were true then, or are more/less true/false now, depends on how 'wealth', 'power', and 'respect' are defined and measured. A key phrase here, from an NPL perspective, is "the primacy of right over might," in which 'primacy' means "the most important thing" (*CALD*, 2021), 'right' refers to correct action, and 'might' refers to military strength. That raises the critical question of *who* gets to decide when it is right to use force—as it is almost never those on whom that force is unloaded and unleashed. Another important phrase at P26 is, "to resist the lure of fascism and tyranny." 'Resistance' can mean, more generally, "the refusal to accept or comply with something; the attempt to prevent something by action or argument" (*OED*, 2021) or more specifically, in relation to WWII: "the Resistance: The underground movement formed in France during World War II to fight the German occupying forces and the Vichy government" (*OED*, 2021). In addition, the use of 'lure' as a noun here refers to something that can act as bait to attract animals, or people, so they can be caught, trapped or ensnared.

A thorough discussion of Fascism is beyond the scope of this book, as it is such a large, complex, multifaceted political concept, starting with the all-purpose definition: "a political system based on a very powerful leader, state control, and being extremely proud of country and race, and in which political opposition is not allowed" (*CALD*, 2021). However, within the large volumes of literature written about fascism, there are the more specific definitions given by authors such as Michael Mann, in his 2004 book, titled simply *Fascist*: "Most concisely, *fascism is the pursuit of a transcendent and cleansing nation-statism through paramilitarism*" (p. 13, original emphasis). Mann spends the next several pages unpacking that definition, which we do not need to do here, other than to highlight the fact that this particular 'F-word' would have registered strongly with some members of BHO's audience. A 'tyrant' is "a ruler who has unlimited power over other people, and uses it unfairly and cruelly" (*CALD*, 2021) and the two—fascism and tyranny—have become synonymous with each other. (For more on this, see Christopher Hutton's *Linguistics and the Third Reich: Mother-Tongue Fascism, Race and the Science of Language*, 1999).

Later in P26, BHO talked about the building of a "post-World War II Order," reference to which is used to begin P27: "That order is now being challenged—first by *violent fanatics* who claim to speak for Islam; more recently by autocrats in foreign capitals who see free markets, open democracies, and civil society itself as a threat to their power" (emphasis added). Although chaos is not mentioned anywhere in the OFA, many people, if asked 'What is the opposite of order?' would probably say, 'chaos'. In that case, the allusion to chaos may be a good example of what could be called a 'subliminal antonym', i.e., creating an image in the mind of the listener/

reader by referring to the opposite, but as that opposite has not been explicitly identified and named, it occurs at the subconscious level.

"Violent fanatics" may count as a kind of tautological descriptor, or as a form of deliberate repetition-for-emphasis, as a 'fanatic' is defined as someone "who has very extreme beliefs that may lead them to behave in unreasonable or *violent ways*" (*CALD*, 2021, emphasis added). Although the jump from unreasonable to violent is quite a large leap, clearly the sense of 'fanatical' can incorporate resorting to violence, especially as 'peaceful fanatic', 'peacefully fanatical' or 'fanatically peaceful' would all appear to be contradictions in terms. Also, BHO made a key distinction by distinguishing between those who *claim to* speak for Islam, and those who *actually* speak for Islam, which may have been an attempt to avoid the mistaken connotation—either deliberately or accidental—of [Islamic = Extremist = Terrorist].

In other cognitive-linguistic connotations, "foreign autocrats" (P27) appear to be equated with "violent fanatics," at least regarding their threat to free markets, and democratic, civil societies. The concluding "threat to their power" is the fourth of seven uses of 'threat' and 'threatened' in this address, with three instantiations before P27, and three after. The three before are:

P10: There have been moments throughout our history that *threatened* to rupture that solidarity

P15: There's a second *threat* to our democracy—one as old as our nation itself

P23: This trend represents a third *threat* to our democracy (emphases added)

And the three after are:

P28: ISIL will be destroyed, and no one who *threatens* America will ever be safe

P29: our own freedoms will eventually be *threatened*

P31: our democracy is *threatened* whenever we take it for granted (emphases added)

It seems clear, then, that BHO was highlighting, perhaps to an almost excessive extent, the scale and scope of a series of potential threats, which might relate to an earlier caution about the need to "remain vigilant against external aggression" (29.3, see below).

An In-Depth NPL Deconstruction of a Single Paragraph

An NPL analysis of P29 illustrates a number of important points, one of which is that NPL goes into much greater linguistic depth than previous language analyses that have been referred to as 'PL', as discussed in Chapter 4 (here, for example, an approximately 2,000-word analysis of a 150-word piece of text). The deconstruction of P29 is an example of that kind of in-depth analysis, however, not analysis for the sake of analysis, as in 'Pure Linguistics', but analysis that peels away the many layers and levels of meaning, to unearth what lies beneath. Another aspect of NPL analyses illustrated by the following detailed deconstruction of P29 is the non-linear relationship between quantity and quality of language, in which a great deal of meaning can be expressed in relatively few words, as discussed in Chapter 6.

Paragraph 29, which can, for analytic purposes, be divided into ten sentences, is worth looking at in this level of detail, as this paragraph illustrates many areas that are of particular interest to NPL practitioners, in a single, densely-packed chunk of text, including some of the warist discourse and other kinds of discourse areas introduced and explored earlier, such as:

- military might
- democratic ideals
- citizens and citizenship
- terrorism and torture
- civil liberties
- expanding democracy and human rights
- extremism, sectarianism and authoritarianism
- freedom and the rule of law
- the likelihood of war

The first point that needs to be noted is that most (or even all) of the areas above may be subject to geopolitical definition, for example, 'democracy' and 'democratic ideals' as well as 'citizenship' and 'civil liberties' may be defined differently, depending on the country, the context and on who is doing the defining. Paragraph 29 began:

P29.1: But protecting our way of life requires more than our military.

P29.2: Democracy can buckle when we give in to fear.

P29.3: So just as we, as citizens, must remain vigilant against external aggression,

P29.4: we must guard against a weakening of the values that make us who we are.

P29.5: That's why, for the past eight years, I've worked to put the fight against terrorism on a firm legal footing.

P29.6: That's why we've ended torture, worked to close Gitmo, and reform our laws governing surveillance to protect privacy and civil liberties.

P29.7: That's why I reject discrimination against Muslim Americans, who are just as patriotic as we are.

P29.8: That's why we cannot withdraw from big global fights—to expand democracy, and human rights, and women's rights, and LGBT rights

P29.9: no matter how imperfect our efforts, no matter how expedient ignoring such values may seem.

P.29.10: For the fight against extremism and intolerance and sectarianism are of a piece with the fight against authoritarianism and nationalist aggression.

There are a number of key words and phrases in P29 that catch the eye and ear of the NPL practitioner. A more obvious example is 'military' (P29.1), as one of the cognitive associations that most readily comes to mind with that is 'armed forces', which in turn carries with it words and phrases such as 'weapons' and 'use of force'. The phrase "when we give into fear" (P29.2) is likely to have been an echo or a linguistic 'callback' to the inaugural address given by the 32nd President of the United States, Franklin D. Roosevelt (1882–1945), who won a record four presidential elections, and served as President for 12 years, from 1933 until his death in 1945. In 1933, Roosevelt famously said: "the only thing we have to fear is... fear itself"—with a brief but effective, dramatic pause between "fear is" and "fear itself." Such pauses were also put to good use by BHO throughout the speeches he gave during his time in office, from his first address as the President of the USA (see Chapter 6) to his last.

At P29.3, there are two words that should also be noted in an NPL analysis: vigilant and aggression. The latter may be more obvious, as the phrase 'acts of aggression' usually refers to one country behaving in a hostile manner towards another, often entailing the use of armed forces. Here, the implication appears to be that the aggression is coming from elsewhere, somewhere outside of the USA, as it is described as an "external aggression." That description could have been an allusion to foreign powers, such as Russia, who were at that time being investigated for attempting to interfere with the 2016 presidential election in the USA, and other elections in other countries as well, including the UK (Oliker, 2017). 'Vigilant' may count as a less obvious item in the NPL lexicon, but it should be noted, as it means: "being very careful to notice things, *esp.* [especially] *signs of danger*" (*CALD*, 2021, emphasis added). At P29.4, "we must guard against a weakening of the values that make us who we are," it would have been tempting to contrast weak with strong, for example: we must guard against a weakening of the values that make us strong. However, such a juxtaposition of opposing forces might have seemed too obvious a contrast and perhaps too forceful. Also, the use of "the values that make us who we are" rather than 'the values that make us strong' is a more effective appeal to a collective sense of identity.

There is some rhythmic alliteration at P29.5 with the three-part, f-word [fight + firm + footing], and more important here is the reference to "fight against terrorism," as fighting is generally frowned upon. However, fighting for something that is perceived to be desirable, for example, fighting for 'a good cause', such as Freedom, is received positively, and encouraged. But on other side of the same coin, fighting against something that is perceived to be undesirable, for example, fighting against Terrorism, is also received positively and encouraged. Therefore, whether fighting is labelled as good or bad largely depends on what is being fought for or against, and who is doing the fighting. Furthermore, the use of "a firm legal footing" may have been to give the "fight against terrorism" some sort of legal validity, perhaps in an international court of human rights, such as The International Criminal Court (ICC)—validity which such fighting may or may not have had in reality. Also, as discussed below, P29.5 is one of the instances in which BHO signals the taking of personal responsibility, with "I've worked."

The earlier reference to "protecting our way of life" (P29.1) appears again at P29.6: "to protect privacy and civil liberties." We can also see the third part of an elongating sequence describing achievements over the previous eight years; from the two-word "ended torture," to the four-word "worked to close Gitmo," to the five-word, "reform our laws governing surveillance." 'Gitmo' is the short-form for the Guantanamo Bay detention camp and military prison, operated by the US government, in Cuba, where inmates could be detained indefinitely, without trial, and tortured. The camp is, therefore, considered by organizations such as Amnesty International to be a major violation of human rights. Gitmo was opened in January 2002, after the attacks by the Islamic terrorist group al-Qaeda against the United States on September 11, 2001. Here, the difference between "worked to close" and 'closed' is a considerable one, as the BHO administration did attempt to have Gitmo closed down, but were met with strong bipartisan resistance. Although, as of late 2021, Gitmo is still officially open, the number of inmates is reported to have been reduced from more than 200 to fewer than 50. In January 2018, BHO's successor, DJT, signed an executive order to keep Gitmo open indefinitely (see Swain, 2019). However, there is the possibility that the administration of DJT's successor, under the 46th President of the USA, may follow through on the plans for closure.

Pronoun-switching can be examined as a distinctive feature between P29.1 and P29.7, including the notion of 'ouring' (see Chapter 5), in which collective pronouns are used to include rather than exclude. This section of the text starts with the possessive pronoun 'our', twice at P29.1, with "our way of life" and "our military," implying, firstly, a shared set of values, beliefs and attitudes, which may be key for living together peacefully, and secondly, the collective ownership of the armed forces. However, the armed forces of the USA are not, in fact, collectively owned, as they are under the auspices of the Commander-in-Chief, i.e., the President of the USA—but they are collectively paid for, as they are funded by tax-payers. The use of the shared-ownership pronoun 'our' then switches to 'we', four times at P29.2, P29.3 and P29.4: we + "give into fear" [preceded by 'when'] + "as citizens" + "must guard against" + "who we are," showing a range of uses of group pronouns, while incorporating "guard against," which is often a preemptive response to an anticipated attack of some kind. The next 'we' is the contracted form of 'we have', i.e., 'we've', which gives the OFA a more informal and conversational tone. Contractions can also be used to blur the distinctions between written and spoken forms of the language. Here, contractions are used together with the explanatory, "That's why," repeated a second time, and two more times at P29.7 and P29.8, making four uses of "That's why" in four consecutive sentences, between P29.5 and P29.8. That repetition creates a rhythm, and gives the text a forward-flowing momentum, while also giving reasons for some of the decisions BHO had made and the actions he had taken over the previous eight years when he was in office.

There are only two first-person singular references in these ten sentences: "I've worked to put the fight against terrorism on a firm legal footing" (P29.5) and "I reject discrimination against Muslim Americans" (P29.7). Those appear to have been carefully constructed, to show BHO taking personal responsibility for those two particular policies and actions, rather than the earlier expressions of shared responsibility. At P29.8 the pronoun reverts to 'we': "That's why we cannot withdraw from big global fights" (P29.8), using the more direct and perhaps more emotive 'fight', rather than 'global conflict' or the gentler-still 'global tensions.' There is no indication of which specific "global fights" are being referred to, but the use of the present simple tense, i.e., 'that is why' (used in its contracted form, "that's why") alludes to conflicts that were taking place at the time the OFA was being delivered. One other aspect of P29.7 is also noteworthy;

the characterization of "Muslim Americans" as being "just as patriotic as we are" (P29.7), indicating a form of 'ouring'.

REACT 7.2: *How aware are you of your own use of pronouns, and how other people around you use pronouns? For example, do you use 'we' more when you want to be more inclusive? For one or two days, pay careful attention to your use of pronouns, and the use of pronouns by those around you. You might be surprised by what you find.*

Although details of where, when, and who is the 'enemy' are missing from the mention of "global fights," details of what those fights are about was given at P29.9: "to expand democracy, and human rights, women's rights, and LGBT rights," linking the notion of democracy closely and repeatedly to the notion of rights. Also, a superordinate categorization is used, starting with 'human', followed by 'women', followed by members of the LGBTQIA+ community.

Sentence P29.9 continued: "no matter how imperfect our efforts, no matter how expedient ignoring such values may seem," which appears to be a combination of different speech acts, starting with an implied apology, i.e., we are sorry [if/that] our efforts were less-than-ideal. Alternatively, that could be read as less of an apology, and more of an insistence on pursuing a current course of action, even if or when it goes badly, i.e., we will keep fighting for these rights, even when we get it wrong. The reason for that continuation of efforts is given, with a doubling of "no matter how," as being the importance of values, linking back to P29.4: "we must guard against a weakening of the values that make us who we are," and extending the connection to make another three-part relationship: [Democracy = Rights = Values]. Or [Democracy = Rights + Values]. Or [Values = Democracy + Rights]. That is also an echoing of a statement made during BHO's inaugural address as President of the USA, in 2009, when he said: "As for our common defense, we reject as false the choice between our safety and our ideals... Those ideals still light the world, and we will not give them up *for expedience sake*" (P18, emphasis added). As noted above, it is highly unlikely that audiences listening to such speeches will be consciously aware of such echoing or 'callbacks', which is when NPL analyses can help make longitudinal connections between the language use of an individual over time, thereby identify recurring and shifting themes and patterns.

At P29.10, "[a]uthoritarianism and nationalist aggression" are presented as subsets of "extremism and intolerance and sectarianism." The use of unusual phrases such as "are of a piece with," together with the sentence-initial, low-frequency use of "For," rather than "Because," may be one of the reasons why BHO's speaking style has been referred to as 'aloof' or 'distant' (Bouie, 2013). Furthermore, the sentence-initial use of words like 'for' may, for those listening carefully, even have been a distraction from the main content and purpose of sentence P29.10, i.e., "the fight against extremism and intolerance and sectarianism . . . against authoritarianism and nationalist aggression." Each of those five vocabulary items—[extremism + intolerance + sectarianism + authoritarianism + nationalist aggression]—are loaded with meaning, all of it negative, to explain or justify (some might say, to excuse) the fighting that is repeatedly referred to throughout P29.

Immediately after P29, at P30, BHO said: "So let's be vigilant but not afraid. ISIL will try to kill innocent people." The repeated warning to be vigilant here at P30, echoes the earlier warning, at P29.3, about the need to "remain vigilant against external aggression." But at just seven words, it is the second sentence that is most potentially shocking: "ISIL will . . . kill," which is one of the shortest sentences in this entire OFA, but the one with the most impact, not only because of the word 'kill', but also because of the rhyming definiteness of 'will/kill', somewhat ameliorated by "try to." Also, the contradiction between being told to not be afraid, while at the same time being told people are coming to kill you may have caused some confusion. The climactic ending to this high impact line is the reference to the "innocent people," which is an echoing from eight years earlier, in 2009, during his inaugural address, when BHO warned: "those who seek to advance their aims by inducing terror and *slaughtering innocents*" (emphasis added, see Chapter 6, P22 of the OIA). The "ISIL will . . . kill" statement at P.30 is also a parallel structure with the equal and opposite statement made by BHO at P28 (discussed above): "ISIL will be destroyed."

There was at the time a great deal of discussion about the difference between the abbreviations 'ISIS', standing for 'The Islamic State of Iraq and al-Sham', and 'ISIL', standing for the 'Islamic State of Iraq and the Levant', which includes Cyprus, Israel, Jordan, Lebanon, Palestine, Syria, and Turkey (see, for example, Kahn, 2016; Sanchez, 2017; Kauffman, 2017). However, according to Jonathan Hogeback, writing for the *Encyclopedia Britannica* online: "the acronym ISIL is the more-accurate name, as it recognizes these areas that the group affects and targets, while ISIS refers exclusively to Iraq and Syria" (no date). A third name has also emerged, 'Daesh', which is also an acronym, but with a phonetic or phonological twist, as "the sound of the acronym is intended to be unpleasant, and the rare use of an acronym in Arabic is meant to attribute disrespect to the group and to ignore the meaning behind its longer name" (Hogeback, n.d.). And regarding the relationships between languages and cultures, it is interesting to note that in situations such as this ISIS–ISIL-Daesh distinction, abbreviating can be perceived not as a neutral shorthand but as a deliberate insult.

Concluding Comments and Closing Statements

We can now examine some of BHO's concluding comments, starting with, at P38: "I've seen the youngest of children remind us of our obligations to care for refugees, *to work in peace,* and above all to look out for each other" (emphasis added). This repeating three-part pattern, given here in the form of three infinitive verbs—"to care . . . to work . . . to look out for"—includes the third explicit reference to peace. The two previous references were at P8: "In 10 days, the world will witness a hallmark of our democracy: *the peaceful transfer of power* (as discussed above), and at P19: "when they wage *peaceful protest,* they're not demanding special treatment," referring to times "when minority groups voice discontent [who are] not just engaging in reverse racism or practicing political correctness" (emphases added). It is important to note that, in the OFA, the references to peace appear to be significantly outnumbered by the references to armed conflicts, such as war. There may be many reasons for that imbalance, one of which could be reflecting the perception, in the mind of the speaker and/or the listeners, that there is much more war in the world than there is peace, whether or not that was the case in actuality (see Pettersson & Eck, 2018, and Chapter 1).

The use of the preposition 'in' in the phrase "to work in peace" (P38) is linguistically noteworthy, because it is a somewhat unexpected grammatical construction, as 'to work peacefully' or 'to work towards peace' may have been anticipated. However, "in peace" may have been to contrast 'in war-time'. Likewise, "to wage peace" might have been somewhat unexpected, as the more common collocations are 'to wage war' and 'to make peace'. The "youngest of children" is likely to have been a reference to one of the news reports in 2016, when a six-year old named Alex, who lived in New York, wrote to BHO, asking the President to invite a Syrian child, Omran Daqneesh, into Alex's home, after a devastating airstrike in Aleppo, the previous month. Alex was responding to: "The photograph of a traumatised Omran, covered in dust and blood after a bombing raid in Aleppo [which] captivated the world's attention and became a symbol for the suffering of Syria's children in the civil war" (Blair, 2016) which has ravaged the country for more than ten years (since 2011). Alex and his family were invited to the White House and met with President Obama and his family.

In one of the closing paragraphs, at P43, BHO spoke about the future, specifically addressing the next generation:

> This generation coming up—unselfish, altruistic, creative, patriotic...You believe in a fair, just, inclusive America...and you are willing to carry this hard work of democracy forward. You'll soon outnumber any of us, and I believe as a result that the future is in good hands.

Here we can see a 4 + 3 construction, with four adjectives describing "this generation," followed by three more describing the country they will inherit—albeit a highly idealized view—while echoing the statement made at the beginning of the OFA, at P6: "The work of democracy has always been hard, contentious and sometimes bloody." The four-part adjectival sequence used here, i.e., "unselfish, altruistic, creative, patriotic," can be seen as a blend of a more positive first three adjectives, ending with the complex and potentially less-positive "patriotic," as a 'patriot' can be defined as: "a person who loves their country and, if necessary, will *fight for it*" (*CALD*, 2021, emphasis added).

In the penultimate paragraph, P45, BHO referred to a "creed reaffirmed by those who planted flags from foreign battlefields to the surface of the moon; a creed at the core of every American whose story is not yet written." This is the third use of 'creed', with the previous two being: "a constant widening of *our founding creed* to embrace all, and not just some," at P6, and "America wasn't weakened by the presence of these newcomers; they embraced *this nation's creed*, and it was strengthened," at P20 (as discussed above). And again, we see the reference to armed conflict, on "foreign battlefields"—not domestic—this time connected to the success of the USA's space flight program, and wrapped up with a nod to the power of the personal narrative (see Chapter 6), "at the core of every American *whose story is not yet written*" (emphasis added), which may also have been an allusion to the "newcomers" mentioned earlier.

The invoking of the image of the American flag recalls the expression 'to wrap oneself in the flag', which is defined as showing "great loyalty and support for your country *in a way that does not ask questions*" (*CALD*, 2021, emphasis added). That implies a potentially powerfully destructive kind of mindless nationalism, which can easily cross the thin line into racism, which appears to have been a growing problem in many countries in recent years. The OFA spoken text concluded, at P46, with an echo of/callback to the slogan used in BHO's 2008 presidential campaign, 'Yes We Can', together with a past-tense variation on the theme, this using 'we did'. There is also a concluding note of thanks, and the usual, obligatory call for God to continue blessing that particular country: "Yes We Can. Yes We Did. Yes We Can. Thank you. God bless you. And may God continue to bless the United States of America."

REACT 7.3: *Video and audio recordings of this speech/spoken text are freely available online, for example, on YouTube and C-Span. Look closely and carefully at the last few minutes of this farewell speech. What do you notice about BHO's body language, and do you see any connections (or disconnects) between his verbal and non-verbal language in those last few minutes?*

Suggestions for Further Reading

The Secret Life of Pronouns: What Our Words Say About Us (2011, Bloomsbury Press) by James W. Pennebaker is one of the most through examinations of how pronouns are used in English, and how each person's use of pronouns can reveal a great deal about them.

The Audacity of Hope: Thoughts on Reclaiming the American Dream, written by BHO, was published in 2006 (Crown Publishers), and became an immediate bestseller. Although such books are now *de rigueur* for politicians in the USA attempting to get on the ballot to run for the presidency, the book provides many illuminating examples of BHO's use of language in a written text.

Maya Rhodan wrote an informative piece for *Time* magazine (11 January, 2017), 'In His Farewell Speech, President Obama Returns to His Roots as a Community Leader'. The piece, including a five-minute video, can be read/seen at: http://time.com/4631089/barack-obama-farewell-speech-analysis

Andrew Gallagher (PhD) hosts a website called 'Metaphors in American Politics', and at the link below, he describes the metaphors used in BHO's farewell speech, under eleven main areas: Personification, Vision, Animals, Shapes and Sizes, Strong Chemicals, Literature, Games, Food, Machines, Buildings, and Journey. http://www.politicalmetaphors.com/2017/01/16/obamas-farewell-address

PART III

New Peace Linguistics Analyses of the Language of Donald J. Trump and Joseph R. Biden

8

Manipulating Not Communicating

Bending and Breaking the Rules

According to a 2020 survey of global power and influence: "The US retains its position as the world's most-powerful country" (Baker, 2020). The annual rankings, published by *US News and World Report,* are based on comparing the political, economic and military power of 80 countries, drawing on input from more than 20,000 respondents. According to that report, the USA retained its position as first most powerful in 2020—although that may change in the years ahead (Baker, 2020)—with Russia second and China third most powerful in 2020. However, power is not synonymous with respect, and as Clark (2017) pointed out, there has been declining respect for the leadership of the USA in recent years. For example, by 2019, the annual *Forbes* survey of 'The World's Most Reputable Countries' ranked the USA as 36th out of 55 countries (Valet, 2019), followed by India, South Africa and Egypt, ranked 37th, 38th and 39th, respectively (with Sweden, Switzerland and Norway ranked 1st, 2nd and 3rd, respectively). The report concluded that: "The reputation of the US has been in steep decline since 2016" (Valet, 2019).

The New Peace Linguistics and The Role of Language in Conflict, pages 141–166

In addition to Power and Respect, Trust is perhaps the third most important factor in making such global comparisons, which the *US News and World Report* also provides annual, global rankings of. In 2020, the *Report* stated that: "The world's trust in the United States... has dropped by more than 50% since 2016, *the sharpest drop of any country assessed*" (Drew, 2020, emphasis added). The UK was also found to have "experienced the second-greatest drop in the world's trust since 2016" and as a contrast, Canada is "seen as the world's most trustworthy country... a position the nation has held since the annual global survey was first released in 2010" (Drew 2010). Therefore, because of power rather than respect or trust, no matter who is the President of the USA, whatever he (or perhaps, even one day, she/they) says or writes needs to be paid close attention to by anyone interested in understanding how the language of those in power shapes the world for the rest of us. And that understanding needs to go beyond the superficial surface meanings, to uncover the deeper multilayered meanings of, for example, what the US President says and writes, especially the ways in which their words relate to conflicts such as war and/or peace. History may well judge the 45th President of the USA, DJT, harshly, for many reasons, and the purpose of these chapters is not to critique the DJT administration for their governmental policies. However, given the importance of context in NPL analyses—and the fact that, in this case, DJT is the context—it is necessary to give a few pages to briefly summarizing key aspects of the four years of the DJT presidency, which provided an embarrassment of riches for those of us in the NPL field.

DJT and The Language of Lies

Lies Need Language. It may seem obvious that language is the essential prerequisite for lying, as without language there can be no lies—no language, no lies. As the saying, attributed to Irish playwright Oliver Goldsmith (1728–1774), goes: Ask me no questions and I'll tell you no lies. However, from an NPL perspective, analyzing the language of some of the most powerful people in the world can be vitally important in helping to make it clear when those people are manipulating others through spreading—deliberately or accidentally—misinformation, when they speak and when they write. By the same token, it is tempting to think that great big obvious lies should not fool anyone with any capacity for intelligent thought. However, as political leanings in the USA and elsewhere have shown, disturbingly large numbers of people appear to swallow the lies of their leaders hook-line-and-sinker (as the fishing analogy goes).

'Everybody Lies!' is a common retort from those who lie easily and effortless, without noticing or even thinking about what they are doing, and from those who support others in their compulsive lie-telling. Although that statement may be factually true, there is no way of proving or disproving it. Furthermore, not all lies are created equal. If the most powerful person in the world tells a lie, to the largest audience in the world, then that lie can do incalculably greater damage than, for example, a small child, standing next to a broken object saying: 'Wasn't me!' Furthermore, again from the point of view of NPL, such large-scale lies may not only be morally and ethically dangerous, but they can have deadly consequences. For example, at the end of his four years in office, DJT's "legacy of lies" and a presidency "riddled" with falsehoods (Cathey, 2021) was being described in relation to "how Trump *weaponized mistruths* during his presidency" (Cathey, 2021, emphasis added). That kind of language weaponizing has been part of a pattern in DJT's spoken and written comments. For example, in 2020, DJT gave an example of "weaponizing religion" by attacking the faith of the future-46th President, Joe Biden, claiming that Biden was "against God" (Cathey, 2020). No evidence of any kind was found to support that claim.

In relation to lies and lying, DJT may be remembered as one of the most prolific liars ever to occupy the White House, officially passing the 10,000 mark in the Spring of 2019: "In a truly superhuman feat, *The Washington Post* has tallied all the 'falsehoods' that have spewed from Trump's mouth and fingers since January 20, 2017, to April 27, 2019... that's a whopping 10,111 in 828 days" (Levin, 2019). Not only that, but the rate of lying was increasing to the point of DJT being labelled "a pathological liar [who] after telling a mere 5,000 false and misleading statements during his first 601 days in office... doubled his bullshit in just a third of the time" telling nearly two dozen lies a day in the seven-month period between October 2018 and April 2019. (see Curtis, 2018j, for a linguistic analysis of the first 6,000 lies told by DJT during his first two years in office).

The DJT presidential lying, on a record-breaking, apparently pathological scale continued into 2020. For example, of a number of websites that were created to do nothing but fact-check DJT's statements, *The Washington Post* tracker was widely accepted as the most complete and the most reliable. By the Summer of 2020, the number of false and (deliberately, knowingly) misleading claims had doubled, from the 10,000 falsehoods in the Spring of 2019, to more than 20,000 (Kessler, Kelly, Rizzo & Lee, 2021). Earlier in 2020, before *The Washington Post* updated count was published, *The Huffington Post* senior White House correspondent, S.V. Dáte, wrote that after more than 30 years as a journalist, which included 12 years covering the Florida legislature, he had: "never encountered a public official, a candidate for office, a bureaucrat, a defense lawyer or, frankly, an actual criminal who is as regularly and aggressively dishonest as the current president of the United States" (Dáte, 2020). Not only the sheer number of lies but also the scale and scope of DJT's lies led Dáte to conclude that: "the defining feature of this White House" will be a president who will "spew falsehoods about nearly everything... He lies in one-on-one interviews, in formal news conferences, and standing beside other world leaders. He lies in official government speeches and at campaign rallies" (Dáte, 2020).

As NPL includes understanding and analyzing what might appear to be subtle differences between the meaning of closely related words, a note on the difference between a lie and a falsehood is necessary here. A 'lie' is defined as: "something you say that you know is not true" (*CALD, 2021*), whereas a 'falsehood' is defined as: "a lie or a statement that is not correct" (*CALD, 2021*). Clearly, there is considerable overlap between the two, with more in common between them than aspects that distinguishes them. One potential difference is the question of intent, i.e., if the speaker *knows* that what they are saying is not true, but they say it anyway. However, this definition of a falsehood omits the agent of the action, and only refers to the statement itself. Therefore, one way of distinguishing between the two is to look at how often the untrue/false statement is repeated, in spite of the untrue/false nature of the statement having been pointed out and proved. As we will see from the discussion below, one of the many things that DJT may be remembered for in the years to come is how many lies he repeated and how often he repeated them. As discussed below, in analyzing the lies told by DJT up to 2017, *Wired* reporter Emily Dreyfuss (2017) asked and answered the question in the title of her article: 'Want to make a lie seem true? Say it again, And again. And again' (2017).

By the end of his one-term four years, DJT had racked up well over 30,000 falsehoods, as collecting and analyzed by the same *Washington Post* team (Kessler, Kelly, Rizzo & Lee, 2021), and reported in new outlets around the world. But by January 2021, tracking DJT falsehoods had become, in some ways, a cottage industry, in which independent fact-checkers were working full-time, around-the-clock, just to keep up. *The Washington Post* team created what is probably the most thorough representation and record of the 30,000-plus falsehoods, starting with a graph that shows 15 false claims on DJT's first full day in office, January 21, 2017. Within one month, the total number of falsehoods had grown exponentially, to 149 by February 22 (2017), and to well over 2,000 after 12 months in office (by January 21, 2018). After 24 months in office, the total number had grown to well over 8,000 (by January 22, 2019)—a four-fold increase over the previous 12 months—which continued to grow exponentially, up to nearly 16,500 false claims by January 22, 2020. However, while campaigning during the 2020 US presidential election year, the number of falsehoods rose even more rapidly, growing by 50% in just nine months, up to more than 25,000 false claims made by mid-October 2020, peaking at a grand total of 30,573 falsehoods by DJT's last full day in office, 19 January 2021 (Kessler, Kelly, Rizzo & Lee, 2021).

The 30,000-plus false claims were arranged by the *Washington Post* team into no fewer than 18 categories: the economy, immigration, jobs, foreign policy, taxes, Russia, healthcare, the 2020 election, the environment, DJT's own biographical record, crimes, terrorism, guns, education, trade, Ukraine probe, Coronavirus, and a miscellaneous category. The *Washington Post* team even counted how many times each false claim was made by DJT, with "We also built the greatest economy in the history of the world... Powered by these policies, we built the greatest economy in the history of the world"—a lie repeated nearly 500 times over the four years, meaning it was repeated on average every three days, over a period of approximately 1,460 days. The second most-repeated lie, said nearly 300 times, and which DJT was saying up his last morning in office (January 20, 2021) was: "We also got tax cuts, the largest tax cut and reform in the history of our country, by far" (Kessler, Kelly, Rizzo & Lee, 2021).

Even within such a mountainous pile of lies, some lies live long after they have been told, especially when they result in people killing and being killed, such as the deadly attack on the US Capitol in January 2021, during which five people were killed—when, once again, language played a key role. For example, Calvin Woodward and Deb Riechmann reported on 'How Trump's words, rhetoric have incited violence, including Capitol breach' (2021). Reporting for the BBC, Sam Cabral noted the importance of DJT's words at a rally that ignited the Capitol attacks, as he: "exhorted them [the crowd] to march on Congress where politicians had met to certify Democrat Joe Biden's win. *The attack began moments after he took the applause.* Those words have now played a central part in his second impeachment" (Cabral, 2021, emphasis added). Five key phrases from DJT's speech that day were discussed by University of Baltimore professor Garrett Epps (who was interviewed by Cabral), starting with: "We won this election, and we won it by a landslide" (Cabral, 2021)—a claim for which not a single shred of evidence was ever provided. But such a claim, no matter how false, may have played a critical role in turning a group of disgruntled and frustrated protestors into an angry, armed mob—angry enough to kill. The second phrase followed the same lie: "We will stop the steal," as nobody 'stole' anything from anyone, followed by a three-part: "We will never give up. We will never concede. It doesn't happen." It is not clear which 'it' DJT was referring to here, but he was most likely referring to the 2020 election results being officially and finally certified. As Epps pointed out, DJT's use of 'we' is "exhorting his supporters to join him . . . saying in the clearest terms yet that he will never accept Joe Biden's win" (Cabral, 2021) (see Chapter 5 on the use of such pronouns).

The most direct call to arms from DJT came when he said: "If you don't fight like hell you're not going to have a country anymore," followed by the contradictory: "Peacefully and patriotically make your voices heard." Such immediate contradictions, from one phrase to the next, are one of the hallmarks of DJT's speeches, as Michael Kruse and Noah Wieland (2016) pointed out early on: "Trump has talked about every imaginable subject: gun rights to germs . . . love and sex, self-promotion and politics. And on every one of those topics, he has taken positions that directly contradict *exactly what he has previously said*" (original emphasis). In their report for *Politico*, Kruse and Wieland (2016) also provide well over 100 examples of such contradictions, going back to the 1970s, showing just deeply ingrained in DJT is this pattern of verbal behavior. Furthermore, returning to the events of January 6, 2021, it is clear from the death-toll that none of the hundreds of people who attacked the Capitol paid any attention to DJT's contradictory and apparently insincere call for peace. The last of the five phrases discussed by Cabral/Garrett is "We are going to Capitol," again employing the collective 'we', although DJT himself stayed well away from the Capitol that day.

Another one of the many other accounts of DJT's speech on January 6, 2021 was presented by American University School of Communication professor, Kurt Braddock, whose piece in *The Conversation* was titled: 'At impeachment hearing, lawmakers will deliberate over a deadly weapon used in the attack on Capitol Hill—*President Trump's words*' (Braddock, 2021, emphasis added). Braddock, whose research focuses on the role of disinformation and far-right domestic terrorism in the USA, reported that: "decades of research on social influence, persuasion and psychology show that the messages that people encounter heavily influence their decisions to engage in certain behaviors . . . *Words have consequences*" (Braddock, 2021, emphasis added). In the case of DJT, one of the consequences of his words that day in January is that he will go down in history as being the only president in the quarter-century history of the USA who has ever been impeached *twice*.

In terms of the potentially deadly consequence of repeated, large-scale lying by powerful people to massive audiences, and how NPL analyses may be able to help make such lies less damaging and less deadly, it is necessary to the turn to the global COVID-19 pandemic. As of November 2021, the pandemic had taken the lives of more than 5 million people worldwide, with the largest number of those, by far, being in the USA, which had exceeded

750,000 COVID deaths by that time, with a daily death toll as high as 3,000 to 4,000 Americans in the USA at the beginning of 2021. In reflecting on the four years of DJT's presidency, the question of how many of those lives might have been saved if a different leader had used different language, and had told the truth about the severity of the pandemic, was considered by many. For example, DJT was shown to have: "repeatedly spread misinformation about coronavirus testing, masks, unproven treatments—once claiming that injecting bleach might treat the virus—while attacking public health experts along the way who disputed his view that the virus wasn't just going to 'disappear'" (Cathey, 2021).

Unfortunately, neither NPL nor any other branch of applied linguistics could have done much to help in those circumstances. But more in-depth analyses of the language used by leaders during COVID-19 may help when the next pandemic comes—which according to the World Health Organization will be far sooner than most people realize or may even dare to think (Besheer, 2020). And from an NPL perspective, perhaps the most succinct reason such a field is necessary—perhaps needed now more than ever—is the fact that, as Braddock (2021) stated so clearly and concisely: words have consequences. In wrapping up this section of the destructive power of powerful people telling lies, to hundreds of millions of people, over and over again, a comparison between the lies of different US presidents was presented by US history professor, Eric Alterman, author of *Lying in State: Why Presidents Lie—And Why Trump Is Worse* (2020), who was interviewed for the BBC (Sheerin, 2021). Alterman concluded that: "Donald Trump is the Frankenstein's monster of a political system that has not merely tolerated lies from our leaders, but has come to demand them" (Sheerin, 2021).

REACT 8.1: *Do you agree or disagree with idea that 'Everybody lies'? Why or why not? When was the last time someone lied to you? Do you remember what they lied about and why they lied? When was the last time you lied to someone else? Do you remember what you lied about and why you lied?*

DJT's Contributions to Language, Literature, and Linguistics

As explained above, the 45th President's rhetoric was conclusively identified as one of the most influential factors in fomenting the deadly violence during the Capitol riots in January 2021; rhetoric which will likely be remembered long after the 45th President has faded from memory and passed away. Going back several centuries, comparisons with tragic figures in the plays of William Shakespeare were a recurring theme throughout DJT's four years in office. In fact, articles comparing DJT and characters created by Shakespeare started appearing even before DJT occupied the White House (Cohen-Wade, 2016). However, an unexpected aspect of DJT's legacy may be the inadvertent boost his one-term presidency gave to the world of language and literature, as well as to the evolution of NPL.

One of the first full-length literary works in this vein was published in 2018, written by Pulitzer Prize-winning author Stephen Greenblatt and titled *Tyrant: Shakespeare on Politics*, in which Greenblatt argues that "Shakespeare understood how those unfit for political office gain and hold on to power," and he explained 'How Shakespeare explains Donald Trump's rise to power' (Bethune, 2018). This particular area of interest continued to grow, and by 2020, Harvard University writing professor, Jeffrey Wilson, had gathered enough literary comparisons to write an entire book, *Shakespeare and Trump* (Wilson, 2020a). Wilson also wrote a piece describing '10 scenes from Shakespeare that fit Donald Trump's presidency' (Wilson, 2020b). Also in 2018, the DJT-inspired children's story book, *Whose Boat Is This Boat? Comments That Don't Help in the Aftermath of a Hurricane* (Colbert, 2018) was published, and 2020 also saw the publication of the DJT-inspired book of poetry by the multi-award-winning actor-turned-author, John Lithgow, *Trumpty Dumpty Wanted a Crown: Verses for a Despotic Age* (Lithgow, 2020). Those tragically Shakespearian comparisons continued into 2021. For example, Peter Herman, professor of English literature at San Diego State University and author of *Unspeakable: Literature and Terrorism from the Gunpowder Plot to 9/11* (2020), wrote a piece, 'Shakespeare and the Catastrophic End of Donald Trump's Presidency' (Herman, 2021), in which stated simply that: "In the end, Trump's presidency followed the general arc of a Shakespearean tragedy."

Even after years of being compared to so many deeply flawed figures, doomed to die dishonorable deaths, from the tips of Shakespeare's feather-quill pen, some new comparisons were still being found, at the end of his presidency. For example, *The New York Times* writer, Jesse Green (2021), suggested that 'It's Time to Turn the Page on the Trump-Shakespeare Comparisons', but not before proposing one more DJT comparison; this time to Shakespeare's lesser-known and rarely-performed play, Timon of Athens (which appears to have been co-authored with Thomas Middleton (1580–1627), published in the 1620s and first performed in the 1670s, more than 50 years after Shakespeare's death). Green (2021) describes the play, with a modern-twist ending, thus: "the Shakespeare tragedy in which a bankrupt businessman, deserted by his sycophants and bereft of power, renounces society with wild curses . . . to take up a miserly life by the sea at Mar-a-Lago." Some of the most oft-cited lines from Shakespeare, in connection with DJT, come from what many consider to be the most tragic of all such characters, Macbeth, in which he describes: "a poor player, That struts and frets his hour upon the stage, And then is heard no more . . . a tale, Told by an idiot, full of sound and fury, Signifying nothing" (Act 5, Scene 5).

By the Fall of 2019, DJT was being described by writers such as Peter Wehner, an editor at *The Atlantic* and a senior fellow at Ethics and Public Policy Center, who "served in the White House for seven years in three administrations and worked for three presidents," as "temperamentally unfit to be president . . . erratic . . . unprincipled . . . unstable . . . [with] a personality disorder" (Wehner, 2019). That view of DJT continued throughout 2020, including a book, *Too Much and Never Enough: How My Family Created the World's Most Dangerous Man* (2020), written by Dr. Mary L. Trump (PhD), a clinical psychologist, and DJT's niece. Other in-depth explorations of DJT include, for example, *A Very Stable Genius: Donald J Trump's Testing of America* (Rucker & Leonnig, 2020), *Fear: Trump in the White House* (Woodward, 2018) and *Rage* (Woodward, 2020), which focuses on how poor presidential leadership during a global pandemic resulted in the deaths of hundreds of thousands of Americans.

Such fatally fundamental character flaws may make someone dangerously "unfit to be president"—especially of the world's most powerful country (even if they are no longer trusted or respected). However, one of the by-products of those flaws is the production of more language for NPL analyses than that provided by any other world leader, coming from the 45th President President's on a daily basis—and sometimes even hourly. For example, DJT tweeted or re-tweeted: "approximately 3,500 times in 2018, 7,700 times in 2019 and on over more than 12,000 occasions in 2020. His most prolific day came on June 05, 2020 when he sent 200 tweets or retweets" (McCarthy, 2021). However, tweeted texts are limited to 280 characters, including spaces and punctuation, which may be a maximum of a single 50-word sentence, assuming mostly short, mono-syllabic words, as used by DJT. Therefore, given the potential impact of spoken and written texts from the President of the USA, and to show what in-depth NPL analyses can uncover, the remainder of this chapter is based on an analysis of a single, very long sentence spoken by DJT, said in the Summer of 2015, while he was campaigning to become the next President of the USA.

An NPL Analysis of a Single Sentence Spoken by Donald J. Trump (July, 2015)

Although it is one, single sentence—albeit a long and winding one—at least ten aspects of language use that are of interest to NPL practitioners were found, including:

- appealing to the 'losers', i.e., those who feel they have lost everything they value
- cries for attention (narcissism)
- claims of greatness
- claims of superiority (genetic, educational, etc.)
- misrepresentations of the self/the speaker (deliberate or accidental)
- self-aggrandizing claims
- the myth of the self-made man
- presenting insults as compliments
- negative stereotyping based on race, ethnicity
- labeling entire cultures and civilizations as 'killers'

For a single-sentence, which took just 90 seconds to say, to reveal so much about the speaker, through an NPL analysis, may be unprecedented. And such an utterance shows how even relatively little language (in this case, fewer than 300 words) can be used by those in power to manipulate their audience in unexpectedly and disproportionately large and varied ways. Lastly, it is possible that, had such analyses been carried out in 2015, far more clues and warning signs of where this would lead may have been revealed.

On July 21, 2015, Donald J. Trump (DJT) held a US presidential campaign rally in South Carolina, which has been a Republican stronghold for many decades. DJT was, then, playing to something of a 'home crowd', in the same way that BHO was when he gave his Farewell Address in Chicago, in 2017 (see Chapter 7). That historical-political sense of security may have been one reason why DJT ended up going so-far off-track that he produced one of the single longest sentences uttered in public, on record by a world leader. However, in spite of the rambling, think-aloud, stream-of-consciousness nature of the sentence, an NPL analysis can tell us much about how people in power use language to manipulate their audiences, rather than communicate with them.

As reporter Tara Golshan (2017) wrote in her report for *Vox* magazine, the sentence said by DJT was so difficult to understand that the magazine *Slate* asked its readers: 'Help Us Diagram This Sentence by Donald Trump!'

(Golshan, 2017). None of their readers apparently took up the challenge, and as far as we know, this is the first in-depth, systematic, linguistic analysis of what the linguist, John McWhorter (2018) called "this famous Trump utterance from July 2015." In this chapter, this now-(in)famous DJT sentence will be referred to as the 'South Carolina Commentary', abbreviated to 'SCC'—using 'commentary' in the sense of: "a spoken description of an event on the radio or television that is broadcast as the event happens" (*CALD*, 2021). As Golshan surmised, although the overall message was relatively simple and straightforward, i.e., "the Iran deal is bad for the United States" (Golshan, 2017), that message became a collection of "musings on his uncle's education, his own education, the power of nuclear energy, prisoners, the intelligence of women... the negotiating prowess of Iranians" (Golshan, 2017). She also noticed that in the SCC and in other talks by DJT: "We get a lot of fractured, unfinished sentences, moving quickly from thought to thought—what Trump calls a 'beautiful flowing sentence'," which DJT claims are distorted and misrepresented by the media. Transcripts of the sentence appeared in a number of news reports, including *Vox* (Golshan, 2017):

> Look, having nuclear—my uncle was a great professor and scientist and engineer, Dr. John Trump at MIT; good genes, very good genes, okay, very smart, the Wharton School of Finance, very good, very smart—you know, if you're a conservative Republican, if I were a liberal, if, like, okay, if I ran as a liberal Democrat, they would say I'm one of the smartest people anywhere in the world—it's true!—but when you're a conservative Republican they try—oh, do they do a number—that's why I always start off: Went to Wharton, was a good student, went there, went there, did this, built a fortune—you know I have to give my like credentials all the time, because we're a little disadvantaged—but you look at the nuclear deal, the thing that really bothers me—it would have been so easy, and it's not as important as these lives are—nuclear is powerful; my uncle explained that to me many, many years ago, the power and that was 35 years ago; he would explain the power of what's going to happen and he was right—who would have thought?—but when you look at what's going on with the four prisoners—now it used to be three, now it's four—but when it was three and even now, I would have said it's all in the messenger; fellas, and it is fellas because, you know, they don't, they haven't figured that the women are smarter right now than the men, so, you know, it's gonna take them about another 150 years—but the Persians are great negotiators, the Iranians are great negotiators, so, and they, they just killed, they just killed us.

REACT 8.2: *Take a few minutes, and re-read the above sentence, which took 90 seconds for DJT to say. Mark any words or phrases that you think are noteworthy, from an NPL perspective, with a brief note about why those particular words/phrases are especially relevant to NPL.*

To try to understand the discourse of DJT, including the think-aloud, 285-word single sentence above, Golshan (2017) interviewed a number of professional linguists and historians, including professor George Lakoff, who is famous for his work, with Mark Johnson, on metaphors (*Metaphors We Live By*, 1980). Based on those interviews, Golshan concluded that:

> when Trump's audience finishes his sentences for him, the blanks are filled with sentiments that resonate: fears of joblessness, worries about the United States losing its status as a major world power, concerns about foreign terrorist organizations. Trump validates their insecurities and justifies their anger. (Golshan, 2017)

As we can see from the SCC transcript above, there are so many opportunities for the listeners to attempt to fill-in-the-blanks when listening to the words of DJT. One major problem with that blank-filling is that there is no way to know if the blanks are being filled-in correctly. However, making sense, which may be thought of an essential principle of communication, may not be the point of such texts. Instead the main point may be to feed off the fear, for example, as we saw in Chapter 5, 'Fear of the Other', which may be part of all three of the fears listed by Golshan, i.e., individuals losing jobs, the country losing its status, and organizations wanting to harm the USA (see Gellman, 2010, on 'Our addiction to anger and fear'). NPL analyses of the spoken and written texts of DJT show that the focus on loss is an essential aspect of the language of DJT, which is designed to resonate most loudly with the 'losers', i.e., those who have lost, for example, their jobs, and who feel they have been left behind in the rush to globalization of markets and products. That idea of targeting losers is discussed in more depth in Chapter 8, in an NPL analysis of a speech given by DJT four years after the SCC, in early 2019, showing what an important part that loser-focused messaging played in his use of language.

To better understand statements such as the SCC, it is helpful to look briefly at the work of the British philosopher of language, Paul Grice (1913–1988), who is best-known for his Cooperative Principle (1975), which states: "Make your conversational contribution such as is required, at the stage at which it occurs, by the accepted purpose or direction of the talk exchange in which you are engaged" (1975, p. 45). From that principle, and building on the work of the German philosopher, Immanuel Kant (1724–1804), Grice derived four categories, which he referred to as "Quantity, Quality, Relation, and Manner" (Grice, 1975, p. 45). In the category of 'Quantity', Grice stipulated two 'maxims': "1. Make your contribution as informative as is required (for the current purposes of the exchange). 2. Do not make your contribution more informative than is required" (p. 45). Although such advice might seem obvious, as we will see in the analyses of the texts of DJT, such advice is often not followed. Why would such common-sense advice not be followed, especially by a world leader, in a public, recorded and televised speech of the kind that gave rise to the SCC? As pointed out above, although such spoken texts may *appear* to be for the purposes of communicating, it is entirely possible that that is not at all their main purpose. Instead, such speeches may be designed primarily to manipulate audiences, not to communicate with them. That use of language—to so something *to* people rather than to communicate *with* them—may constitute a new Uncooperative Principle.

In the category of 'Quality', Grice proposed two more maxims: "1. Do not say what you believe to be false. 2. Do not say that for which you lack adequate evidence" (1975, p. 46). As postulated above, DJT will be remembered for making tens of thousands of statements that are false and for which there is no evidence—two features which characterize much of what he said and wrote during his time in office (Curtis, 2018j). Under 'Relation' Grice had one relatively straightforward maxim: "Be relevant" (p. 46), but under 'Manner', Grice listed four maxims: "1. Avoid obscurity of expression; 2. Avoid ambiguity; 3. Be brief (avoid unnecessary prolixity); 4. Be orderly" (p. 46). Once again, all of these maxims were constantly violated in the texts of DJT, especially the spoken texts, which reiterates the idea that his speeches were designed not to communicate—as they break all of the rules of effective communication—but to manipulate.

From a communicative competence perspective, perhaps Golshan's most pertinent conclusion is that: "People understand Trump on *an emotional level*" (emphasis added), which would explain "Why Trump's speeches are incomprehensible to some—and make perfect sense to others" (Golshan, 2017). That kind of verbal behavior continued long after DJT was elected, throughout his four years as president—in spite of his promises to his audience that he would be "so presidential you will be bored" (Detrow, 2016). Like many of DJT's promises, that one was broken too, and instead DJT later claimed, to excuse his promise-breaking, that his fans "would be so bored" if he "acted presidential" (Seipel, 2018). That is a good example of using language to promise one thing, then delivering the complete opposite, but claiming that what you promised is the opposite of what the people really wanted. So, you are now giving them the opposite of what you promised, because that is what they *really* wanted. Needless to say, there is no truth in such self-serving pseudo-arguments, but such twisted language and logic may be extremely effective at consolidating power over people.

Critically Deconstructing DJT's SCC

The SCC could have been transcribed as a series of sentences. However, as there are no clear breaks that could constitute a period (or 'full stop'), from a discourse analytic perspective, it does indeed appear to have been one, long sentence. Therefore, before we can attempt an NPL analysis, we first need unravel or unpack the stream of words transmitted to the listeners during those 90 seconds in 2015—which turned out to be an important indication of what was to come, although those 'warning signs' were apparently not noticed at that time.

In grammatical terminology, a clause is defined as containing a subject and a verb, while a dependent clause, as the name suggests, cannot be free-standing, as it needs an independent clause to create a complete a sentence. A case can be made for labeling some of the 'word chunks' in the SCC as 'clauses' and some as 'phrases', which can be defined as "a group of words without a subject-verb component" (grammarbook.com). But for ease-of-reference, all of the chunks of language in the SCC will be referred to as 'phrases', and for notational purposes, 'P + Number' indicates which phrase is being referred to.

P1: Look

P2: having nuclear

P3: my uncle was a great professor and scientist and engineer, Dr. John Trump at MIT

P4: good genes, very good genes, okay, very smart

P5: the Wharton School of Finance, very good, very smart

P6: you know, if you're a conservative Republican

P7: if I were a liberal

P8: if, like, okay

P9: if I ran as a liberal Democrat

P10: they would say I'm one of the smartest people anywhere in the world—it's true!

P11: but when you're a conservative Republican they try—oh, do they do a number

P12: that's why I always start off: Went to Wharton, was a good student

P13: went there, went there, did this, built a fortune

P14: you know I have to give my like credentials all the time

P15: because we're a little disadvantaged

P16: but you look at the nuclear deal

P17: the thing that really bothers me

P18: it would have been so easy

P19: and it's not as important as these lives are

P20: nuclear is powerful; my uncle explained that to me many, many years ago, the power, and that was 35 years ago;

P21: he would explain the power of what's going to happen and he was right—who would have thought?

P22: but when you look at what's going on with the four prisoners

P23: now it used to be three, now it's four—but when it was three, and even now

P24: I would have said it's all in the messenger

P25: fellas, and it is fellas because, you know,

P26: they don't, they haven't figured that the women are smarter right now than the men

P27: so, you know, it's gonna take them about another 150 years

P28: but the Persians are great negotiators,

P29: the Iranians are great negotiators

P30: so, and they, they just killed, they just killed us.

From this breakdown we can see 30 phrases, which could have been further sub-divided, but using a discourse analysis approach, each of these 30 phrases contains what can be considered as a unit of expression, with the shortest units being between one and four words, e.g., "like, having nuclear, if, like, okay." The next size of unit, known in linguistics as 'mean length of utterance' (MLU, see, for example, Miller and Chapman, 1981), is between five and ten words, e.g., "but you look at the nuclear deal," "the thing that really bothers me," and "it would have been so easy." The next largest size of MLU is between 11 and 15 words, e.g., "you know I have to give my, like, credentials all the time" and "my uncle was a great professor and scientist and engineer, Dr. John Trump at MIT," then 16 to 20-word units, e.g., "he would explain the power of what's going to happen and he was right—who would have thought?." There were only a few phrases more than 20 words long. e.g., "nuclear is powerful; my uncle explained that to me many, many years ago, the power, and that was 35 years ago." As stated above, the case can be made for further sub-dividing some of the phrases in the SCC, such as P11, P20 and P21, but the opposite case also be made, for example, two antecedent uses of 'that' in P20, i.e., "that to me" and "that was 35 years ago," means that P20 can be analyzed a single phrase or unit of expression. Therefore, applying the idea of MLUs and units of expression gives us these 30 pieces of language. However, some of the SCC phrases have anywhere between no clear meaning, at one end, and too many possible meanings to count, at the other.

This brings us to the question: Why Bother? Or, to pose the question in its fuller form: Why bother to analyze a sentence that seems to make such little sense? One reason for examining the SCC in this way is because an NPL analysis at this level can tell us a great deal about the mind and the motivations of the speaker, in this case, the future-president of the most powerful country in the world (at least, based on military might, as discussed earlier). Second, as noted above and in previous chapters, everything that the most powerful people in the world say and write has the greatest potential to alter the state of the world, for better or for worse, towards peace or towards war, and therefore requires in-depth, systematic, linguistic analysis. Third, a detailed examination of a single sentence can show how such NPL analyses can peel away layers of meaning, to show what may be hidden within and between the words and phrases. Another function of NPL text analyses of this kind is to highlight the fact that not all words and phrases are created equal; some can carry much more semantic weight—in terms of direct and indirect, explicit and implicit, surface and hidden meanings—than others. That unequal weighting may perhaps seem somewhat obvious, but the concern of NPL practitioners relates to, for example, whether the 'heavier' words and phrases, i.e., those more loaded with meaning, are more or less peaceful.

A fifth aspect of NPL, especially at the micro level, relates to the notion of a 'deep dive', defined as "an in-depth examination or analysis of a topic" (*OED*, 2021). That metaphor appeals to those of us who (like myself) are poor swimmers, as this NPL approach involves soaking in the language, immersing oneself in it, to see what may be lurking beneath the surface. By diving deeper into a text, the goal of NPL practitioners is to uncover meaning that may usually not be seen or heard by the majority of those reading or listening. A sixth aspect of NPL is pattern recognition, where relationships between recurring words and phrases, ideas and images, are identified, analyzed and explained.

A Deep Dive into the South Carolina Commentary

Rather than looking at every one of the 30 sub-texts of the SCC, as this is an NPL analysis, we will focus on those that relate to war and other kinds of conflict, as well as to peace.

2. *"having nuclear"*

Listeners would expect the word 'nuclear' to be followed by, for example, 'weapons' or 'capabilities.' However, "having nuclear" turned out to be what linguists refer to as a 'garden path' phrase, as it did not lead to where the listeners are likely to have been expecting to go (Ferreira, Christianson & Hollingworth, 2001). Usually, applied linguists refer to garden path *sentences*, but this speaker produces here what may be called a garden path *phrase*, as the listener is taken down a linguistic dead end or cul-de-sac, or simply 'left hanging.' Therefore, at just three words into the SCC, this may have served as an early warning that this sentence was going to go off in myriad directions. In relation to warist discourse, it is also possible that 'having nuclear' was an allusion to 'going nuclear', which is defined as: "to become wildly excited or upset: to go berserk" (*Merriam-Webster*, 2021). It is also worth noting that the *Merriam-Webster Dictionary* website published an entire article on DJT, during the 2016 Presidential Elections in the USA, and the use of the phrase 'going nuclear' (*Merriam-Webster*, 2017).

3. *"my uncle was a great professor and scientist and engineer, Dr. John Trump at MIT"*

John George Trump (1907–1985) was indeed an electrical engineer, inventor, and physicist, who was a member of the US National Academy of Engineering. He received the National Medal of Science from President Ronald Reagan for his work on developing rotational radiation therapy, and he was a professor at MIT from 1936 until 1973. Although there does not appear to be any connection of any kind between the work of Dr. Trump and his nephew Mr. Trump, DJT appeared to be claiming that greatness ran in the family—with a version of 'guilt by association' recast or reframed as 'greatness by association'. The grammatically unnecessary repetition of 'and'—"a great professor *and* scientist *and* engineer" –provides some repetition for emphasis. This notion of 'inherited greatness' was made more explicit in the following phrase, immediately below.

4. *"good genes, very good genes, okay"*

For the White Supremacists who supported DJT, before, during and after his election (C. Smith, 2016; Coates, 2017; Fractenberg, 2018; S. Jones, 2019; Lopez, 2020; Bebout, 2021) the reference to "very good genes" may have been an especially important dog whistle, which is defined as a political "expression or statement that has a secondary meaning intended to be understood only by a particular group of people" (*Merriam-Webster*, 2021) (see Chapter 10, also McCutcheon & Mark, 2014). This particular dog whistle related to Eugenics, which equates societal success with inherent, inborn genetic superiority, and vice versa. It was the dominant belief system in Nazi Germany, and as Daniel Kevles explained in his book *In the Name of Eugenics* (1995) "for much of the first half of the 20th century... social distinctions of race and class were commonly attributed to biological merit" (p. vii) (see also Mark Haller's 1963 *Eugenics: Hereditarian Attitudes in American Thought* for early work in this area). And for the third time, in the phrase immediately below, DJT referred to how clever he is.

5. "very smart, the Wharton School of Finance, very good, very smart"

Reporting on the ways in which language was used by the different candidates in the 2016 US Presidential Election, Beth Harpaz pointed out that: "You don't hear Ted Cruz *talk* much about his Princeton degree. Hillary Clinton doesn't often *mention* Yale. But Donald Trump can't stop *trumpeting* his Ivy League pedigree" (2016, emphases added). ('Ivy League' refers to the highest ranked universities in the USA.) The differences between 'talk', 'mention' and 'trumpet' are significant, in quantity and quality, and DJT has also used the Wharton reference to deny his own use of inappropriate (and decidedly un-presidential) language: "Accused of making a vulgar comment, he responded: 'Who would say that? I went to the Wharton School of Finance!'" (Harpaz, 2016), implying that the latter precludes the former, which is, at best, a non sequitur, and at worst, an obvious logical fallacy. There is also the repetition of 'very', three times in just 11 words, and 'smart' twice, making the claim, whatever its veracity (or lack thereof), easier for the listeners to process cognitively, perhaps especially for those with limited cognitive capacities. Lastly, The Wharton School of the University of Pennsylvania is also known as Wharton Business School. There is, however, no Wharton School of Finance.

10. "they would say I'm one of the smartest people anywhere in the world—it's true!"

Following up on the earlier claims about his superior intellect (see P3, P4 and P5, above), here at P10, DJT again employs repetition to add weight to his claims (Dreyfuss, 2017). The phrase-ending reference to the 'truth' could be a case of presenting an opinion—and an extremely biased one at that—as a fact, i.e., I am, indeed, one of the smartest people in the world. Hedging terms are used to make a statement less extreme and all-encompassing, and an example here is, "*one of* the smartest" (emphasis added) rather than simply 'the smartest'. Also, "would say" may be perceived and processed as being less definite and more speculative than 'will say', but with another kind of emphatic marker also being used here, "*anywhere* in the world," with 'anywhere', here, meaning something more like 'everywhere'.

11. "but when you're a conservative Republican they try— oh, do they do a number"

Many language analysts and/or political commentators would likely focus on the fact that being a 'conservative Republican' means many different things to many different people. For example, Friedersdorf (2012) found more than 20 meanings embedded in the phrase 'conservative Republican'. Those cognitive connotations include: "A belief that America is an exceptional nation, a shining city on a hill, whose rightful role is leader of the free world," "Disdain for ... multiculturalism" and "A desire to return to the way things once were." However, as with many of these phrases, there is, from an NPL perspective, more meaning than meets the eye, or in this case, the ear. The phrase 'to do a number on somebody' is defined as: "US slang: to injure someone or something, or to hurt or embarrass someone" (*CALD*, 2021). DJT's claims of being hurt or harmed are marked emphatically by the use of the phrase-initial, exclamatory 'Oh', and the pseudo-assertion/rhetorical question 'do they do', which may also be functioning as an indirect speech act (Schmidt-Radefeldt, 1977, p. 375).

The conservative Republican "desire to return to the way things once were" (Friedersdorf, 2012) is especially important, as it closely relates to the campaign slogan originally used in the 1980 US presidential campaign, which helped Ronald Reagan (1911–2004) become the 40th President of the USA (1981–1989): 'Let's Make American Great Again'. That slogan was co-opted by the DJT campaign team, starting in November 2012, without the inclusive, shared effort of 'Lets', to just 'Make America Great Again' which was, in turn, derived from the book title *Time to Get Tough: Making America #1 Again* (Trump, 2011). (The same book was re-issued in 2015 under the exclamatory title, *Time to Get Tough: Make America Great Again!*). Following that pattern, the DJT campaign team announced in 2018 that the 2020 presidential election campaign slogan would be 'Keep America Great!' which was copyrighted—with and without the exclamation mark.

12. "that's why I always start off: Went to Wharton, was a good student"

By this point, the speaker has started repeating not only descriptions of himself, but also details of his earlier life, in this case, his educational background (see P5, above: "the Wharton School of Finance, very good, very smart"). However, in this second reference to DJT's alma mater, he uses the shorter form, 'Wharton', rather than the full name, as a sign of familiarity, and a deliberate repetition-for-emphasis. Indeed, DJT invoked the name of Wharton so many times—and referred to himself as a 'genius' so many times (see, for example, Frisk, 2018 and Billman, 2019)—that a number of news reports have looked into his academic performance at Wharton, about which still very little is known (see, for example, Spinelli, 2015; Rabin & Tan, 2017; Jenkins, 2017; Vilania, 2019).

In early 2019, during the criminal trial of DJT's longtime personal attorney, Michael Cohen, in his testimony to the US Congress, described DJT as "a racist, a con man and a cheat" (Reilly, 2019). In case the meaning of any of those descriptors was unclear to any members of Congress, Cohen went on to give a specific, education-level example: "'When I say con man, I'm talking about a man who declares himself brilliant but directed me to threaten his high school, his colleges, and the College Board to never release his grades or SAT scores" (Standardize Achievement Tests for entry to colleagues and universities in the USA). Cohen went on to note that: "The irony wasn't lost on me at the time that Mr. Trump in 2011 had strongly criticized President Obama for not releasing his grades" (Reilly, 2019). Therefore, in addition to such language-based strategies as hyperbole, exaggeration, or just 'straight-up lying' (Sung, 2018), within P12 is another strategy used by those in power to deceive others: Accuse your opponent of something you know that you yourself have done, but which your opponent may or may not have done.

Such a strategy may be an example of a kind of inverted *ad hominem* argument, as such arguments are usually in the form of personal attacks on someone for something they said or did. But in this case, DJT appears to be accusing his predecessor, BHO, of doing something that BHO did not do, but that DJT did do. The lower-level logic, perhaps aimed at those more easily led, may then follow the path or pattern of: a. surely, the speaker would not accuse someone of a wrongdoing that they themselves have done, because b. That would be a level of hypocrisy beyond comprehension. Therefore (c) the speaker must be innocent, and (d) the accused must be guilty.

13. "went there, went there, did this, built a fortune"

Like the appeal to the idea of genetic and intellectual superiority, in some of the previous SCC phrases, this is a claim of financial superiority. As this phrase immediately followed the "went to Wharton" reiteration, "went there, went there" may be another (third) reference to DJT's alma mater. Also, because of the vagueness of "went there, went there, did this," there is no way for the audience/listeners to know what, if any, connection there is/was between his goings and his doings, including his "building" of "a fortune." The question of how much of DJT's fortune was 'built' and how much was inherited, in this case, passed from father to son, was the subject of much speculation, because, again, like the Wharton reference, it was mentioned by DJT with such a high frequency.

Reporter Zoe Thomas, asked: 'How did Trump make his fortune?' (2016), and reporter Glenn Kessler reported on 'Trump's false claim he built his empire with a "small loan" from his father' (2016). The use of the diminutizing 'small' here appears to be a calculated and repeated discoursal move, to imply that only a small amount of money was involved. However, a number of news agencies (including Thomas, 2016 and Kessler, 2016) confirmed that the loan was approximately 1,000,000 USD, made more than 40 years ago, in 1978. Therefore, in spite of DJT repeatedly referring to that one million US dollars as "a small loan," even today, such a loan would not be described as 'small'—and 40 years ago, it would indeed have constituted a fortune. Also, contrary to DJT's repeated claims of what an exceptionally successful business man he was, it was in fact reported that DJT "lost more money than nearly any other individual American taxpayer" in the entire country (Holmes, 2019). Based on DJT's tax filings between 1985 and 1994, it was found that he lost, mostly as the result of failed real estate deals, approximately one hundred million US dollars each year for ten years, making accumulated losses of one billion USD over that decade (Holmes, 2019).

Leaving the financial falsehoods aside, and returning to some much subtler uses of language for deceptive purposes, we can turn our attention to the connotational and implicative differences between '*built* a fortune' and '*inherited* a fortune'. The use of the verb 'to build' is especially important here, as it alludes to the notion of 'the self-made man', which is a deeply ingrained myth, perhaps especially in the USA and Canada. For example, Allan Smith (1978) reported on 'The Myth of the Self-made Man in English Canada', between 1850 and 1914, and Richard Hofstadter's 2009 essay is titled 'Abraham Lincoln and the Self-Made Myth'.

Like most powerful myths, this one goes back a long way. For example, more than 60 years ago, in 1956, Wyllie, Diamond, Kilman and Wright published an article, 'The Self-Made Man in America: The Myth of Rags to Riches', and James Catano's 1990 article is on, 'The Rhetoric of Masculinity: Origins, Institutions, and the Myth of the Self-Made Man'. In addition, in the USA, there has been the 100-year influence of Horatio Alger, Jr (1832–1899). According to the Horatio Alger Society, Alger was: "a prolific 19th-century American author, best known for his many formulaic juvenile novels about impoverished boys and their rise from humble backgrounds to lives of respectable middle-class security and comfort through hard work, determination, courage, and honesty" (www.horatioalgersociety). Alger wrote more than 100 rags-to-riches storybooks, which "have had a lasting impact on the American culture and many well-known authors were greatly influenced by his works" (www.horatioalgersociety). Although none of the Alger myths may apply to DJT, he made the most of that mythical connection and connotation, and the publications above are just a few of the many that attest to just how deep-seated this particular American myth still is in the USA, and probably elsewhere as well. That is why DJT's use of "built a fortune" is so important to NPL practitioners, who are sensitized to the potential impact of such seemingly innocuous language choices, but which are, in fact, loaded with more meaning than the recipients of the message may recognize or even realize.

22. "but when you look at what's going on with the four prisoners—

23. now it used to be three, now it's four—but when it was three and even now"

Eventually, DJT returned to the "lives" he mentioned earlier (P19), and it became clear that it was the lives of the prisoners being held in Iran that he was referring to, although he appeared to be confused about the number of prisoners. The use of 'now' three times in the same phrase—"now it," "now it's," "even now"—also creates some potential confusion (again, deliberately or accidentally) regarding what timeframe was being referred to: the past, with "it used to be" and "it was," and/or the present, with "now it's" and "even now." Unfortunately, for the listeners, another garden-path phrase leaves the listener hanging once again: "when you look at what's going on with the four prisoners." Such a phrase would usually be followed by a statement of *what it is that you can know/understand when you see what's happening with these prisoners.* For example: When you look at what's going on with the three/four prisoners... it's great that they were released unharmed. Or: When you look at what's going on with the three/four prisoners... it's terrible that they were held hostage like that. These are, of course, major differences, as the latter phrase could escalate tensions and even lead to another avoidable war, whereas the former could help to bring about a peaceful resolution.

24. "I would have said it's all in the messenger"

Here, DJT referred to the importance of a 'messenger' of some kind, which was the first time such a reference had been made. There are, as with many moments during this telling stream-of-consciousness, think-aloud spoken text, a perplexingly wide range of possible meanings and potential motives. One possible meaning of "I would have said it's all in the messenger" could go back to Shakespeare's *Macbeth* (1606), who, upon hearing a strange and supernatural-sounding report from a character referred to only as 'Messenger', lashes out: "Liar and slave" (Act 5, Scene 5). The Messenger replies to Macbeth: "Let me endure your wrath, if't be not so," to which Macbeth says: "If thou speak'st false, Upon the next tree shall thou hang alive, Til famine cling thee." That dramatic scene, as the corrupt leader's world starts to cave in on him, is one of the sources of the phrase: 'Don't shoot the messenger', although that phrase may be traced as far back as Sophocles' play, *Antigone,* written around 440 BCE. Alternatively, DJT could also have simply meant to say, for example: It's all in the message, the messaging, etc.

28. "but the Persians are great negotiators,
29. the Iranians are great negotiators"

At P28 and P29, we can see some illustrative examples of potential insults presented as apparent compliments. In his article, 'Adding Insult to Inquiry', Lionel Wee (2015), pointed out that "While compliments are usually intended to give credit and insults offense, the latter cannot simply be treated as opposites of the former" (p. 1). That role reversal, in pragmatic terms, does seem to apply here, as, in April 2016, nine months after the SSC took place, DJT gave a lengthy interview to the *Washington Post,* as part of his election campaign activities. In reporting on the interview, Isahaan Tharoor pointed out that: "Trump dabbled in a familiar ethnic stereotype, casting the result of many months of concerted international diplomacy as a clever Persian trick." DJT went on to explain that: "It was negotiated by people that are poor negotiators against great negotiators. Persians being great negotiators, okay?" (Tharoor, 2016). Tharoor went on to point out that that was not the first time DJT has used such language, and that "the idea that 'Persians are great negotiators,' while seemingly flattering, is part of a centuries-old Western cliché of the wily Persian swindler who cannot be trusted" (Tharoor, 2016). (See also Wolfson & Manes, 2009, on linguistic features of complimenting as a social strategy). However, as reported by Tharoor, DJT "was not alone in embracing this stereotype," as "A host of leading US diplomats and commentators from across the political spectrum trade in this lazy shorthand" (Tharoor, 2016). Also, although 'Persian' and 'Iranian' are used interchangeably in the SCC, they do not mean the same thing, as the former may relate to a particular ethnicity, while the later refers to a particular nationality (see Gina Nahai's 'On Being Persian', 2014, for more on this distinction).

30. "so, and they, they just killed, they just killed us."

The string for these last three phrases, P28, P29 and P30 can be represented as:

[(Persians = Iranians) + (Iranians = Persians)] plus
[Persians + Iranians = killer-negotiators]
Therefore [Persians = Iranians = Killers of the USA]

The final phrase in this 285-word, 90-second sentence is almost a kind of denouement, in which the killer in the story is discovered, perhaps as part of some sort of 'big reveal', in which our hero dramatically 'takes down the bad guy'. In the NPL world, there are few more powerfully significant and signifying words than 'kill', which has a long and bloody history in English. Around 1200 CE, it meant, "to strike, hit, beat, knock" (Harper, 2021), and by a century later (1300 CE) it had come to mean, "to deprive of life, put to death." In addition to the literal meanings of 'kill', there are now the metaphorical meanings, including the verb 'to kill it', which is used informally to mean, "to do something extremely well" (*CALD*, 2021) and 'to make a killing', also informal, and used to mean, "to earn a lot of money in a short time and with little effort" (*CALD*, 2021). Added to P30 was another, phrase-initial 'so', which again could be a cause-effect marker, meaning, as a result of being good negotiators, the Persians/Iranians killed us, either literally or metaphorically. However, it is more likely that the 'so' here was again simply serving as a 'filler', while DJT gathered his thoughts, although the implication that the Iranian government killed US soldiers is clearly one possible meaning. And that meaning could have been assigned to those three phrases (P28–30) by some, many, or even most of the listeners at that particular rally in South Carolina, at that time (and perhaps is still being assigned by DJT's supporters today).

In September 2015, soon after the SCC, the US military announced that the Iranian government, officially referred to as the 'Iranian Islamic regime', had been, between 2005 and 2011, "directly involved in the killing of more than 500 American service members in Iraq by supplying Shiite extremists with advanced roadside bombs, rocket-propelled explosives and other munitions" (Scarborough, 2015). Given that, the concluding phrase—"so, and they, they just killed, they just killed us"—made for a dramatic and emotional conclusion to this, perhaps one of the longest and most telling, single sentences uttered publicly by a world leader on record. However, it was not telling in terms of providing insights into foreign policy planning, as presidential candidate's speeches often do, but telling in the sense of revealing so much more about DJT than he himself and perhaps his audience were even aware of.

From an NPL point of view—and I accept the understandable charge of bias and/or overstating the case—it is conceivable that if the kind of analysis of DJT's words presented in this chapter had been available in 2015, that might have helped more people understand what was really being said, and how they may have been manipulated through the language used.

REACT 8.3: *Go back and re-read the original, complete transcript of the SCC. Having gone through it in detail, see if the SCC text looks, sounds, or feels different now, after this NPL analysis. Do you notice anything now that you did not notice before? Do you notice anything that was not described/overlooked in the analysis above?*

Suggestions for Further Reading

Common Discourse Particles in English Conversation (1985, Routledge), by Lawrence Schourup, is more than three decades old now. But it is still one of the few entire books dedicated to a few specific spoken discourse markers in English, including six sections on the use of 'like', eleven sections on the use of 'well', and thirteen sections on the use of 'you know'.

The Conversation is an academic online magazine, written by university experts for a general readership. In 2015, Professor Jennifer Mercieca (Texas A&M University) published an article in *The Conversation*, 'The Rhetorical Brilliance of Trump the Demagogue'. https://theconversation.com/the-rhetorical-brilliance-of-trump-the-demagogue-51984

Talking Donald Trump: A Sociolinguistic Study of Style, Metadiscourse, and Political Identity (2018, Routledge) by Professor Jennifer Sclafani (Georgetown

University) is a collection of brief chapters (each of which is a few pages) on DJT's use of phrases such as 'well', 'by the way' and 'believe me'.

The March 2018 issue of *The Atlantic* magazine published an article by Kurt Andersen, 'How to Talk Like Trump: A short guide to speaking the president's dialect', which lists some of his favorite adjectives, adverbs, nouns, and 'special phrases'. https://www.theatlantic.com/magazine/archive/2018/03/how-to-talk-trump/550934/

9

Using Language to Manipulate, Misrepresent, and Misinform

In Chapter 8, we saw how an in-depth NPL analysis can reveal so many messages in a single, 90-second sentence. Fast-forward nearly four years, to early 2019, and we can deconstruct the opposite of a short, single sentence, i.e., a two-hour speech from DJT, including a question-and-answer session with journalists. That speech event, in February 2019, which was held in the Rose Garden of the White House, was one of the longest public addresses ever given by a president of the USA, and revealed more aspects of language use that are of particular interest to those working in the area of NPL. As always, the February 2019 event—which will be referred to here as the Rose Garden Speech (RGS)—was covered by news agencies all over the world, which may be part of a problem, in which a narcissistic need for attention is fed by the global media, exponentially exacerbating the problem, making it a vicious cycle (Appelbaum, 2021). However, as highlighted in previous chapters, when one of the most powerful people in the world holds court, whatever they say (or write, or do) the world's media feels obliged to give the story the maximum coverage. Of course, it is also

The New Peace Linguistics and The Role of Language in Conflict, pages 167–182

possible that such wall-to-wall, 24/7 coverage saves some of those news agencies from having to report on anything else that day.

One of the many news agencies that covered the RGS was *Vanity Fair,* which described the speech as "a rambling mess" (Nguyen, 2019), while *CNN* reported on: 'The 47 most outrageous lines from Donald Trump's wild national emergency declaration' (Cillizza, 2019). One of those 47 lines related to how illegal drugs are entering the USA, and how that is being reported in the media, about which DJT said: "It's all a big lie. It's a big con game." Explaining that statement, Cillizza stated: "Trump is speaking specifically about the [US/Mexico] border here. But again, this statement is also a decent stand-in for his worldview: *Everyone is lying to you and trying to screw you. Everybody but me*" (Cillizza, 2019, original emphasis). That may be one of the hallmarks of people-in-power using language to manipulate others, i.e., telling their audience that, not only can they trust the speaker with their very lives (especially in the case of COVID-19)—no matter how many lies the speaker has been shown to have told—but that they can *only* trust the speaker, and no one else.

When the most powerful people in the world show themselves to be largely incapable of telling the truth, we are all at risk, as pathological liars will say anything to get what they want, no matter how much damage and destruction that entails. Specifically, in relation to NPL, beyond the usual meaning of 'a deliberate deceit', the word 'lie' has also been defined as: "In mod. [modern] use, the word is normally *a violent expression* of moral reprobation" (Harper, 2021, emphasis added). If we look at lying as a form of verbal violence, its more direct relationship to NPL becomes clearer, and perhaps as a reflection of how much world leaders lie today, a line of research has developed focused on that particular use of language. For example, Simpson (1992) looked at 'Lying, Liars and Language'; Hancock, Curry, Goorha and Woodworth (2008) reported 'On Lying and Being Lied To' using a linguistic analysis of computer-mediated communication; and in 2019, "the first international verbal lie detection workshop," looking at 'the language of lies', was held at Bar-Ilan University, in Israel (Nahari et al., 2019).

Recurring Themes in the Language of DJT

In the previous chapter, in our analysis of part of a speech given by DJT in 2015, we identified at least 10 aspects of language of interest to NPL practitioners. Here, in the RGS, we identify another ten or more, some of which overlap with the aspects identified in the previous chapter:

- Alluding to being at war, including trade wars

- Taking extreme positions, to polarize groups, to an extent that prevents discussion
- Scapegoating/blaming others to avoid having to take/share responsibility for problems/challenges
- Claiming to be disrespected, and therefore having to fight to (re) gain that respect
- Claiming to be taken advantage of, treated unfairly, and stolen from
- Lying, repeating the same lies, and expanding on those lies by exaggerating
- Manufacturing crises and feeding off the fear created by those crises
- Presenting a Winning vs. Losing mutually exclusive dichotomy, in which there are only winners and losers
- Appealing to those who have lost, for example, their jobs, their homes, etc.
- Describing people and places as 'infestations' and 'invasions'
- Invoking images of mythical, satanic beast, such as 'monsters' to refer to 'the Other'

REACT 9.1: *Look for examples, in the speeches of other leaders, of one or more of the aspects of language listed above. Do your leaders use any of the strategies listed above? And if so which ones, when and why?*

An NPL Analysis of an Announcement Made by Donald J Trump Declaring a 'National Emergency' (February, 2019)

After opening with thanks, DJT began by saying:

> We have a large team of very talented people in China. We've had a negotiation going on for about two days. It's going extremely well... we're very much working very closely with China... We're covering everything... whether it was theft or anything. Anything. The unfairness... We're going to be leveling the playing field... The tariffs are hurting China very badly... we're having many billions of dollars pouring into our Treasury. We've never had that before with China. It's been very much of a one-way street... And the relationship with China is very good, but I think they finally respect our country. They haven't respected us for a long time. Not for a long time.

Note: Full transcripts of this speech were published in *The Atlantic* (Paschal, 2019), *The Washington Post* (Blake, 2019) and many other newspapers and new organizations.

From an NPL perspective, several important messages were sent by DJT in the first few paragraphs, about half of which (120 of 240 words) are shown above. First, there is the overall implication that the USA is at war—but without saying those words. In this case, the conflict being alluded to is a trade war—with the rest of the world, including China and Europe. For example, in *Forbes*, Rapoza (2019) reported that: “China is losing the trade war,” and the BBC has an entire collection of news reports on US-China trade talks under a section titled ‘Trade War’. That use of ‘negative warist discourse’ raises the question: Why not refer to ‘trade talks’ rather than a ‘trade war’? According to University of Sheffield professor Tom Stafford (2014): “It may be because we’re drawn to depressing stories without realizing” as a result of a phenomena psychologists call ‘negativity bias’, which refers to “our collective hunger to hear, and remember bad news” (Stafford, 2014). That response is, in turn, the result of humans having “evolved to react quickly to potential threats. Bad news could be a signal that we need to change what we’re doing to avoid danger” (Stafford, 2014). Trade talks usually pose little or no immediate danger, whereas trade wars may be perceived as posing a more potentially serious (economic) threat, which may be why the sensationalist media often prefers to report on ‘trade wars’ rather than ‘trade talks’.

Another important point is that it does not matter against whom the war is being fought, as the purpose of the ‘we’re-at-war’ messaging is designed to bring the audience together—united against a common enemy. Reporting in *Psychology Today*, Steve Rathje (2018a) wrote that: “Political polarization in the US is higher than ever... However, it’s unclear if political polarization is a problem that we actually want to solve.” That comment leads to another question of why anyone would *not* want to solve such a pressing polarization problem, if it was in their power to do so. The answer, according to Rathje and others, is that: “Our political opponents may be filling important needs in our lives, giving us scapegoats to blame, common enemies to unite over, and a simplified cause behind complex problems” (Rathje, 2018a). Those are highly persuasive reasons for being so susceptible to the idea of a common enemy, whether they are an actual enemy or not, as that relieves the audience of the burden of taking responsibility for their own actions, telling themselves: It’s not our fault, it’s their fault (see Chapter 5, on Othering).

Within the more general and over-arching opening themes of ‘we’re-at-war’, DJT then presented the USA as a victim of “theft” and “unfairness” at the hands of China, followed by a standard sporting metaphor: “leveling the playing field,” which means that both sides in a sporting competition have a fair and equal chance of winning. Such metaphors may appear to be just part of the ordinary, everyday language of regular interaction. However, in NPL, such language is also a way of talking about war without specifically referring to it, as we saw BHO do in his 2009 inaugural address (See Chapter 6). Psychologist Azadeh Aalai (2012) pointed out that: "Historically, gaming rituals have oftentimes been either precursors to actual war or ways to prepare young boys for war," highlighting what may be a gender-bias in the use of such sport-as-war, war-as-sport connotations. Aalai (2012) also stated that: "The metaphor of sports as warfare is in no way a new one, and has endured throughout the ages" and that: "American football serves as a prime example of how the notion of sports as war can be taken too far." Reiterating the maleness of the metaphor, and coming to the present day, Aalai (2012) continued: "In this age, where fighting on an actual battlefield is a remote possibility for most males in our society, sports has replaced battle as the ultimate rite of passage for masculinity."

REACT 9.2: *Read or listen to a few descriptions of a sports competition, such as a soccer or football match, and note any references that compare encounters on the sports field with encounters on the battlefield. How does the sports-as-war commentary affect your understanding of the game?*

After the warring-sporting allusion, DJT went on to describe how the USA has been "hurting China very badly" via the tariffs (taxes on imports), as a result of which the USA was: "having many billions of dollars pouring into our Treasury." DJT claimed that such billion-dollar pouring from Chinese to US coffers had never happened before, which may or may not have been true, but regardless, it allowed him to follow-up on his 'we're-at-war' imagery with a 'we're-winning-the-war'. Leaving aside the potential falsity of such claims, it is important to be aware of how one country, in this case, China, is being portrayed not only as the enemy, but as an enemy that is losing the battle, that is being very "badly hurt." Another strategy to employ in this kind of war of words is to portray the speaker's country, in this case, DJT's USA, as not only a victorious victim but also as being disrespected: "I think they finally respect our country. They haven't respected us for a long time. Not for a long time," with the pause-then-repeating of that last point for emphasis. And although "[not] for a long time" has no real historical or chronological meaning, it may have been used by DJT to give the sense of China adding insult to injury, making the claims of America's victory over China all the more (self)satisfyingly grandiose.

Presenting Invalid Arguments

As discussed previously, repeating oneself again and again may be one of the oldest rhetorical tricks in the book, and one that was frequently used by DJT. One reason for the enduring popularity of such a technique is its simplicity—it is easy to do, easy to say, and simple to process. And as we saw in Chapter 8, repeating the same point—*regardless of whether or not it is true*—can be an effective way of making lies seem true, especially for those who would rather believe a lie than the truth, as the truth may upset their perception of reality, whereas a comforting lie may be far more welcome. With some kinds of audiences, whatever their leader tells their followers, it will eventually become 'the truth'—or perhaps, more precisely, '*their* truth', i.e., what the followers chose to believe, regardless of facts, figures, evidence, data, proof, etc. that clearly show the contrary to be true.

The second portrayal of the USA as a victim—but one who is heroically fighting back against an agreed upon arch-enemy—occurred when DJT said, referring to North Korea 'taking advantage' in the same way as China has been doing: "They [North Korea] have really taken advantage of the United States. Billions of dollars has [*sic*] been paid to them. And we won't let that happen." The reference to "billions of dollars" is also a good example of the age-old use of simple but effective exaggeration. As one news agency put it: "Trump may have exaggerated . . . according to a 2014 report by the Congressional Research Service, the US gave over $1.3 billion in aid to North Korea between 1995 and 2008 and very little since" (Young, 2017). That raises the question: At what point does an exaggeration become a lie? And although the answer to that is largely 'it depends', when analyzing language, NPL practitioners distinguish between exaggerating to make a point and lying with the intent to deceive, as the latter can escalate to become the difference between a peaceful disagreement and an armed conflict.

Writing for *The Atlantic,* David Frum (2019) reported that 'Trump is angry that the FBI won't endorse his theory of victimhood', and DJT's comments about China and North Korea also make use of what psychologists refer to as Victim Identity. For example, cognitive therapist Andrea Mathews (2011), described Victim Identity as part of "an allergic reaction to [taking] personal responsibility." According to Mathews, constantly thinking of oneself and presenting oneself as a victim includes some of the following messages: "Life is really, really hard . . . Beware, always beware of trickery; it's around every corner; You can't trust anyone . . . You just don't understand how hard it is for me . . . Everyone is always picking on me." Mathews contrasted the Victim Identify with the Authentic Self, and explained that those who are stuck in the former and unable to grow into the latter are unable to move forward "because there is shame attached to their efforts to manipulate and their history of failures" (Mathews, 2011). That does appear to apply to DJT, and to other leaders too, who also believe that they are in fact the greatly wronged victims of everyone else, no matter how much cruelty they may be inflicting on their own people, thereby relieving those leaders of the need to take any personal responsibility for their own words or actions.

Immediately after the references to North Korea, DJT illustrated another war-talk tactic, equating wars being fought far away with the arrival of immigrants on the shores of the USA: "We fight wars that are 6,000 miles away; wars that we should have never been in, in many cases. But we don't control our own border." It is possible that DJT was correct when he talked about wars that the USA "should have never been in," but he was incorrect in equating armed conflicts on foreign soil with controlling borders, in this case, the USA-Mexico border. After mis-representing border-crossing as an act of war, DJT then referred to the crossings as "the national security crisis on our southern border," which had to be confronted. That statement was followed by another false equivalence logical fallacy: "We're rebuilding the military; our economy is thriving like never before." That is an example of how language can be used to misrepresent multiple relationships; first between armed conflict and border-crossing, then between a national security crisis and border-crossing, then between a thriving economy and military spending.

Those kinds of false equivalences may not make sense in the mind of the listeners whose critical faculties are engaged and who are listening more for content than for emotional appeals. However, for those listeners who are being told what they already believe and what they want to hear, so that their beliefs can be reinforced, they may well believe that immigrants seeking asylum at the borders of the USA are indeed the same as an invading army, and should therefore be met with military force. And that is exactly what happened, when tear gas was fired by US border agents at a group of approximately 150 Central Americans trying to cross from Tijuana into southern California on January 1, 2019. Such groups are described by DJT and his administration as 'migrant caravans'. For example, in the RGS, DJT explained that: "We've *broken up* two caravans that are on their way. They just are *breaking*. They're in the process of *breaking up*. We have another one that we haven't been able *to break up* yet." That makes four references to 'broke(n)/breaking' in just over 30 words, stressing how important it is to at least damage the enemy, before eventually going on to destroy them, regardless of the fact that most migrants at most borders arrive hungry, thirsty, unarmed, and in no condition to fight anyone about anything.

In the RGS, DJT also referred to "these monstrous caravans that have been coming up" to the USA from Mexico, thereby equating immigrants seeking asylum with monsters, making them seem inhuman or subhuman, while also tapping into some of our most deep-seated fears: "fear of nuclear destruction, fear of climate change, fear of the subversive, and fear of foreigners" (Braudy, 2016). Then, to make the migrants seem yet more monstrous, DJT blamed them for a "tremendous amounts of drugs flowing into our country, much of it coming from the southern border" and associated the migrants with "2,000 murders right on the other side of the wall." For some audiences, whether or not such claims are true or accurate is not as important as the conviction with which they are presented, or the extent to which such claims confirm their fears.

Bandying about or throwing out numbers, especially big-sounding numbers, is another strategy that can be used to support points being made—again, regardless of whether or not the numbers can be checked or verified, or even explained. For example, DJT said: "So everyone knows that walls work... Almost everywhere. Take a look at Israel. They're building another wall. Their wall is 99.9 percent effective, they told me—99.9 percent. That's what it would be with us, too." Although figures such as 99.9% are impressive, perhaps even more so when they are repeated, they are largely meaningless, as it is entirely unclear how such a figure could be arrived at. For example, when talking about a wall, what is meant by 'effectiveness' and how is effectiveness being quantified?

'Infectious Infestations' and Good Versus Evil

After warning his audience, again, about the evils of immigrants—"We're talking about an invasion of our country with drugs, with human traffickers, with all types of criminals and gangs"—DJT then gave six paragraphs (approx. 250 words) of his speech to a group referred to as the 'Angel Moms'. That terms refers to "the bereaved parents or relatives of those who have died because of an 'illegal alien'" (Golshan, 2019). Reporting for *Vox*, Golshan explained that: "Trump keeps highlighting 'angel moms' to make the case for his [anti]immigration agenda." In the RGS, DJT said: "Angel Moms, Angel Dads, Angel Families. I have great respect for these people. These are great people. They're fighting for their children that have been killed by people that were illegally in this country." As well as the standard repetition ("great respect," "great people") DJT was also employing guilt by association, in which a small subgroup is presented as being typical of the whole group, in this case, presenting illegal immigrants who kill as being representative of all immigrants, which is demonstrably and completely untrue. The specter of an army of invading migrants was conjured up again, later in the RGS, as a reason for by-passing the usual routes for introducing new laws and instead claiming that a 'national emergency' was happening: "So, we're going to be signing today and registering a National Emergency. And it's a great thing to do because we have an invasion of drugs, invasion of gangs, invasion of people, and it's unacceptable." Contrary to such claims, the data shows that far more people in the USA, during DJT's time as president, were killed by domestic terrorists than immigrants or anyone else from outside of the USA (Byman, 2019).

Regarding overall trends, reporting for the Cato Institute (a US public policy research organization) Alex Nowrasteh presented detailed data on terrorism in the USA by status and nationality over a 43-year period, from 1975 to 2017, for risk analysis purposes. The data showed that, including those killed in the 9/11 terrorist attacks: "the chance of an American being murdered in a terrorist attack by a refugee is about 1 in 3.86 *billion* per year, while the annual chance of being murdered in an attack committed by an illegal immigrant is *zero*" (Nowrasteh. 2019, original emphasis). By contrast, the data showed that the chance of a US citizen being murdered "by a tourist on a B visa, the most common tourist visa, is about 1 in 4.1 million per year [compared with] the chance of being murdered by a native-born terrorist [which] is about 1 in 28 million per year" (Nowrasteh, 2019). Therefore, in spite of DJT's repeated lies or falsehoods about immigrants, an American in the USA is infinitely more likely to die at the hands of a tourist or a domestic terrorist than they are to be killed by an 'illegal immigrant'.

Having used 'invasion' three times in just nine words, DJT went on to repeat his warning again, saying that: "It's very simple: We want to stop drugs from coming into our country. We want to stop criminals and gangs from coming into our country." DJT's language here can be shown as: [immigrants = invasion] + [immigrants = criminals/gang members] therefore [immigrants = invasion of drug-smuggling, gang members]. The repeated use of 'invasion' by DJT was part of his long-term language pattern when referring to immigrants that pre-dated his time as president, when he used the word 'infection' which may create even more powerfully negative thoughts, feelings and images in the hearts and mind of listeners and readers. For example, in 2015, DJT accused Mexicans of being responsible for "tremendous infectious disease... pouring across the border" (Neate & Tuckman, 2015). In 2018, DJT used the noun "animals" while criticizing California's approach to immigration (Simon, 2018), and that same year, he used the verb 'infest' to describe illegal immigration: "They [the Democrats] don't care about crime and want illegal immigrants, no matter how bad they may be, to pour into and infest our country" (Simon, 2018). In *Psychology*

Today, Steve Rathje (2018b) reported on research related to DJT's warning "that immigrants will pour in and infest our country... The are coming from sh*thole countries... these aren't people. They are animals" (Rathje, 2018b). The findings from that research are that "dehumanizing language can have damaging effects" and that "dehumanizing metaphors lead to dehumanizing policies" (Rathje, 2018b; see also Chapter 1, on the language of the Rwandan Genocide of 1994).

According to Ben Zimmer, the language columnist for the *Wall Street Journal*, DJT's use of the language of infestation can be traced all the way back to the early 1990s, when DJT said: "We're looking to get zoning for a piece of land that's unzoned, that's employing no people, that's sitting there rotting. It's rat-infested" (Zimmer, 2019). In the past, DJT has called Jones Beach Park in New York a "rat-infested dump," he has described Atlanta as "crime-infested," and in 2019, he called Baltimore a "disgusting, rat and rodent infested mess" (Zimmer, 2019). Also in 2019, DJT tweeted a message telling four new Democratic members of Congress—all women of color—to "go back and help fix the totally broken and crime infested places from which they came" (Yglesias, 2019). However, three of those four new members were born in the USA, and the fourth one came from Somalia to the US when she was six years old, and has been a US citizen for most of her life. The use of such language is a powerful example of how single words, such as 'invasion' and 'infestation' can have devastating effects on large numbers of people. For example, Yglesias cited the *The New York Times* columnist Charles Blow, who pointed out that, "infestations justify exterminations," and the *Rolling Stone* senior writer Jamil Smith, who observed that: "When Trump speaks of immigrants 'infesting' America, he speaks in the language of genocide, not governance. By likening people to insects or vermin... he provides himself license to be an exterminator. We know that story" (Zimmer, 2019). That last comment by Smith, related to knowing how such stories end, recalls the 800,000 people killed over 100 days in 1994 in Rwanda, as a result of a campaign of hate in which the used of the word 'cockroach' by one group to demonize the other proved to be instrumental (see Chapter 1).

Repeating the Same Story: Making Myths Seem Real

The RGS can be divided into two halves; the first part, which was the speech given by DJT, of approximately 4,000 words, and the second part, which was the question-and-answer with journalists, of approximately 5,000 words (9,000 words in total). As part of his wrapping-up of the first part of his speech, DJT recapped for his audience some of his main points (at approx. 3,000 words into his 4,000-word speech):

> So, that's the story. We want to have a safe country. I ran on a very simple slogan: 'Make America Great Again.' If you're going to have drugs pouring across the border, if you're going to have human traffickers pouring across the border in areas where we have no protection, in areas where we don't have a barrier, then [it's] very hard to make America great again.

Again, we can see the appeal to/appeal of simplicity, in DJT's "very simple slogan," and on one level, the slogan may look and sound simple—based on a superficial acceptance of the message. However, NPL practitioners peel back the layers of such slogans, and look at the deeper-level meanings, which is one of the goals of NPL, as stated in earlier chapters. Starting at the end of the slogan, the use of 'again' implies that America is no longer 'great', which should, in the minds of critical consumers of such messages, raise many questions including:

- Assuming it is no longer great, what is America now?
- Was it great before? And if so, in what ways was it great?
- How is greatness, as it is used here, being defined, described or measured?
- If there are no objective measures of greatness, then is it just about feeling powerful? And if so, powerful in what ways? Having what kind of power over whom? And so on.

Such analyses require time and thought; cognitive engagement which requires stepping-back and asking questions, rather the unquestioning acceptance and uncritical embracing of such slogans, which is where NPL can help, by giving listeners and readers the tools to help them deconstruct such simple-sounding language and look deeper. By going deeper, we can better understand the implications of such language, and those who follow such speakers with the kind of faith that may be associated with religious zeal, and other kinds of cultish behavior (see Ruth Graham's piece in *Politico,* published in 2018, on the 'Church of the Donald').

DJT's restatement of the MAGA slogan (Make America Great Again) was followed by two lots of "If you're going to have" together with two lots of "pouring": "If you're going to have drugs pouring across the border, if you're going to have human traffickers pouring across the border." That kind of if-then appeal to some kind of (il)logical conclusion can be represented as: [drugs + human traffickers = America Not Great]. That kind of 'logic' is appealing as it absolves the listeners/followers of any responsibility for America not being great anymore, as the reason for that fall from greatness is not anything that anyone in the USA has done—and certainly not due to the (in)actions of the country's leaders. It is all the fault of those others, i.e., the drug-smugglers and the human traffickers, those who infect and invade, and were it not for those others, America indeed would still be great—or possibly even greater.

As part of his wrapping-up of the RGS, DJT thanked a specific group, mentioned earlier, while laying another 'language trap':

> I want to thank, in particular, the Angel Moms and Dads for being here. Thank you very much. We have great respect for you. The real country, our real country—the people that really love our country, they love you. So, I just want you to know that. I know how hard you fight and I know how hard a fight you're having.

The 'language trap' laid here is based on the notion of 'reality', which is mentioned three times in a single, short sentence, making it an even higher concentration of DJT-repetition than usual: "The *real* country, our *real* country—the people that *really* love our country, they love you" (emphases added). The fallacious logic here is the implication that anyone that does not love the Angel Moms and Dads does not love their country, the USA. Furthermore, the sequence of: "real *country*, our real *country*—the people that really love our *country*" equates 'reality' with 'love of country', and by extension implies that anyone who does not love America without question is 'un-American'. However, it is entirely possible to love one's country—whatever that may mean to the individual—while still asking critical questions, as the two are not mutually exclusive.

Making Winners Out of Losers: Promising Victories

The remainder of the conclusion to this part of the RGS focused on winning, again implicitly invoking notions of a battle. For example, referring to his attempts to push through laws banning certain groups from entering the USA, and laws to secure funding for 2,000-mile border wall between the USA and Mexico, DJT said:

> So the [executive] order is signed... And we will have a National Emergency, and then we will then be sued... And then we'll end up in the Supreme Court... And *we'll win* in the Supreme Court, just like the ban. They sued us in the Ninth Circuit, and *we lost,* and then *we lost* in the appellate division, and then we went to the Supreme Court, and *we won.* (emphases added)

The win–lost–lost–won sequence gives the sense of a heroic battle being fought by the forces of good—the USA—against the forces of evil—anyone who does not love the USA unquestioningly, and/or who does not fear/hate immigrants. The implication here is also that, in spite of earlier defeats of the USA—which are important to show that it was a hard-fought battle, and not an easy win—the forces of good emerge triumphant over evil. Using an NPL approach, we can see just how important this idea of winning has been for DJT, going back to a speech he gave in the Spring of 2016. While he was on the campaign trail, when he boasted loudly, to cheering crowds:

> We're going to *win*. We're going to *win* so much. We're going to *win* at trade, we're going to *win* at the border. We're going to *win* so much, you're going to be so sick and tired of *winning*, you're going to come to me and go, 'Please, please, we can't *win* any more' (Crilly, 2017, emphasis added).

That makes no fewer than seven 'wins' in little more than 50 words, or one 'win' every seven words.

This notion of Winners vs. Losers may have been more important in the language of DJT than realized, as it goes back many years (see Chapter 8). For example, in 2015, the Canadian news magazine, *Maclean's*, published a list of approximately 60 occasions when DJT publicly called someone a 'loser', between 2013 and 2017 (Gilmore, 2017). From his predecessor, the 44th President of the USA, Barrack Obama (2009–2017), to reporters and journalists, to actors and actresses, radio hosts, writers and novelists, even including his own former advisor, Roger Stone, who was deemed worthy of the emphatic additional accolade of 'Stone Cold Loser' (Gilmore, 2017). In addition to those 60 or so 'losers', 'stone cold losers' and 'evil losers' (the latter reserved for the ISIS terrorist group), within that same time-frame (2013–2017) at least another 40 or so other recurring insults were hurled by DJT, including repeated name-calling of others as: Dumb, Dummy, Moron, Fool, Idiot, Failure, and other verbal abuses. But by far, DJT's favorite insult has been 'Loser' (Gilmore, 2017). Consequently, when DJT lost the US presidential election in 2020, he was unable to accept that fact publicly, as he had, by his own words, become the biggest loser of them all.

Of particular interest to NPL practitioners is the ratios of attacking language to praising language as used by some of the most powerful people in the world, as their words can set the tone, literally and metaphorically, for more 'negative warist' or more peaceful discourse. In the case of DJT, an outstanding example of the kind of 'journolistics'—in which journalists dabble in linguistics—(discussed in the following chapter) is the analysis of more than 11,000 tweets sent by DJT over a 34-month period, from January 2017 to October 2019, carried out by a team of *New York Times* journalists (Shear et al., 2019). During those 34 months, the journalists classified most of those 11,000 tweets as 'attacking something or someone'—approximately 5,900. Most of those attacks were against members of the opposition Democratic Party (2,400), news agencies that were critical of DJT (1,300), immigrants (570) and previous US presidential administrations (450). On the other hand, approximately 4,900 of DJT's tweets 'praised something or someone'. However, more than 2,000 of those positive tweets were DJT praising himself for the excellent work he had done. In addition, approximately 750 of those tweets were in praise of Conservative media that publicly supported DJT and publicly attacked anyone who disagreed with DJT (for example, Fox News), with approximately 130 tweets categorized as 'praising dictators', for example Kim Jung-un (Shear et al., 2019).

To return to DJT's scorn for losers and his fixation on winners and on being a winner himself, that can be explained at least in part by a simplistic but nonetheless appealing black-white worldview, in which there are only winners and losers, the victors and the vanquished, the heroes and the villains. It is also possible, then, that that focus on losers may make the supporters of DJT 'the Party of Losers', in the sense of those who feel they have 'lost out'. The phrasal verb 'to lose out' is defined as: "to not have an advantage that other people have" or "to not get something that you expected or wanted" (*CALD*, 2021). Therefore, the constant name-calling of 'losers' by DJT may be understood as a strategy targeting those people in the USA who feel that they have lost their jobs to 'the others', who feel that, after enjoying centuries of privilege, due to being part of the dominant White culture, their position is now being undermined and irreversibly eroded. But with DJT as their leader, they may have been able to finally feel like 'winners' once again.

Continuing in the same winner-takes-all vein, DJT continued:

> We have a ban on certain areas, certain countries, depending on what's going on in the world. And *we won*... And then it went to the Supreme Court and *I won*. Didn't want to take it that far. But *we won* on the ban and *we won* on other things, too. (emphases added)

That feeling of going from being the winners to being the losers, to wanting to be the winners again, which was reflected in so much of what DJT said and wrote, was captured in the book title, *That Used to Be Us: How America fell behind in the world it invented and how we can come back* (2011), by Thomas Friedman and Michael Mandelbaum. Leaving aside the fact that no country can claim to have invented the world, Friedman and Mandelbaum wrote about the belief that "Britain owned the nineteenth century, America dominated the twentieth century, and China will inevitably reign supreme in the twenty-first century" (p. 7). Although Friedman and Mandelbaum made it clear that they did not agree with such a characterization, they also recognized the fact that many of their fellow Americans may feel that way, which explains the thousands of winner-loser references made by DJT over the years.

REACT 9.3: *A saying in English is:* Everybody loves a winner. *Does that saying exist in other languages or contexts that you know, and if so, what happens to those who do not win? What kind of language is used to talk about not winning in those contexts? What are some of the challenges of a 'For me to win, you must lose' mindset? How can those kinds of challenges be met?*

In the final paragraph of DJT's RGS spoken text, before going on to an extremely long, drawn-out question-and-answer session with journalists, he repeated once again some of his main themes: winning, invasions, evil people, and monsters, while giving as an example "one of the world's most brutal street gangs" (*BBC*, April 2017), called 'MS-13':

> The probably easiest one to *win* is on declaring a national emergency, because we're declaring it for virtual *invasion* purposes: drugs, traffickers, and *gangs*. And one of the things, just to finish: We have removed thousands of MS-13 *gang monsters*. Thousands. *They're out* of this country. *We take them out* by the thousands. And they are *monsters* (emphases added)

Although it is not entirely clear what the "easiest one to win" was referring to, it may have been another allusion to another battle fought and won by DJT. Likewise, it is not clear what a "virtual invasion" is, or if the removal of "thousands of MS-13 gang monsters" ever actually happened, or if 'take out' here means 'kill', as used by BHO in his farewell address (see Chapter 7), or deported. However, as discussed above, the point here may not be to tell the truth or to inform, but to use language in ways that build support, ensure compliance, and feed off the fear and distrust sown.

Suggestions for Further Reading

In *Reality Lost: Markets of Attention, Misinformation and Manipulation* (2019, Springer), University of Copenhagen professor, Vincent Hendricks and Mads Vestergaard, look at phenomena such as 'Attention Speculation and Political Bubbles', 'Alternative Facts, Misinformation, and Fake News', and 'Fact Resistance, Populism, and Conspiracy Theories'.

In the current affairs magazine, *Quartz*, in the article 'Know how fake your news is with this lexicon of lies', Ephrat Levini (August 14, 2017) compares and contrasts, 'misinformation, 'disinformation' and 'misdirection', as well as propaganda, gas-lighting and other ways of misleading. https://qz.com/1051397/know-how-fake-your-news-is-with-this-lexicon-of-lies

In a report published by the Pew Research Center, *The Future of Truth and Misinformation Online* (2017) Janna Anderson and Lee Rainie conclude that: "Experts are evenly split on whether the coming decade will see a reduction in false and misleading narratives online." https://www.pewinternet.org/2017/10/19/the-future-of-truth-and-misinformation-online

10

"The Pen is Mightier than the Sword"

Warring Words in Writing

"The pen is mightier than the sword" is a saying attributed to the English writer and politician, Edward Bulwer-Lytton (1803–1873), who served as the Secretary of State for the Colonies of the British Empire in the late 1850s. Applied linguists call Bulwer-Lytton's statement a 'metonymic adage', meaning it is a saying or proverb of some kind, in which indirect reference is made to the main point, in this case, 'pen' is used figuratively to refer to 'the written word', and 'sword' to refer to any kind of armed conflict. For many people, computer keyboards and mobile multimedia devices such as smartphones have largely replaced pen and paper. However, the fact that words can be weaponized has not changed, and it is that weaponization of language that is of particular concern and interest to NPL practitioners, as we have seen in previous chapters. For example, in Chapter 4, we read Sartre's comment that "words are loaded pistols" (cited in Dedaić, 2003, p. 1), and Tishkov's (2004) conclusion that, "words can kill no less than bullets" (cited in Wenden, 2007, p. 163). Therefore, in this chapter and in the following one, we will look at NPL analyses of two written texts, from the former US president, Donald J. Trump (DJT).

The New Peace Linguistics and The Role of Language in Conflict, pages 183–197

The first of the two written texts is a letter sent, in the Spring of 2018, from DJT to Chairman Kim Jung-un (KJU, the leader of North Korea since 2011), cancelling a high-profile, much-anticipated, and historic meeting between them. The meeting was to discuss the denuclearization of North Korea, and an official end to the conflict between the two Koreas. Therefore, pre-meeting expectations were very high—higher than they had been for many years—especially following the first face-to-face official meeting between the leaders of North and South Korea in more than a decade, the previous month (April, 2018). With great ceremony and symbolism, the April 2018 meeting was held at the Inter-Korean Peace House—also known as the House of Peace and/or the Home of Peace, on the south side of what is called the 'Military Demarcation Line', dividing the two Koreas. The tagline or motto for that meeting was 'Peace, A New Start'. Given the global concerns regarding North Korea's nuclear capability and the hope for a less nuclear-weapons-armed world, the possibility of a peace-keeping/ peace-building deal between the two Koreas, brokered by the USA, made headlines around the world. Consequently, when in May, the letter (henceforth, in this chapter, the Letter) was sent from DJT to KJU, cancelling the meeting between them, which was scheduled to be held the following month (June, 2018) in Singapore, the Letter was published, read and reported on by news agencies all over the world.

In the previous two chapters, based on NPL analyses of DJT's 2015 SCC and of his 2019 RGS, we identified a total of more than 20 strategies and aspects of language use of particular interest to NPL practitioners. Here, with an NPL analysis of the Letter, we identify ten more, including:

- Semiotic mixed messages
- Self-aggrandizing
- Egocentric expressions
- Dissing and Disrespecting
- Turning the tables
- Emphatic discourse markers
- Exaggerating
- Threatening and accusatory warnings
- False charm
- Content-free, garrulous verbiage

The New Peace Linguistics and 'Journolistics'

In the Spring of 2018, the BBC reporter Anthony Zurcher published a piece titled 'Analysing Trump's letter to Kim Jong-un'. Zurcher reported that:

> Donald Trump called off the upcoming US-North Korea summit on Thursday morning [24 May 2018], catching much of official Washington, and the world, by surprise. How he did it—in a personal letter to North Korean leader Kim Jong-un—offers revealing insight at [*sic*] Trump-style diplomacy and what might happen next.

Zurcher's (2018) one-page (450-word) analysis of the Letter is a good example of not only the linguistic insights that some reporters and news agencies can bring to such texts, but also of some of the limitations of what might be called 'journalistic linguistics', or 'journolistics'. Zurcher pointed out a possible "passive-aggressive dig" by DJT at KJU, when DJT pointed out that it was KJU who proposed the meeting. Using a carnivorous metaphor, with some rhythmic, four-part, plosive-p alliteration [paragraph + president's + pen + poison], to build to a climactic finish, Zurcher reported that: "The real meat of the letter comes at the end of the paragraph, however, as the president's pen turns poison."

Continuing with his analysis of the opening paragraph, Zurcher (2018) described DJT as firing off "another round of 'fire and fury' style language, boasting about the massive and powerful US nuclear arsenal," which Zurcher identified as "a return to the rhetoric of last summer [2017]" when a previous round of "nuclear sabre-rattling" took place. Zurcher (2018) concluded his analysis of the first paragraph by noting that: "The start of the letter may be diplomat-speak, but this [threatening language] is Mr. Trump's voice coming through." In his analysis of the second paragraph, Zurcher (2018) rolled a number of metaphors into one: "the diplomatic gloves are back on," "the recent thaw," and a "hint that the door has not been fully slammed shut." Zurcher (2018) also commented on DJT's writing of "wonderful dialogue" (for some reason, written with a UK spelling, rather the usual USA spelling of 'dialog'), to describe the back-and-forth between the USA and North Korea at that time, and on DJT's use of the phrase "beautiful gesture" to describe the release of three American prisoners. Commenting on the use of "beautiful gesture," Zurcher (2018) concluded that: "There will certainly be some critics who question whether this is an appropriate place to turn on the charm"—that is, assuming that DJT's words were read by KJU as being charming.

Zurcher's analysis of the third and final paragraph of the Letter stated that: "The business letter template kicks in again in the closing paragraph, albeit with somewhat tortured prose." The tortured line in the Letter that he was referring to is: "If you change your mind having to do with this most important summit, please do not hesitate to call me or write," to which Zurcher added, playfully: "We have operators standing by!" In conclusion,

Zurcher described the Letter as finishing "on a wistful note," although DJT's apparent melancholia may have been more to do with his hopes of being awarded the Nobel Peace Prize having been dashed than with anything else (Zurcher, 2018).

Another good example of 'journolistics' was provided by *The New York Times* reporter, Alexander Burns, who presented an annotated account of the speech in which Mr. Peter Paul Buttigieg (PPB) announced, in the Spring of 2019, that he would be running for the Democratic Party nomination in the 2020 presidential elections in the USA. PPB's candidacy-announcement speech was approximately 3,600 words, with 11 sets of annotations provided by Burns, totaling approximately 900 words of commentary. Although most of Burn's annotations do not analyze the language used by PPB, as Burn's piece was focused on the political implications of the speech, there are some insightful language-based observations. For example, early on in the speech (approx. 200 words in), PPB says: "Thanks to my mom who is here physically and my dad who is here in more ways that he could have imagined. And Chasten, my love, for giving me the strength to do this and the grounding to be myself as we go." Burn's notes on those lines from PPB explained that: "This understated line is the first acknowledgment of the historic nature of Mr. Buttigieg's bid, as the first openly gay presidential candidate to achieve national prominence." Burns also noted, in his commentary on those same lines: "Mr. Buttigieg has not framed his campaign in terms of identity—the word 'gay' does not appear in the speech—but the proud display of a same-sex marriage is unique in American political history" (Burns, 2019).

Burns (2019) compared the language used by PPB to the language used by Barack Obama (BHO), as PPB's supporters "often liken him to Barack Obama, because of his youth and persona as a cerebral outsider" and because PPB used "Obama-esque flourishes throughout, including more than half a dozen references each to 'hope' and 'change'" (Burns, 2019). PPB made a number of comments about Washington, including: "The horror show in Washington is mesmerizing, all-consuming. But starting today, we are going to change the channel." Burns' notes on those lines explained that: "This rhetoric about the importance of Washington may sound de rigueur for a presidential candidate, but it represents a shift from the message that helped make Mr. Buttigieg a national figure in the first place."

One of the concluding paragraphs of spoken text said by PPB was: "If you and I rise together to meet this moment, one day they will write histories, not just about one campaign or one presidency, but about the era that began here today…where past, present, and future meet." In 'journalisticing' those lines, Burns again drew comparisons with BHO: "As the speech builds to a conclusion, Mr. Buttigieg again evokes Mr. Obama, casting his campaign in epochal terms, as a turning point for the country. This passage recalls Mr. Obama's 2008 speech, upon clinching the Democratic nomination" (Burns, 2019). A great many news reports have been cited in this book, along with many books written by reporters, media personalities and other non-linguists, which I hope illustrates how much I appreciate (and enjoy reading) such reports and books. However, there are understandable limitations to such analyses, some of which are beyond the control of the journalists themselves, such as word-length, as news reports and books for mass-consumption tend to have to be shorter. Those limitations reiterate the need to establish a New Peace Linguistics, where more in-depth and detailed linguistic analyses of the words of the world's most powerful people can take place.

An NPL Analysis of a Written Text: The Letter Sent by DJT to KJU (May 2018)

The Seal

In the case of the Letter, an NPL analysis begins even before the text begins. With a letter from the President of the USA that beginning would be The Official Seal of the President of the United States, the image of which appears at the top of the page. Semiotics is a branch of linguistics that looks at the uses and interpretations of signs and symbols, and from a semiotic and NPL perspective, the Presidential Seal is more important than may be initially realized. Firstly, because, like DJT himself, the Seal is highly contradictory, as the Seal's American Eagle holds, in its right talons, an olive branch, which is recognized worldwide as a symbol of peace (as in the English expression 'to extend an olive branch'). However, in its left talon, the Eagle holds a bundle of 13 arrows, representing not only the 13 original states of the USA, but with a bow, that part of the Seal also represents one of the oldest forms of sharpened, human-made weapons of war, going back to prehistoric times. The torso of the American Eagle is protected by a shield, with a banner of some kind in the Eagle's mouth, on which is written the Latin expression *E PLURIBUS UNUM* (all in full-caps). That expression is usually translated into English as 'Out of many, one' or 'One out of many', which is stamped onto every single coin of currency in the USA in use today. However, as Niose (2011) pointed out, although *E Pluribus Unum* was "intended to represent the federal nature of the nation—out of many states, one country," the Religious Right in the USA considered the phrase "almost un-American," preferring instead the motto 'In God We Trust' (Niose, 2011). Therefore, before even the first word of written text of the Letter is read, a number of powerful messages may already have been sent.

The main text of the Letter begins with an opening salutation and continues:

> Dear Mr. Chairman:
>
> We greatly appreciate your time, patience, and effort with respect to our recent negotiations and discussions relative to a summit long sought by both parties, which was scheduled to take place on June 12 in Singapore. We were informed that the meeting was requested by North Korea, but that to us is totally irrelevant. I was very much looking forward to being there with you. Sadly, based on the tremendous anger and open hostility displayed in your most recent statement, I feel it is inappropriate, at this time, to have this long-planned meeting. Therefore, please let this letter serve to represent that the Singapore summit, for the good of both parties, but to the detriment of the world, will not take place. You talk about your nuclear capabilities, but ours are so massive and powerful that I pray to God they will never have to be used.
>
> I felt a wonderful dialogue was building up between you and me, and ultimately, it is only that dialogue that matters. Some day, I look very much forward to meeting you. In the meantime, I want to thank you for the release of the hostages who are now home with their families. That was a beautiful gesture and was very much appreciated.
>
> If you change your mind having to do with this most important summit, please do not hesitate to call me or write. The world, and North Korea in particular, has lost a great opportunity for lasting peace and great prosperity and wealth. This missed opportunity is a truly sad moment in history.
>
> Sincerely yours,
>
> Donald J. Trump
>
> President of the United States of America

REACT 10.1: *Read the first paragraph of the Letter again. How would you describe the different feelings being expressed by the writer, DJT? What do you think are some of the ways the reader, KJU, might have responded to that first paragraph?*

The Letter

Unpacked and unraveled, the main text of the Letter looks like this:

Paragraph 1 [P = Paragraph, S = Sentence]

P1.S1: "We greatly appreciate your time, patience, and effort with respect to our recent negotiations and discussions relative to a summit long sought by both parties, which was scheduled to take place on June 12 in Singapore.

P1.S2: We were informed that the meeting was requested by North Korea, but that to us is totally irrelevant.

P1.S3: I was very much looking forward to being there with you.

P1.S4: Sadly, based on the tremendous anger and open hostility displayed in your most recent statement, I feel it is inappropriate, at this time, to have this long-planned meeting.

P1.S5: Therefore, please let this letter serve to represent that the Singapore summit, for the good of both parties, but to the detriment of the world, will not take place.

P1.S6: You talk about your nuclear capabilities, but ours are so massive and powerful that I pray to God they will never have to be used."

Paragraph 2

P2.S1: "I felt a wonderful dialogue was building up between you and me, and ultimately, it is only that dialogue that matters.

P2.S2: Some day, I look very much forward to meeting you.

P2.S3: In the meantime, I want to thank you for the release of the hostages who are now home with their families.

P2.S4: That was a beautiful gesture and was very much appreciated."

Paragraph 3

P3.S1: "If you change your mind having to do with this most important summit, please do not hesitate to call me or write.

P3.S2: The world, and North Korea in particular, has lost a great opportunity for lasting peace and great prosperity and wealth.

P3.S3: This missed opportunity is a truly sad moment in history."

The Opening Paragraph

After the opening salutation, the text begins with a collective 'we': "We greatly appreciate your time, patience, and effort..." That first 'we' may have been referring specifically to DJT's administrative team who were making the meeting arrangements, or more generally to the American people. Or, that 'we' may even have been some sort of global reference to the world's population, and perhaps even a worldwide desire for peace (assuming such a desire exists). The Letter continued: "with respect to our recent negotiations and discussions relative to a summit long sought by both parties..." which marks the end of the first sentence. Here, we can see a three-part alliteration, based on the effect created by [respect + recent + relative], which might help to explain the long-winded, cumbersome wording. Instead, that line could have been written, more effectively and more efficiently as, for example: "regarding the summit, long-sought by both parties," rather than: "with respect to our recent negotiations and discussions relative to a summit long sought by both parties."

The use of 'summit', as opposed to 'meeting', or even 'historic meeting', is potentially important, as a 'summit' is defined as: "an important formal meeting between leaders of governments from two or more countries" (*CALD*, 2021), and if the meeting is of the highest importance, then, by implication, so too must be those who are attending the meeting. 'Summit' also carries with it ideational connotations and mental images of the highest point that can be reached when climbing a mountain; the pinnacle, or the peak (of achievement). Although 'long sought' (unhyphenated here, although 'long-planned', later in the Letter, is hyphenated) is a chronological reference, it is the use of the simple past tense 'was' that rings loudly in the mind of the NPL practitioner. In the phrase, "which was scheduled to take place on June 12 in Singapore," many readers would normally and naturally focus on details such as names and numbers (Bredart, Brennen & Valentine, 1997)—in this case, the date and the place of the meeting. However, in the mind of the NPL reader, alarms bells of the *Whoa! Wait! What-Just-Happened?* kind ring loud-and-clear. The reason is that the phrase "which *was* scheduled to take place" (emphasis added) can mean one thing, and one thing only, i.e., the meeting is (now) not taking place (anymore).

To briefly recap, the first sentence of the Letter is: "We greatly appreciate your time, patience, and effort with respect to our recent negotiations and discussions relative to a summit long sought by both parties, which was scheduled to take place on June 12 in Singapore." Those 36 words, divided by punctuation, into three phrases, may seem respectful (an impression perhaps helped by the use of "with respect to") and may seem informational in some neutral manner. However, to use the militaristic language so widely-used by DJT (see, for example, Michael Wolff's 2018 book, *Fire and Fury: Inside the Trump White House*), those 36 words may have been an opening salvo in a 'negative warist discourse' (see Chapter 3)—thinly disguised as an expression of appreciation (see also Wolff's 2019 book, *Siege: Trump Under Fire*).

The second sentence of P1 of the Letter states: "We were informed that the meeting was requested by North Korea, but that to us is totally irrelevant." One NPL question that arises from that statement is: Why draw attention to something that is described by the writer as not just "irrelevant" but "*totally* irrelevant"? Clearly, that detail, of who requested the meeting, is *highly* relevant. Indeed, it the only real content conveyed in the entire sentence, which tells the reader that, firstly, the writer is lying, when he writes, "that to us is totally irrelevant" and secondly, that the writer, DJT, may assume that the reader, KJU, will not notice such an obviously contradictory statement. That statement may, in turn, have signaled to KJU that DJT thought KJU was a gullible fool. Sending such messages, from one country-leader to another—both of which possess world-ending nuclear weapons—may be one way to start a war, or at least, a conflict that could escalate to a war.

The purpose of P1.S2 seems to be something along the lines of: You [KJU] requested this historic mountain-top meeting, but I [DJT] am now cancelling it, which (by the way) shows that I have (much) more power than you. Strategically, P1.S2 may also have been designed to show KJU that DJT is willing to walk away from the negotiation table, perhaps in the same way that a tourist haggling at a souvenir stand walks away, to see if the seller can be pressured into reducing the price (further). However, while such strategies may work in the business of buying-and-selling real estate, they do not work well when trying to bring about world peace. There is also DJT's use of 'totally', for emphasis, which was described by the *National Geographic* reporter Marcus Woo (2013) as the word used by "the stereotypical ditzy, young, well-to-do, white women" in southern California.

REACT 10.2: *For one or two days, observe and make notes on your own use of emphatic discourse markers, or on the use of emphatic discourse markers by someone else. Do you see any patterns in your/their use of such markers? If so, why, where and when are you/they using those kinds of markers?*

The third and fourth sentences in the first paragraph can be considered together, as they are both based on emotions, while the pronouns switched from the collective 'we' in the first two statements to the individual 'I' in these second two: "I was very much looking forward to being there with you. Sadly, based on the tremendous anger and open hostility displayed in your most recent statement, I feel it is inappropriate, at this time, to have this long-planned meeting" (P1.S3 and P1.S4). A four-part expression of emotions is set-up here, starting with positive, anticipatory emotion, expressed by DJT, i.e., "very much looking forward to," changing to sadness ("Sadly"), which is followed by references to "anger" and "hostility," but this time, on the part of KJU, as accused by DJT, who concludes with "I feel it is inappropriate…" Here, rather than 'totally', the emphatic marker used is 'tremendous', to describe the magnitude of KJU's presumed/assumed anger, with 'open' used to describe KJU's 'hostility'. These two adjectival modifiers—totally and open—are different in linguistically important ways. 'Totally' can refer to scale and scope, i.e., completely, whereas 'open' refers to mood and manner. 'Open' may also be seen to imply that 'closed' or 'hidden' hostility might have been somehow more acceptable, or at least less unacceptable. But being openly hostile crosses some invisible line, perhaps in a way that might be verbally analogous to an incursion of some kind.

From a text analysis and critical discourse analysis perspective, the Letter then takes a turn for the worse, at the fifth and sixth sentences of Paragraph One (P1.S5 and P1.S6):

> Therefore, please let this letter serve to represent that the Singapore summit, for the good of both parties, but to the detriment of the world, will not take place. You talk about your nuclear capabilities, but ours are so massive and powerful that I pray to God they will never have to be used.

The sentence-initial, cause–effect marker, "Therefore," implies a logical progression, however, what follows appears to be anything but logical: "please let this letter serve to represent." The use of that phrase makes little sense, apart from the politeness-permission marker ("please"), although permission is not, in fact, being sought by DJT. A rule-of-thumb, related to the notion of textual redundancy that is taught in basic composition classes, can be expressed as: If the phrase can be cut, without altering the meaning of the sentence, then cut it. Let us see what happens if we apply that logic to P1.S5: Therefore, the Singapore summit, for the good of both parties, but to the detriment of the world, will not take place. The repeated and definitive 'will', in "will not take place," is retained. But cutting "please let this letter serve to represent that" does not appear to alter the meaning of the sentence in any way, leaving the reader to wonder what the motivation for such garrulous verbiage could be, as phrases like "serve to represent that" are almost entirely content-free, from a linguistic or communicative purpose perspective. The verboseness of such phrasing may have been designed to impress the reader, but such superfluous writing might only impress a reader, if that reader was less literate than the writer.

The first of the three paragraphs concluded by turning accusatory and threatening, as pointed out by Zurcher (2018), together with an appeal to a Higher Power: "*You* talk about *your* nuclear capabilities, but *ours* are so massive and powerful that *I* pray to God *they* will never have to be used" [emphases added]. The use of "ours are so massive" was picked up by several international news agencies. For example, the headline in *The Australian* newspaper on 3 January 2018 was: 'Trump Turns North Korea Nuclear Crisis into "Mine's Bigger Than Yours" Contest'. Callum Watson, at the Geneva Centre for the Democratic Control of Armed Forces, concluded his gender analysis of decision-making by the USA's National Security Council during the Cuban Missile Crisis, titled *My Missile is Bigger than Yours*, with the finding that: "masculine norms and gendered power dynamics are reflected in final policy outcomes" (Watson, 2012, p. 81). Furthermore, in considering this machismo focus on size matters, Cook & Stambaugh (1997) discussed the politics of male "pissing contests" (p. 63) online, and Harwood (2011) considered the use of "big guns" to compensate for 'small penis syndrome' amongst "the most outspoken advocates of 'the right to bear arms' in a country [the USA] that has no need of a civilian militia" (p. 479).

As noted in previous chapters, viewing DJT's uses of "ours are so massive" through an NPL lens highlights aspects that may not have been as obvious to some readers. For example, reporting for NPR, on the 2016 US presidential elections, Danielle Kurtzleben (2016) described 'Trump and the Testosterone Takeover of 2016'. Kurtzleben noted that: "The most blatant example of Trump's manliness as a focal point was the debate over his hand size in this election [when] he became the first presidential candidate to, in a debate, bring up the size of his penis." Four years later, in 2020, Kurtzleben (2020), reiterated the fact that: 'Trump has weaponized masculinity as president' and she reported that: "Trump has been blatant about amping up his particular, aggressive and pugilistic brand of masculinity. After four years, that machismo has manifested itself in seemingly every area of his presidency." Furthermore, such toxic presidential masculinity "has potential political and even policy impacts that may last well beyond [DJT's] tenure in office" (Kurtzleben, 2020).

The last part of the sixth and final sentence of the first paragraph concluded with the characteristic appeal to a Higher Power: "I pray to God they will never have to be used." The reference to praying may be some kind of dog whistle (see Chapter 8, also McCutcheon & Mark, 2014) for the "80% of white evangelicals [who] reported voting for Trump" in exit polls after the 2016 presidential election, and whose "approval of his presidential performance has been double the national average" (Myers, 2017). Given that White evangelical support, that last part of the sixth sentence may also have been a nod to The Four Horsemen of the Apocalypse—Pestilence (or the Anti-Christ), War, Famine, and Death—as described in the Book of Revelation, the final book of the New Testament of the *Bible.* It is also possible that the "I pray to God" reference may have been for the benefit of those DJT-supporting White Christian evangelicals who believe that Communist leaders like Chairman Kim Jong-un, and Communist countries like North

Korea, are atheists who reject their White, Christian God (Wilson-Hartgrove, 2018). Four years later, in the 2020 elections, that figure of 80% support for DJT from that group of White Christian evangelicals was found to be steady: "Trump's reputation in moral terms hasn't changed all that much during his time in office, but there is little evidence of slippage among these faith voters" (Gjelten, 2020). As Gene Demby and Shereen Meraji put in, in their NPR report, 'The White Elephant in the Room' (2020): "a group whose support for Donald Trump hasn't wavered [is] white evangelical voters."

REACT 10.3: *In your context, is there a relationship between religion and politics? If so, what is the nature of that relationship? For example, do religious leaders there talk about politics, and/or do political leaders talk about religion? If so, what kinds of language do those leaders use when talking about religion/politics?*

Paragraphs Two and Three

The second and third paragraphs of the Letter's main text are a total of 114 words; 62 and 52, respectively, making P2 and P3 combined significantly shorter than P1, at 147 words. After the threatening and accusatory warning at the end of the first paragraph, at the beginning of the second, the tone switched abruptly to: "I felt a wonderful dialogue was building up between you and me." That line was followed by perhaps the most egotistical phrase of the Letter, describing the dialog between DJT and KJU as being "the only... dialogue that matters," completely ignoring all the other discussions that have been taking place around the world, about relations with North Korea, going back more than sixty years.

At P2.S2, the Letter continued: "Some day, I look very much forward to meeting you" (P2.S2), and "In the meantime, I want to thank you for the release of the hostages who are now home with their families" (P2.S3). The hostages released were three citizens of the USA, of Korean origin, imprisoned in North Korea, who were being held on charges of committing espionage or unidentified 'hostile acts' against North Korea. Paragraph Two concluded with: "That was a beautiful gesture and was very much appreciated" (P2.S4), which Zurcher (2018) interpreted as an attempt to "turn on the charm," but which may have been read as being more 'smarmy' than 'charming', i.e., "extremely polite or helpful or showing a lot of respect in a way that is annoying or *does not seem sincere*" (*CALD*, 2021, emphasis added). The possibility of smarminess is reflected in a poll conducted in the Spring of 2019, in which 'insincere' was one of the words used most often to describe DJT (Karni, 2019).

The third and final paragraph is made up of three sentences:

P3.S1: If you change your mind having to do with this most important summit, please do not hesitate to call me or write.
P3.S2: The world, and North Korea in particular, has lost a great opportunity for lasting peace and great prosperity and wealth.
P3.S3: This missed opportunity is a truly sad moment in history.

The sentence-initial conditional 'If', used at the beginning of P3, implies an openness to the possibility of the summit still taking place. However: "If you change your mind," meaning 'the ball is in your court' and/or 'we are extending the olive branch', completely ignores the fact that it was DJT, not KJU, who changed his mind. With "you" and "your" the writer, DJT, puts the onus—or the blame—on the reader, KJU, although the reader was not the one who decided to cancel the summit. At P3.S1 DJT continued: "having to do with this most important summit, please do not hesitate to call me or write." The phrase, "having to do with" appears to be the same kind of content-free, garrulous verbiage we saw at P1.S5, i.e., "please let this letter serve to represent that." It could have been written more concisely and more clearly as, for example: 'If you change your mind about a summit meeting, please do not hesitate to call or write to me'. And similar to "please let this letter," we have "please do not hesitate," giving the *appearance* of politeness, although it is not possible to know how (in)sincere such politeness might actually have been (see Karni, 2019, above)

Closing Lines

One of the reasons that NPL appears to be emerging as an increasingly important branch of applied linguistics is the ways in which world leaders, and others in power, refer to peace, in their written and spoken texts, which need to be analyzed closely and carefully, to find the deeper and sometimes contradictory meanings within their messages. Here, the Letter reads: "The world, and North Korea in particular, has lost a great opportunity for lasting peace and great prosperity and wealth" (P3.S2). In language education, 'the three Ps' refers to the traditional sequence of presentation of a language item by the teacher, followed by the learners practicing the item, with help from the teacher, then the learners produce the language item independently. An analogous three-part, three-p alliteration appears to exist in politics, for example, 'Peace, Progress, and Prosperity', which was the campaign slogan of George White (1872–1853), who served as Chairman of the US Democratic National Committee from 1920 to 1921. Nearly a century later, two of its three parts appeared in the Letter as: "The world... has lost a great opportunity for lasting peace and great prosperity and wealth" (P3. S2). The repeated use of 'great' twice in just eight words may have been an illusion to the slogan of the Trump campaign in the 2016 Presidential Election, i.e., 'Make America Great Again' and/or to the 2020 re-election campaign slogan, 'Keep America Great'. However, it is equally possible that such repetition may simply reflect a limited vocabulary. The last sentence of the last paragraph is: "This missed opportunity is a truly sad moment in history" (P3.S3). A three-part time-span switch can be seen, between 'lasting', in the previous sentence (P3.S2), referring to a long period of time, which is contrasted with 'moment', in the concluding sentence, which usually refers to a brief or passing period, and finally 'history', which is usually reserved for longer periods. Also, the 'sadness' is emphasized with the use of the adverbial modifier 'truly'.

One of the differences between spoken texts and written texts is that the former may result in 'slips of the tongue', in which a speaker accidentally says something that they did not mean to say. However, that is not the case with written texts, especially those between two country-leaders (with nuclear capabilities), as those kinds of written text are carefully constructed to communicate specific meanings to—and to create specific responses in—the reader. As we can see from this NPL analysis of DJT's letter to KJU, a wide array of language-based strategies was used to appear to state one thing while seeming to mean something else.

Suggestions for Further Reading

Some aspects of the relationships between reading and writing were discussed in earlier chapters. In 2017, after just a month of DJT being in office, Michelle Moyd and Yuliya Komska reported on how 'Trump's redundant, 'post-literate' way of speaking is changing our language'. https://www.businessinsider.com/trumps-redundant-post-literate-way-of-speaking-is-changing-our-language-2017-1

Later in 2017, Jeet Heer's essay in *The New Republic* (2017) was published, 'The Post-Literate American Presidency'. In his essay, DJT is described as "the first TV [television] president" of the USA, and Heer discusses what that might mean for the language and literacy levels of the presidency in the years to come. https://newrepublic.com/article/144940/trump-tv-post-literate-american-presidency

After one year in office, in early 2018, David Graham's *Atlantic* piece was published, 'The President Who Doesn't Read', in which Graham describes DJT as 'America's first post-text president', regarding reading and writing. https://www.theatlantic.com/politics/archive/2018/01/americas-first-post-text-president/549794

A piece in the *Huffington Post,* in 2011, written by a best-selling author, Jason Pinter, is titled 'An Open Letter to Donald Trump: You Are Not A Good Writer'. It is a rebuttal of DJT's claims to be a great writer and voracious reader, and although it was written many years before DJT became President of the USA, Pinter concluded by stating: "Writing, like running the country, in my opinion, needs a modicum of humility and (more than a modicum) of honesty." https://www.huffingtonpost.com/jason-pinter/an-open-letter-to-donald-_b_847875.html

11

Fear-Mongering and Feeding Off the Fear

The Foreign Policy Statement on the USA 'Standing With Saudi Arabia' (Nov, 2018)

In the Fall of 2018, the Government of the USA issued what it called a 'Foreign Policy Statement from President Donald J. Trump on 'Standing with Saudi Arabia' (henceforth, in this chapter, the Statement). The Statement was in response to the brutal, pre-meditated murder of the journalist, Jamal Khashoggi, which was widely believed to have been ordered by Crown Prince Mohammad bin Salman of Saudi Arabia, as retribution for the public criticism of the Crown Prince by Khashoggi. The murder was internationally condemned by countries around the world—but not the USA, in spite of the fact that DJT's own intelligence agencies, including the CIA, reported to DJT their conclusion that "the Saudi crown prince ordered Jamal Khashoggi's assassination" (Harris, Miller & Dawsey, 2018). Furthermore, that CIA report was repeatedly confirmed in a series of further investigations carried between 2019 and 2021, which found the murder to be a "state-sponsored assassination of *Washington Post* journalist Jamal Khashoggi

The New Peace Linguistics and The Role of Language in Conflict, pages 199–212

at the Saudi consulate in Istanbul, Turkey" based on "damning evidence against Saudi crown prince Mohammed bin Salman" (Fraley, 2021).

At a little over 630 words, the Statement, published on the White House website, was relatively short. However, in addition to the 30-plus language strategies of interest to NPL practitioners identified in the previous three chapters (DJT's 2015 SCC, his 2019 RGS, and his 2018 Letter) a dozen more such strategies were identified in an NPL analysis of DJT's Statement. That makes a total of more than 40 distinct but closely connected ways of using language by a world leader, influencing and affecting hundreds of millions of people in the USA, and many more all over the world. The language strategies found in the Statement through an NPL analysis include the following:

- Making excuses
- Appealing to supporter self-interest
- Obfuscating versus Communicating
- Scaring the audience and Feeding off the Fear
- Over-Dramatizing and Over-Emphasizing
- Exaggerating figures to distort facts
- Heroizing the in-group, while demonizing the out-group
- Using descriptors such as 'defense contractors', rather than 'mercenaries'
- Claiming to be defending one thing, e.g. 'Democracy', while actually protecting something else, e.g., oil supplies and arms sales
- Claiming that war is not only good for, but a vital part of, an economy—as long as the war is somewhere else
- Blaming the victim through the use of 'reverse innuendo'
- Making 'non-statements' and 'false promises'
- Using 'doublespeak' and 'doublewrite'

The Statement begins with two short sentences; one of just two words, and the other of seven: "America First!" and "The world is a very dangerous place!"

REACT 11.1: *Do you agree with the statement that: "The world is a very dangerous place!" If so, why do you agree? If not, why do you disagree?*

Even without the customary, over-emphatic exclamation mark, a whole book could be written on that two-word phrase 'America First'. In fact, one has been written, *Behold, America: The Entangled History of 'America First' and 'the American Dream'*, by University of London professor Sarah Churchwell. (or, approximately, half a book, at least). In her book, which won the *Smithsonian Magazine* Best History Book of 2018, Churchwell began by pointing out that: "received wisdoms" about 'America First' are often "misunderstood or delimited," even those offered by some "eminent historians" (p. 4)—and even more so by those who are not historians (eminent or otherwise), such as conservative reporters, political pundits and certain presidents of the USA. By way of correction, Churchwell explained that the phrases 'American dream' and 'America first' "were born almost a century ago" (p. 5). And specifically in relation to language, she pointed out that: "When what's on the table are national values, and *our language obscures us from important truths* about those values, the stakes grow very high" (p. 5, emphasis added). The italicized text is a timely reminder of how language can be used in equal and opposite ways, when it comes to communicating versus obfuscating, as we have seen in previous chapters.

Although Churchwell is an historian, she shows an impressive and somewhat atypical sensitivity to the importance of language in shaping history. For example, she noted that: "Phrases can form chains of association, conceptual paths that the mind follows intuitively, even unconsciously, as one word, or idea, seems to lead naturally to another" (2018, p. 5). Whether or not the conceptual paths followed by our minds are in fact intuitive and/or unconscious is open to debate, as the associative chains of meaning may be the result of habitual exposure and conditioning, as well as perhaps being more subconscious than unconscious. However, Churchwell highlighted that fact that the words and phrases we read and write, say and hear, the messages which we transmit and receive: "help define political and social realities, and it's only by *tracing the words,* how people skip from one to the next without necessarily even being aware of it, that we understand how these ideas have evolved" (pp. 5–6, emphasis added). It is that 'skipping' which enables us to make meaning from language, at a conscious level, but it is the not "being [consciously] aware of it" that gives language its underlying power—which is a feature employed, and sometimes exploited, by those in power.

Churchwell's observation, about our lack of conscious awareness of words and ideas, recalls a similar observation made by David Nunan, presented in Chapter 2: "most of us remain largely ignorant [at the conscious level] of this phenomena [language] that defines us as humans" (2013, p. 200). The importance of written and spoken language in nation-building is one of the recurring themes in Churchwell's book, and she stated that: "In an origin story about the ideas of a nation, *words matter*—especially because their *rhetoric* informs so much of our own *political reality*" (p. 10, emphases added). Although we may be living through times of an ever-widening gap, in many countries and contexts, between the political rhetoric and the political reality (see, for example, Klein, 2015 and Kich, 2015), Chuchwell's book is an unexpected source of support for the development of the field of NPL.

Danger!

According to the BBC, one-sentence paragraphs such as, "The world is a very dangerous place!" can be used for a variety of reasons, including: "to slow the reader down; to create a shock; to make something stand out; to change the flow of the writing; to repeat something; to remind the reader of something" (*BBC Bitesize,* 2019). Some of those reasons do not apply in this case, for example, "to change the flow of the writing" and "to repeat something" may not be reasons, as the Statement is just beginning at that point. However, making the reader pause, before getting to the main body of the text, may be designed to create dramatic impact, and to remind the reader that, in this case, 'danger is everywhere'. However, for most people, danger is not in fact lurking around every corner, waiting to pounce on us, the minute we drop our guard. One obvious reason for that kind of (melo) dramatic, one-line opening is to spread fear, as people are far more susceptible to believing and doing what they are told, without question, when they believe they are in danger (Weir, 2017) which then allows the speaker/writer to present themselves as the protector of the listener/reader.

Given the fear factor, it is no coincidence that the title of one of the most discussed books of 2018 about the government of the USA is, *Fear: Trump in the Whitehouse,* by Bob Woodward, followed by his book *Rage* (2020). Over more than 45 years, Woodward has interviewed more Presidents of the USA than any other reporter in the world—nine, starting with Richard Milhous Nixon (1913–1994). Nixon presided from 1969 until he became the only President of the USA (so far) to resign, in 1974, to avoid being impeached, and it is worth noting that DJT has been compared many times to Nixon. For example, the *Maclean's* reporter, Charlie Gillis, pointed out the "parallels in the two leaders' popular appeal and personal idiosyncrasies—from their paranoid musings to their exploitation of the politics of grievance," and concluded that: "as clashes between the White House and those investigating Trump's associates intensify, the similarities are getting downright eerie" (Gillis, 2017. See also, Kruse, 2018; Glanton, 2018; Rothkopf, 2018).

On one of the first pages of Woodward's (2018) book is a quote from an interview with DJT in the Spring of 2016, when he was a presidential candidate. The interview was carried out by Bob Woodward and Robert Costa, at the Trump International Hotel in Washington, DC. "Real power," said DJT "is fear" (Woodward, 2018, p. xvi). *Fear* was published on September 11, on the seventeenth anniversary of the 9/11 terrorist attacks (see Chapter 5). A few days before *Fear* was published, one of Woodward's lead assistants on two of his previous books, Bill Murphy, published a piece, 'Here's the 1 Question Every Leader Must Answer Now', which started with what Murphy called a "crucial question": "Are people afraid of you?" (Murphy, 2018).

Fear may be one of the most effective and efficient ways of controlling people. In 'Seven Things You Need to Know About Fear', neuropsychology professor, Theo Tsaousides explained that "You don't need to be in danger to be scared" (2015). Tsaousides distinguished between 'conditioned fear', which is a habitual response, for example, to a raging inferno in front of us, and 'anticipatory fear', in which we fear that which is "not even present" (Tsaousides, 2015). Number five on the list of seven is: "The more scared you feel, the scarier things will seem," which is the result of a process called 'potentiation' in which "your fear response is amplified if you are already in a state of fear." For example, if a nervous flyer is on board a plane that encounters even mild turbulence, the nervous flyer will expect the worst. In 1933, Franklin D. Roosevelt (1882–1945), the four-term 32nd President of the USA (from 1933 to 1945), uttered during his inaugural address what would become one of his most famous lines: "So, first of all, let me assert my firm belief that the only thing we have to fear is fear itself—*nameless, unreasoning, unjustified* terror which paralyzes needed efforts to convert retreat into advance" (Rosenman, 1938, emphasis added) (see also Chapters 6 & 7). The three italicized adjectives exemplify the notion of 'anticipatory fear', and of employing 'potentiation'.

REACT 11.2: *Some people enjoy watching scary movies, while others do not. If you enjoy such movies, what do you enjoy about being scared? If you do not enjoy such movies, what are some other things that scare you? How do you cope with fear, whether in the movies or in real life?*

Before moving onto the rest of this text, and having considered the opening and exclamatory, one-sentence paragraph, "The world is a very dangerous place!," it is worth considering some questions that arise from that statement. Firstly, for whom is the world such a dangerous place? For the speaker, for the listeners, for everybody, everywhere? Such imprecise language may be deliberate, by design, so as to include as many people as possible. Secondly, what kinds of dangers are being referred to here? Thirdly, who or what is the cause and the source of these dangers? Some clarification was provided by DJT:

P2.1: The country of Iran, as an example, is responsible for a bloody proxy war against Saudi Arabia in Yemen, trying to destabilize Iraq's fragile attempt at democracy, supporting the terror group Hezbollah in Lebanon, propping up dictator Bashar Assad in Syria (who has killed millions of his own citizens), and much more.

P2.2: Likewise, the Iranians have killed many Americans and other innocent people throughout the Middle East.

P2.3: Iran states openly, and with great force, 'Death to America!' and 'Death to Israel!'

P.2.4: Iran is considered the world's leading sponsor of terror.

The 90-word, four-sentence second paragraph above (P2.1-P2.4) may actually say less than the opening two lines, of just nine words in total: "America First! The world is a very dangerous place!" To put P2 more clearly and concisely: 'Iran is the Enemy', as far as DJT and the USA was/is concerned, which may well be true. However, the statement that the President of Syria (since 2000) Bashir al-Assad has "killed millions of his own citizens" appears to be one of the usual DJT exaggerations (Juneau, 2018). The number of those who have died in Syria, during the war there, appears to be in hundreds of thousands (CNN Library, Syrian Civil War Fast Facts), which is still an incomprehensible and heart-breaking loss of life, much of which does indeed appear to have been on the orders of President Assad himself. The phrase "Death to America," or 'Marg bar Amrika' in Farsi, which dates back 40 years to 1979, may be more accurately translated into English as 'Down with America'. However it is translated, that phrase has been said and heard much less in recent years than previously, following the historic meeting (by phone) between President Barack Obama and Ayatollah Rouhani in 2013 (Mason & Charbonneau, 2013). But referring to such phrases is an extremely effective way to demonize 'the other', as discussed in previous chapters. As for Iran being called by DJT "the world's leading sponsor of terror," that characterization could also be applied to other countries as well (Herman, 1987; Fayazi, 2017).

Moving onto P3, we see who is, according to DJT, the Opposite of the Enemy, i.e., Saudi Arabia, as indicated by opening with the contrasting transitional phrase "On the other hand":

P3.1: On the other hand, Saudi Arabia would gladly withdraw from Yemen if the Iranians would agree to leave.

P3.2: They would immediately provide desperately needed humanitarian assistance.

P3.3: Additionally, Saudi Arabia has agreed to spend billions of dollars in leading the fight against Radical Islamic Terrorism.

Before DJT was elected, in 2016, he called Saudi Arabia "the world's leading state sponsor of terror" (Williams, 2018). However, by 2018, after his election, he was presenting Saudi Arabia as The Friend of the USA. That re-labeling may have been an attempt to tap into the ancient idea that, 'The enemy of my enemy is my friend', with Saudi Arabia being presented by DJT as some kind of humanitarian hero. Such heroizing of Saudi Arabia and its leaders by DJT is in stark contrast to how the country is being perceived elsewhere. For example, in the Summer of 2018, writing in *The Guardian* newspaper, Arwa Mahdawi reported that: "Saudi Arabia is not driving change—it is trying to hoodwink the west," and in the Spring of 2019, it was reported that Saudi Arabia had, "imprisoned two US citizens as part of a fresh crackdown on dissent in the country" as well as arresting 11 "women activists who were advocating for a woman's right to drive in the country" (Ward, 2019). The women "remained under arrest even after Saudi Arabia lifted the ban on women drivers" (Ward, 2019).

Regarding the spending of billions of US dollars, that was a reference to Saudi Arabia agreeing, in the Spring of 2017, to buy 110 billion dollars' worth of weaponry from the USA. However, those deals appear to have been more to do with Saudi Arabia's attempts at diversifying their hitherto oil-dependent economy and boosting the economy of the USA than fighting terrorism (Abdo, 2017). And the closing reference, at the end of P3, to capitalized "Radical Islamic Terrorism," employed one of DJT's most commonly employed fear-mongering phrases, as pointed out by a number of observers, such as *Vox* journalist, Zack Beaucham, who wrote that "Trump loves saying 'radical Islamic terrorism'" (2017). NPL practitioners also observe that all terrorism is, by definition, 'radical', as 'moderate terrorism' is a contradiction in terms. Furthermore, although only a very small proportion of followers of Islam are terrorists (Lipka, 2017), by repeating phrases such as 'radical Islamic extremism' and 'radical Islamic terrorism', those hearing and seeing such messages are being encouraged—and perhaps conditioned—to believe that most followers of Islam are indeed terrorists. For example, in 2015, DJT proposed a "*total and complete shutdown of Muslims* entering the United States" (Lipka, 2017, emphasis added)—not some Muslims, such as those identified as credible threats, but all Muslims—even though there may be as many as nearly *two billion* Muslims in the world today, which constitutes negative stereotyping and over-generalizing on a global scale that defies reason or logic.

Excusing Murder in the Name of Money

At P4, DJT made the economic case for excusing what most countries in the world saw as the state sanctioned assassination by a Saudi prince:

> **P4:** After my heavily negotiated trip to Saudi Arabia last year, the Kingdom agreed to spend and invest $450 billion in the United States. This is a record amount of money. It will create hundreds of thousands of jobs, tremendous economic development, and much additional wealth for the United States. Of the $450 billion, $110 billion will be spent on the purchase of military equipment from Boeing, Lockheed Martin, Raytheon and many other great US defense contractors. If we foolishly cancel these contracts, Russia and China would be the enormous beneficiaries - and very happy to acquire all of this newfound business. It would be a wonderful gift to them directly from the United States!

In P4, two other competitors are identified, Russia and China. Based on DJT's illogical statement above, if the USA did not sell billions of dollars of weapons to Saudi Arabia, then other countries would do so instead. That would, in turn, rob the USA of the opportunity to profiteer from war, via "the purchase of military equipment," sold by "great US defense contractors"—a phrase indicating that, while others may 'wage war', the USA 'defends peace'. However, Tekingunduz (2018) asked the question: "Are private military contractors any different from mercenaries?" and reported that: "The global market for mercenaries and private military contractors is worth more than $100 billion, and the lines that differentiate the two are blurry" (Tekingunduz, 2018).

From an NPL perspective, the use of 'defense' as an inverse euphemism for 'attack' is unoriginal and unsubtle. However, such language substitutions may still go un-noticed by a significant number of readers, if they are not paying close and careful attention to the ways in which the language is being used, and the ways in which they are potentially being manipulated by the use of that kind of language. To reiterate a recurring theme throughout this book, it is in these kinds of situations where NPL can help to uncover deeper meanings, which can have serious implications for war and/or for peace. Furthermore, it is, of course, possible that, for various reasons, neither China nor Russia would sell such weapons of war to Saudi Arabia. But completely and conveniently ignoring that possibility allowed DJT to exonerate the Saudi Arabian leader, while at the same time, shifting the focus to Russia and China, by foregrounding them as countries who would do harm to the USA, militarily and/or economically, as opposed to countries like Saudi Arabia, portrayed as American's new best friend.

One of the main and most troubling overall messages in P4 is the idea that: War is great for the US economy—*as long as the war is somewhere else*—and not in the USA. Another message appeared to be that war—*as long as it is not on US soil*—may even be an essential part of 'Making America Great Again', even if it is at the expense of the death and destruction of countless others—especially if those others are Muslims. Following the language of these first few paragraphs to their logical conclusion, more Muslims killed in far-away wars would mean fewer "Muslims entering the United States," making it a win-win for the USA, as envisaged by DJT and his supporters, who could see such a situation as 'killing two birds with one stone', i.e., both Islam and Immigration.

REACT 11.3: *'To kill two birds with one stone' would be considered by some people to be a violent or 'killing' saying. Do you know of other phrases in English or in other languages that are similarly violent or 'killing'? What would be non-violent or non-killing ways of expressing the same meanings?*

In the following two paragraphs, the main reason for the Statement becomes clearer, which appears to be to excuse the USA from taking any action as result of the murder, while other countries around the world were condemning such a killing:

> **P5:** The crime against Jamal Khashoggi was a terrible one, and one that our country does not condone. Indeed, we have taken strong action against those already known to have participated in the murder. After great independent research, we now know many details of this horrible crime. We have already sanctioned 17 Saudis known to have been involved in the murder of Mr. Khashoggi, and the disposal of his body.

A key word in P5 is "condone," meaning "to accept or allow behaviour that is wrong" (*CALD*, 2021) as not condoning is significantly different from not condemning, and one of the main reasons for the Statement appears to have been to avoid publicly criticizing the de facto ruler of Saudi Arabia, in case that derailed multi-billion-dollar arms deals between the two countries. Also, the sanctions mentioned by DJT appeared to have been largely for show, as the 17 Saudis had already been sentenced to death by then, making sanctions of any kind against those individuals irrelevant. The dead cannot be sanctioned (unless in some hellish afterlife). However, the sanctions allowed DJT to claim that "strong action" had been taken against those who had committed the "terrible... horrible crime," based on the "great independent research" that was claimed to have been carried out. However, as stated above, the CIA report clearly identified the Crown Prince as being behind the killing.

> **P6:** Representatives of Saudi Arabia say that Jamal Khashoggi was an 'enemy of the state' and a member of the Muslim Brotherhood, but my decision is in no way based on that—this is an unacceptable and horrible crime. King Salman and Crown Prince Mohammad bin Salman vigorously deny any knowledge of the planning or execution of the murder of Mr. Khashoggi. Our intelligence agencies continue to assess all information, but it could very well be that the Crown Prince had knowledge of this tragic event—maybe he did and maybe he didn't!

Blaming the Victim

In P6, DJT employed another ago-old but still effective strategy of blaming the victim, referring to the murdered journalist as "an 'enemy of the state' and a member of the Muslim Brotherhood," thereby reiterating the Evils of Islam theme in DJT's longstanding Islamophobic comments. However, DJT reversed the strategy, claiming that those claims had been made by unnamed "Representatives of Saudi Arabia" and that he himself rejected such claims, as his "decision is in no way based on that." Claiming that something is not important, while at the same time giving it prominence, is one way of using language, in this case, to denigrate and blame the victim.

The Washington Post reporter, Aaron Blake, was one of a number of journalists and fact-checkers who challenged some of the statements made by DJT, and who "criticized Trump for mentioning Saudi Arabia's description of Khashoggi as an enemy of the state,'" observing that "this is a baseless smear against a slain journalist, and the president is repeating it while insisting that it doesn't matter to him. Then why include it?" (cited in Rozsa, 2018). That is a good question, the answer to which can be found in the victim-blaming approach, employed here by drawing the reader's attention to an important point, then stating that that point is not, in fact, important. Again, to those reading closely and carefully, looking for linguistic clues, these strategies can appear to jump off the page. However, that kind of reading is labor-intensive, time-consuming and requires a degree of critical thinking that is actively discouraged—or even forbidden—in authoritarian regimes. Blake concluded by observing that: "Trafficking in this kind of innuendo in a presidential statement is remarkable" (Rozsa, 2018). However, that kind of victim-blaming language is part of a long-established pattern of DJT's use of such language, as we saw in his letter to the leader of North Korea, when DJT wrote: "We were informed that the meeting was requested by North Korea, but that to us is totally irrelevant" (See Chapter 10).

In the second half of P6, DJT willingly and uncritically accepted the "vigorous" denials of the Saudi leaders, who claimed that they had nothing whatsoever to do with the murder—even though denying involvement in a crime would seem to be a standard criminal practice, i.e., denying committing a crime, as opposed to admitting it. Then, after acknowledging that the Crown Prince probably did at least know about "this tragic event," saying "it could very well be that," DJT delivered his verdict: "maybe he did and maybe he didn't!" know about the murder. The main message here is: Whether or not the Crown Prince was involved in "this tragic event" did not matter to DJT—either way was fine with him. And for added protection of the Crown Prince, DJT was careful not to write, for example, "any involvement in," opting instead for the far more innocent-sounding and innocuous "any knowledge of," showing the significant difference choice of vocabulary—including prepositions—can make in such phrases.

P7: That being said, we may never know all of the facts surrounding the murder of Mr. Jamal Khashoggi. In any case, our relationship is with the Kingdom of Saudi Arabia. They have been a great ally in our very important fight against Iran. The United States intends to remain a steadfast partner of Saudi Arabia to ensure the interests of our country, Israel and all other partners in the region. It is our paramount goal to fully eliminate the threat of terrorism throughout the world!

P7 began with "That being said," although it is unclear what was being referred to, and continued: "we may never *know all of the facts* surrounding the murder of Mr. Jamal Khashoggi" (emphasis added). That statement ignored or side-steeped the fact that "all of the facts surrounding the murder" *of anyone* can never be known, as the primary witness to the crime is, by definition, dead. P7 continued: "In any case, our relationship is with the Kingdom of Saudi Arabia." Most readers might focus on the main clause, "our relationship is with the Kingdom of Saudi Arabia." However, for NPL practitioners, it is the sentence-initial "In any case," which is defined as: "in spite of everything" (*Merriam-Webster*, 2021). Therefore, from an NPL point of view, "in any case" is of at least as much significance, as that phrase reiterates the implicit position of DJT and his administration, i.e., I/we do not care if the Crown Prince was directly involved in the pre-meditated murder.

After DJT repeated himself, about what "a great ally" Saudi Arabia had been to the USA, an empty declaration, or 'non-statement' followed: "It is our paramount goal to fully eliminate the threat of terrorism throughout the world!" Such sentences can be considered 'non-statements' as they are logically impossible. Like the impossibility of ever knowing "all of the facts surrounding the murder" of anyone, fully eliminating "the threat of terrorism throughout the world"—fully eliminating the threat of anything "throughout the world"—is a task that can never be 100% completed, once and for all. New and different threats will always be emerging, in different places, at different times, and from different sources.

Concluding Statements

The eighth and final paragraph reads:

> **P8:** I understand there are members of Congress who, for political or other reasons, would like to go in a different direction—and they are free to do so. I will consider whatever ideas are presented to me, but only if they are consistent with the absolute security and safety of America. After the United States, Saudi Arabia is the largest oil producing nation in the world. They have worked closely with us and have been very responsive to my requests to keeping oil prices at reasonable levels—so important for the world. As President of the United States I intend to ensure that, in a very dangerous world, America is pursuing its national interests and vigorously contesting countries that wish to do us harm. Very simply it is called America First!

In his conclusion DJT presented one of his trademark contradictory statements, when he said: "I will consider whatever ideas are presented to me, *but only if* they are consistent with the absolute security and safety of America" (emphasis added). That statement is the equivalent of saying: I will consider all ideas presented to me, as long as *they comply with my criteria for consideration.* In this case, the criteria are "the absolute security and safety of America." However, nothing is absolute, and the safety and security of nowhere and no one can be 100% guaranteed. Therefore, the impossible criteria effectively nullify any openness to alternatives, thereby making a statement and contradicting that statement in the same breadth—taking a position in one phrase, then negating that same statement in the immediately following phrase. In other words: I am saying that I will consider alternatives. But in reality, I have no intention of doing so. Such texts lead us back to the notion of 'doublespeak', which came from the British writer George Orwell's dystopian novel, *Nineteen Eighty-Four,* published more than 60 years ago, in 1949, but still relevant today. 'Doublespeak' is defined as: "language used to deceive usually through concealment or misrepresentation of truth" (*Merriam-Webster,* 2021), referring to the gap between what someone says and what they really mean. Here at P8, in DJT's Statement, we have an example of the written equivalent of 'doublespeak', i.e., 'doublewrite'.

After the opening 'doublewrite' in P8, Saudi Arabia, the Great Friend of America—and perhaps even the Great Friend of the World, according to DJT—was praised again: "They have worked closely with us and have been very responsive to my requests to keeping oil prices at reasonable levels—so important for the world," i.e., so important for the USA under DJT. That ingratiating P8 phrase, "the Great Friend of America," also used the definite rather than the indefinite article, i.e., "*the* Great Friend of America," to reiterate just how great is Saudi Arabia. That was followed by a repeat of the opening fear-mongering claim that: "The world is a very dangerous place." But this time with an inversion to form "a very dangerous world," with a repeat of the "America First!" tagline/campaign slogan. Lastly, the idea of "vigorously contesting" a country, in "vigorously contesting countries that wish to do us harm," makes little or no sense, as the verbal use of 'to contest' means to oppose an argument, or "to claim that a particular action is not fair or is not legal" (*CALD,* 2021). Claims, not countries, are contested.

Suggestions for Further Reading

In February 2020, the BBC published a detailed and updated report, 'Jamal Khashoggi: All you need to know about Saudi journalist's death'. In that account, the BBC explained that: "After the murder was confirmed by the Saudis, President Trump described it as the 'worst cover-up in history'. However, as the story has unfolded, he has persistently defended America's ties to the kingdom, a key trading partner in the region." https://www.bbc.com/news/world-europe-45812399

In 'What Is Trump Getting for Sucking Up to Saudi Arabia?' (August 2018) *Politico* writers Aaron Miller and Richard Sokolsky stated that: "In our 65-plus years of experience working on US Middle East policy, we've never seen anything like the Trump administration's willingness to prostitute American interests to Saudi Arabia." https://www.politico.com/magazine/story/2018/08/29/trump-mbs-saudi-arabia-yemen-middle-east-foreign-policy-219617

As the essay by George Orwell, 'Politics and the English Language' was published more than 70 years ago (1946), the essay can be found freely available online. In spite of the age of the essay, and some of Orwell's negative feelings about 'foreign' words being used in English, much of the essay is still relevant to the use of language by politicians today.

12

Calling for Unity, Recognizing Wrongs, and Promising Positive Change

In the previous four chapters, we carried out NPL analyses of four texts from the 45th president of the United States; two spoken texts and two written, based on which more than 40 language strategies of interest to NPL practitioners were revealed. Unfortunately, from the perspective of world leaders communicating in ways that make peaceful outcomes more likely than conflict outcomes, DJT's language strategies were found to be (far) more likely to lead to the latter than the former. For example, as we saw in Chapter 9, of approximately 11,000 tweets sent by DJT over a 33-month period between 2017 and 2019, nearly 6,000 of those messages were classified as 'attacking something or someone' (Shear et al., 2019). By contrast, in this chapter we have an opportunity to identify and analyze more positive language from DJT's successor and 46th US president, Joseph Biden, while bearing in mind that inaugural addresses are a kind of non-financial 'promissory note', in which the speaker makes promises that can only be assessed retrospectively, with the chronological benefit of hindsight.

The New Peace Linguistics and The Role of Language in Conflict, pages 213–231

An NPL Analysis of President Joseph Biden's Inaugural Speech (January 2021)

On January 20, 2021, the 46th President of the United States, Joseph R. Biden (JRB) began his Inaugural Address (in this chapter, referred to as the Biden Inaugural Address, abbreviated to 'BIA') with the standard welcome message to the assembled dignitaries. But with the exception of his predecessor, DJT, who chose not to attend, which recalls a saying in English: Actions speak louder than words (from the 1620s, attributed to UK parliamentarian, John Pym (1584–1643)). The actual truth of that saying (perhaps like most sayings) is open to debate, as the words of a president, for example, can do far more damage or result in far more healing than the actions of, for example, an applied linguist!

In 'Trump's Terrible fall from Triumph: A story about a sore loser', sports psychology professor Katie Sparks (2021) drew on the early work of John Dollard and his co-researchers (1939), who developed a Frustration-Aggression hypothesis, to explain DJT's absence, i.e., frustration at losing the presidential election, resulting in DJT's passive-aggressive non-attendance at the inauguration. Sparks concludes: "Having such a presence in the world, you would have hoped [DJT] would have set an example for everyone to follow, unfortunately the moral of this story is to do quite the opposite of Trump when you don't succeed" (Sparks, 2021). Grammatically speaking, the repeated use of the past modal form 'would have' shows why such modals are also known as the 'modals of lost opportunity'. The first step towards addressing injustices and inequities is to explicitly recognize that they exist. As the Black American author, James Baldwin (1924–1987) put it: "Not everything that is faced can be changed. But nothing can be changed until it is faced" (Maass, 2017).

Early on in the BIA, JRB referred indirectly to the 400-year history of US slavery, and directly to racism in the USA in relation to the rise of White supremacists and domestic terrorists in the USA, as well as acknowledging the global climate crisis and the ravages wrought by the worldwide COVID-19 pandemic. The BIA also contains examples of how religious and revered texts shape the language of such leaders. The most prominent feature of the BIA is the different ways in which JRB used language to call for unity, to describe the damage caused by lack of unity during the previous four years, and to warn of the dangers of on-going disunity. The language used in the BIA was to encourage the people of the USA to set aside their differences, and instead focus on their commonalities—to come together, to work together.

In the first paragraph (P1), after the official salutations, JRB began his inaugural address with some opening alliteration and rhythmic repetition—"This is democracy's day. A day of history and hope. Of renewal and resolve, followed by, "The will of the people has been heard and the will of the people has been heeded" (P2). Then came JRB's first reference to the deadly violence on Capitol Hill, that had taken place on the same spot just two weeks earlier (See Chapter 8), with JRB contrasting that violence with a peaceful transfer of power on 'sacred soil': "on this hallowed ground where just days ago violence sought to shake this Capitol's very foundation, we come together as one nation, under God, indivisible, to carry out the peaceful transfer of power" (P3). In making that statement, JRB was drawing on the words of the US Pledge of Allegiance: 'I pledge allegiance to the flag of the United States of America, and to the republic for which it stands, one nation under God, indivisible, with liberty and justice for all.' With the use of 'hallowed', JRB may also have been echoing the words of Abraham Lincoln's Gettysburg Address, given in November 1863, when he said: "we cannot dedicate, we cannot consecrate—we cannot hallow—this ground" (Feulner, 2016). Lincoln (1809–1865) served as the 16th President of the USA from 1861 until he was assassinated in 1865.

An incidental but important example of how language and society shape each other is the addition of "under God," which was not in the original Pledge, and which was not added until more than 60 years after the original Pledge was written (J. Jones, 2003), under President Eisenhower (1890–1969), who served as the 34th President of the USA, from 1953 to 1961. One of the main reasons for adding "under God" to the Pledge in the 1950s was the fear of Communism that drove so much of US-government policy-making at that time (J. Jones, 2003). It is also important to note this first reference to unity, "we come together . . . ," which became one of the most prominent and pronounced recurring themes throughout the BIA. The use of that coming-together phrase may also have been influenced by the address given by President George Bush on September 20, 2001, following the 9/11 terrorist attacks. In that address, Bush used the phrase "we will come together" no fewer than five times in little more than 100 words (see Chapter 5).

After speaking about "the resilience of our Constitution and the strength of our nation" (P4), JRB said: "Over the centuries through storm and strife, in peace and in war, we have come so far. But we still have far to go" (P6). That was JRB's second peace-war contrastive pairing, after his reference to the "violence [that] sought to shake this Capitol's very foundation [and prevent the] peaceful transfer of power." But this time, at P6, there is a more explicit peace-war juxta-positioning, using 'in' twice, for parallelism, rather than just 'in peace and war', which would have been more efficient but less rhythmic. That in-peace-in-war phrase was preceded by a third paired contrast, alliteratively combining a meteorological metaphor with another word for "violent or angry disagreement," (*CALD*, 2021) i.e., "storm and strife," starting with a long-time chronological reference, "Over the centuries," and ending with the classic metaphor of the journey, "come so far . . . still have far to go." Those 24 words are a good example of the concept of lexical density discussed in Chapter 6, which refers to a great deal of meaning being compacted into relatively little language, as shown by this representation:

["over the centuries" = historical-time reference] + ["through storm and strife" = storm-war metaphor, with double-s alliteration] + ["in peace and in war" = peace-war parallel contrast] + [we have come so far, but we still have far to go" = bidirectional metaphor of movement and journey]

Deconstructing and re-presenting language in this way, firstly reminds us of the power of language to unite as well as to divide, and secondly helps us understand more deeply how language works and how it can be employed, in this case, to try to begin a healing process after years of dangerously divisive them-vs-us US presidential language and ideology (see Chapter 5 and Chapters 8–11).

Still at P6, JRB continued with a warning of the 'dangerous season' kind: "We will press forward with speed and urgency, for we have much to do in this winter of peril and significant possibilities." That was followed by a five-part [much + to] rhythmic construction: "Much to repair. Much to restore. Much to heal. Much to build. And much to gain" (P6), with brief but effective pauses between each [much + to] phrase. At P7, the tone of JRB became more specific and more somber:

> Few periods in our nation's history have been more challenging or difficult than the one we're in now. A once-in-a-century virus silently stalks the country. It's taken as many lives in one year as America lost in all of World War II. Millions of jobs have been lost. Hundreds of thousands of businesses closed.

Describing COVID-19 as a "once-in-a-century virus," while effectively highlighting the extraordinary—but not unprecedented—nature of the pandemic, was not entirely accurate. Although the previous global pandemic, the mis-named Spanish Flu—which was neither Spanish nor flu (Zelazko, 2020)—happened between 1918 and 1920, at the end of 2020, the World Health Organization was warning the world to prepare for the next global pandemic, which they forecast will be coming (much) sooner, rather later, based on their worldwide infectious disease data (Besheer, 2020).

The comparison to war, specifically the US death-toll in WW II, the reference to job losses and the businesses closing all echoed some of the comments made by President Obama (BHO) at his inaugural address 12 years earlier, in 2008, when BHO said: "Our nation is at war... Our economy is badly weakened... Homes have been lost, jobs shed, businesses shuttered" (P5 of the OIA, see Chapter 6). Few in the audience that day in January 2021 may have made that connection between the two inaugural addresses, except perhaps for BHO himself (who attended his former vice-president's inauguration along with a number of other past US presidents, as is the customary show of civility). However, such echoes or call backs may be an important part of the rhetorical patterns of such speeches, over long periods of time and across different speakers, giving the same kind of ceremonial address on the same kind of occasion.

At P6, the alliterative, sibilant "viru<u>s</u> <u>s</u>ilently <u>s</u>talks" carries the line and the listener forward. But in this case, using an alternative form of alliteration in which the *end* of a previous word reinforces the same sound at the *beginning* of the following words, in this case, the sibilant ending of 'virus' followed by the two word-initial s-sounds of 'silently' and 'stalks.' There is also the personification of COVID-19 through employing the verb-form of 'stalk', which indicate death and danger: "to follow an animal or person as closely as possible without being seen or heard, usually in order to catch or kill them... If something unpleasant stalks a place, it appears there in a threatening way" (*CALD*, 2021).

<u>REACT 12.1</u>: *What kind of language was used to discuss the COVID-19 pandemic in your context? Was that language more scientific and technical? Was it more anecdotal and narrative? Was the pandemic politicized in your context, in which, for example, mask-wearing or refusing to wear a mask was correlated with which political party people voted for? If so, how was that politicizing of the pandemic reflected in the language used in the media.*

A Problem-Solution Approach

At P8 a series of problems are highlighted, and at P9 a solution is identified and proposed; a solution which took the initial mention of coming together (P3), discussed above, and encapsulated that in a single word that defined the first half of the BIA: Unity. But before the solution comes the problem, in this case, four centuries of slavery and racial injustice in the USA, the potentially extinction-level damage that we are doing to our planet, and the rise of far-right extremists, neo-Nazis and domestic terrorists in the USA:

> **P8:** A cry for racial justice some 400 years in the making moves us. The dream of justice for all will be deferred no longer. A cry for survival comes from the planet itself. A cry that can't be any more desperate or any more clear. And now, a rise in political extremism, white supremacy, domestic terrorism that we must confront and we will defeat.

According to the US Library of Congress: "August 2019 marks 400 years since a group of about 20 Africans were brought to the new colony of Virginia and traded as slaves for food" (Hall, 2019). Although the significance of 1619 as the beginning of the African slave trade in the USA has been disputed (Guasco, 2017), many experts in that aspect of US history appear to agree that the US version of slavery was markedly different to slavery in other parts of the world at that time. For example, University of Houston history professor Steven Mintz explained that: "Slavery in the United States was especially distinctive" with many important differences "between Latin America and the United States [based on] conceptions of race" (Mintz, no date). Therefore, the relationships between race, racism and slavery may be especially strong in the USA, which explains JRB's reference to: "A cry for racial justice some 400 years in the making moves us. The dream of justice for all will be deferred no longer." That first 'cry' is followed by a second one, as a way of referring to the urgent need for planet-wide environmental damage to be addressed, and at least ameliorated. An interesting example of the linguistic limits of word processing technology is the fact that the Microsoft Word program wants to change "more clear" (in "A cry that can't be any more desperate or any more clear") to 'clearer'. However, although the meaning of the line would not be changed in any way, the way in which that phrase would have been heard, read, and said is tangibly different, i.e., the parallelism of "any more desperate or any more clear," compared with the asymmetry of 'any more desperate or any clearer'.

In the last part of P8, JRB specifically identified the "rise in political extremism, white supremacy [and] domestic terrorism," which he said must be confronted and defeated. Those three forms of violence may be where the majority of listeners and readers would focus their attention, as they represent life-threateningly violent actions and potentially deadly consequences, of the kind that took place in the Capitol riots two weeks earlier. However, the impact of the sentence- initial "And now, a rise" should not be underestimated, as that phrase signals to the audience that the threats from "political extremism, white supremacy [and] domestic terrorism" have all increased, and increased recently, which raises the question of who and what is behind that increase. In terms of cause-and-effect, according to sources such as the Center for Strategic and International Studies (Gross, 2021), and US intelligence agencies (Hesson, Cooke & Hosenball, 2020) the activities of political extremists, White supremacists and domestic terrorists grew considerably and measurably during the four years of DJT's presidency (2017–2021).

One of the recurring themes in this book has been the fact that what we call things matters (see, for example, Chapter 1), in spite of Juliet's famous line in Shakespeare's play, when she says: "What's in a name? That which we call a rose, By any other name would smell as sweet" (Act II, Scene II). However, the fact remains that, if some renegade rogue rose grower decided to name their new bloom, A Pile of Steaming Horse Sh*t, then very few of us would risk bending down to smell that particular rose—no matter how pretty it looked! JRB's P8 comment may well have been carefully crafted to be in opposition to his predecessor, who was described as "a Commander in Chief whose rhetoric appears to mirror, validate and potentially inspire that of far-right extremists" (Bergengruen & Hennigan, 2019). It was also found that DJT's election and re-election campaigns had, "run some 2,200 Facebook ads warning of an 'invasion' at the border, according to a CNN analysis. It's a term [DJT] regularly uses in tweets and interviews." Furthermore, connecting Juliet's claim with DJT's language, "Reuters reported that Trump had tried to *change the name* of the Countering Violent Extremism program to Countering Radical Islamic Extremism program" (Bergengruen & Hennigan, 2019, emphasis added). Experts such as Mark Pitcavage, a senior research fellow at the Anti-Defamation League's Center on Extremism who has been studying far-right extremism since the mid-1990s put it like this: "This language matters... If we cannot call an evil by its name, how can we hope to defeat it?" (Bergengruen & Hennigan, 2019).

REACT 12.2: *Have you seen or heard, read or listened to 'extremist language'? If so, what kinds of words and phrases identify that language as being 'extremist'? What are some alternatives to using such language, and how do you respond to such language?*

United, Union, Unity

To recap, the opening paragraphs of the BIA covered a great deal of ground, including political, social, economic, environmental and race-related matters of urgency. In those paragraphs, the BIA went from the "violence [that] sought to shake this Capitol's very foundation" (P3) to "storm and strife, in peace and in war" (P6) to "A cry for racial justice... A cry for survival the planet itself" to the recent "rise in political extremism, white supremacy [and] domestic terrorism" (P8). Having laid out a clear, concise kind of SWOT summary—an analysis of Strengths, Weaknesses, Opportunities and Threats once fashionable in the business world—JRB then gave the next eleven paragraphs, from P9 to P19, to the theme of Unity, allocating more than 550 words and more than 20% of his Address to that topic. Unity was also mentioned in P8 of the OIA (see Chapter 6), when the 44th US President said: "On this day, we gather because we have chosen hope over fear, unity of purpose over conflict and discord."

Following up on JRB's opening statement that "we come together as one nation" (P3), at P9 JRB started by offering a solution to the problems listed in the previous paragraph: "To overcome these challenges—to restore the soul and to secure the future of America—requires so much more than words. It requires that most elusive of things in a democracy: Unity. Unity" (P9). It is perhaps ironic that JRB chose to say how "much more than words" was required to counter those threats—while basing the next ten paragraphs of his Address on a single word, 'Unity', and variations of that word, such 'united' and 'union'. At P10, JRB said that his "whole soul" was committed to: "Bringing America together. Uniting our people. And uniting our nation." P10 was followed by the first direct call to action by JRB, when he asked: "every American to join me in this cause. Uniting to fight the common foes we face: Anger, resentment, hatred. Extremism, lawlessness, violence. Disease, joblessness and hopelessness" (P11). In that way, at P11, JRB followed up on his "cry for racial justice [and] cry for survival [from] the planet itself" with his own rallying cry to his audience, asking them to set aside their differences.

The use of the somewhat Shakespearian 'foe', in the double f-word alliterative "the common foes we face," instead of the more modern but also more aggressive-sounding 'enemy', was discussed in Chapter 6, in the NPL analysis of BHO's 2009 Inaugural Address. From the NPL analysis of BHO's address, we can see that the concerns about global environmental damage were also being expressed then: "With old friends and former foes, we'll work tirelessly to lessen the nuclear threat, and roll back the specter of a warming planet" (P21). Twelve years later, the double-f alliteration was in the form of [fight + foe], while the call to come together to fight those foes was presented as 'a cause', in the sense of "a socially valuable principle that is strongly supported by some people" (*CALD*, 2021) such as 'a good cause'. (See Chapter 7 for a discussion of the language formulation, fighting = bad, but fighting against something bad = good.)

In the following paragraph, P12, JRB presented the potential benefits of unity, of the American people fighting their common foes together:

> **P12:** With unity we can do great things. Important things.
> We can right wrongs.
> We can put people to work in good jobs.
> We can teach our children in safe schools.
> We can overcome this deadly virus.
> We can reward work, rebuild the middle class, and make health care secure for all.
> We can deliver racial justice.
> We can make America, once again, the leading force for good in the world.

With more callbacks and echoes, the seven sentence-initial uses of "We can" was likely a reference to both BHO's 2008 presidential campaign tagline, 'Yes, we can', and to BHO's 2017 Farewell Address, which ended with: "Yes We Can. Yes We Did. Yes We Can" (P46 of the OFA, see Chapter 7). In the BIA, the pattern of what can be done with unity built up, from three very general items: "we can do great things. Important things. We can right wrongs," to two specific sites, i.e., workplace and schools, to the COVID-19 pandemic and healthcare, to achieving "racial justice," and ending where P12 started, with the very general item of making America "once again, the leading force for good in the world." The use of the time marker "once again" is a clear indication of the belief that the USA is a worldwide "force for good," that that role has been diminished, but that it can be taken on again by the USA.

The questions of whether or not the USA has actually been "the leading force for good in the world" is open to debate, depending on who is asking and who is answering that question, about which time period, about which part of the world, etc. And even if that characterization of the USA were proved to be true (for some populations, at some times, in some places), from an NPL perspective the use of the definite article instead of the indefinite—*the* force vs *a* force—is at best, unfortunate, and at worse, a reflection of the kind of US-centric view of the world which has led to so much 'bad' in the world. For example, former US Deputy Secretary of State (2015–2017) Antony Blinken and Robert Kagan, a senior fellow at the Brookings Institution (a US non-profit public policy organization) described DJT's 'America First' policy as "making the world worse" (Blinken & Kagan, 2019).

Blinken & Kagan's explanation for the world-worsening first-place positioning of the USA is that "whatever tolerance most Americans had for the global role the United States embraced after World War II began to fade with the collapse of the Soviet Union." That fading embrace was eventually broken, "shattered by the wars in Iraq and Afghanistan and the 2008 financial crisis" (Blinken & Kagan, 2019). And whatever the political explanation, presenting the USA as *the* one and only "force for good in the world," instead of describing the USA as '*a* leading force for good in the world', i.e., one of a number of countries, was potentially extremely unfortunate. But unfortunate in ways that few listeners or readers may have been consciously aware of, as the difference between the definite and indefinite article in English often goes un-noticed, making that another good NPL example of how a seemingly small, almost incidental, change in the language can result in a potentially much larger change of meaning.

REACT 12.3: *Look around you for examples of small changes in language which can lead to big changes in meaning, for example, in the use of articles (definite/indefinite), pronouns (inclusive/exclusive) and other seemingly 'small' pieces of language which can nonetheless significantly change the big picture, and result in large overall shifts in meaning.*

Moving Forward Together

At P13, JRB described the history of the USA as having been: "a constant struggle between the American ideal that we are all created equal and the harsh, ugly reality that racism, nativism, fear, and demonization have long torn us apart. The battle is perennial and victory is never assured." That contrasting of the ideal with the reality may constitute an example of 'positive warist discourse' using war-related language to, in this case, acknowledge the significant gap between what is believed, in theory, and what is experienced, in practice. That kind of discourse continued into the next paragraph, where JRB said: "Through the Civil War, the Great Depression, World War, 9/11, through struggle, sacrifice, and setbacks, our 'better angels' have always prevailed" (P14), compacting references to two wars, an economic collapse and the 9/11 attacks with a triple s-alliteration, ending with an expression made famous by Abraham Lincoln.

In 'Honest Abe Reminds Us of The Power of Words', Lincoln biographer Ronald White (2011) described Lincoln's first inaugural address, in March 1861, at the US Capitol, which was still under construction at the time. According to White: "Lincoln pared away superfluous words" and changed the original speechwriter's version of his address, from "the guardian angel of the nation" to "the better angels of our nature," which White describes as changing the last line of the address from sounding "impersonal [to sounding] deeply personal" (White, 2011). The speech writer was William Seward (1801–1872), a former governor of New York, who Lincoln appointed as the 24th Secretary of State (1861–1869). In relation to writing, re-writing, giving and receiving feedback, White found that, when asked by Lincoln for feedback on his draft of his address: "Seward responded with a seven-page letter containing 49 suggestions, including an instruction to forget the final paragraph and choose one of two new paragraphs Seward supplied." Fortunately for the USA, for history and for the language of leadership, Lincoln did not follow Seward's feedback, which resulted in some of the most memorable, most-cited and most-quoted closing lines of any US presidential address:

> The mystic chords of memory, stretching from every battlefield and patriot grave, to every heart and hearth-stone, all over this broad land, will yet swell the chorus of the Union, when again touched, as surely they will be, by the better angels of our nature. (quoted in White, 2011)

P14 closed with another reference to the theme of unity: "History, faith, and reason show the way, the way of unity." That was followed by practical advice from JRB on how to achieve such unity, and why it is so important to strive for unity, with references to the consequences of non-unity, i.e., division, while making use of the 'we can' phrase three more times:

> We can see each other not as adversaries but as neighbors.
> We can treat each other with dignity and respect.
> We can join forces, stop the shouting, and lower the temperature.
> *For without unity, there is no peace, only bitterness and fury.*
> No progress, only exhausting outrage.
> No nation, only a state of chaos (P15, emphasis added)

Highlighting the negative consequences of the deep divisions in the USA (and elsewhere) continuing was most likely an appeal to some members of the audience to change their behavior, and to stop engaging in destructive verbal and physical attacks. Appealing instead for audience members to come together to, as JRB put it, "lower the temperature," i.e., for everyone to calm down and to stop using inflammatory language of the kind used by JRB's predecessor immediately before the deadly attacks on the US Capitol (and throughout DJT's presidency).

After P15, the following three paragraphs, P16, P17 and P18, expanded on JRB's calls for unity:

P16: This is our historic moment of crisis and challenge, and unity is the path forward.
And, we must meet this moment as the *United* [emphasized] States of America.
If we do that, I guarantee you, we will not fail.

P17: We have never, ever, ever, ever failed in America when we have acted together.
And so today, at this time and in this place, let's start afresh. All of us.
Let us listen to one another. Hear one another.
See one another. Show respect to one another.

P18: Politics doesn't have to be a raging fire, destroying everything in its path.
Every disagreement doesn't have to be a cause for total war.
And, we must reject the culture in which facts themselves are manipulated and even manufactured.

These three paragraphs total around 130 words, i.e., the equivalent of just a few 50-word sentences, but within those words and sentences, the power of the collective and the need for peaceful communication are both emphatically reiterated. At P16, JRB said: "This is our historic moment of crisis and challenge, and unity is the path forward. And, we must meet this moment as the *United* [stressed for emphasis] States of America," connecting unity and united, crisis and challenge, followed by claims that America has "never, ever, ever, ever failed... when we have acted together" (P17). Apart from the over-use of 'ever', it is not clear what JRB was referring to, as all countries have failed in some ways, at one time or another, regardless of how united they were. However, P17 may be an example of deliberate, strategic hyperbole, to drive home a point.

P17 continued with a proposal to reset the timeline, the tone and the temperament: "And so today, at this time and in this place, let's start afresh. All of us," followed by a number of language-based verbs of communication, i.e., listen, hear, see, show: "Let us listen to one another. Hear one another. See one another. Show respect to one another." An important distinction is made between listening and hearing, which for older members of the audience may have harkened back to a couple of lines from the 1965 song, The Sound of Silence, performed by Paul Simon and Art Garfukel and released in 1965: "People talking without speaking. People hearing without listening." The double-s alliteration of see + show also helped to create a rhythm, concluding P17 with perhaps the most pressing message, i.e., for audience members to show each other respect.

At P18, JRB first employed the metaphor of the "raging fire destroying everything in its path," conjuring images of an all-consuming inferno, culminating in the third explicit reference to war, after "through storm and strife, in peace and in war" (P6) and comparing, at P7, the "American [lives] lost in all of World War II" with the US pandemic death-toll in 2020. At P18, JRB went on to say: "Every disagreement doesn't have to be a cause for total war," while warning against the fabrication of lies and the manipulation of factual truths. JRB concluded this part of his speech focused on unity with the standard honorific of 'My Fellow Americans' (see Chapter 6), while emphasizing the importance of doing things differently in the future, and of everyone doing better and being better: "My fellow Americans, we have to be different than this. America has to be better than this. And, I believe America is better than this" (P19). The combination of [have to be + has to be + is] could be confusing, as 'have/has to be' are speculative imperatives, whereas 'is' indicates that the desired state of being/doing better already exists. That combination may, therefore, have been an aspirational expression, implying: we are not doing well + we can do better + we must do better.

At P20, JRB mentioned the "Civil War," which was a way of showing an assumption of shared knowledge between the speaker and the audience, as he used the short form to refer to the American Civil War, which was a civil war in the United States, fought from 1861 to 1865, between the northern and southern states. At P22, JRB connected the US Civil War in the 1860s with the attacks on the Capitol two weeks earlier, two events spanning more than 150 years:

> **P22:** Here we stand across the Potomac from Arlington National Cemetery, where heroes who gave the last full measure of devotion rest in eternal peace. And here we stand, just days after a riotous mob thought they could use violence to silence the will of the people, to stop the work of our democracy, and to drive us from this sacred ground.

Two other speeches were also connected by JRB here: Presidents Abraham Lincoln's 1863 Gettysburg Address and Barack Obama's 2009 Inaugural Address, also separated by nearly 150 years. In 1863, Lincoln spoke of: "these honored dead [who] gave the last full measure of devotion" (Feulner, 2016). In 2009, Obama said: "we remember with humble gratitude those brave Americans who . . . have something to tell us, just as the fallen heroes who lie in Arlington whisper through the ages" (P27 of the OIA, see Chapter 6). The description of "a riotous mob [who] thought they could use violence to silence the will of the people [and] . . . drive us from this sacred ground" highlighted the relationships between small-scale wars, such as the deadly Capitol attack, and large-scale wars, such as the US Civil War.

In addition to connecting words and wars over a century-and-a-half, JRB also contrasted violent protests and wars with peaceful disagreement, when he talked about, at P23: "The right to dissent *peaceably*, within the guardrails of our Republic" (emphasis added) which he described as "perhaps our nation's greatest strength." That statement was followed by a succinct and more forceful reiteration of the same point in the following paragraph: "Yet hear me clearly: Disagreement must not lead to disunion" (P24), using 'dis' x 2 to contrast the emphasis on unity with the notion of disunity. However, somewhat conspicuous by its absence was peace on JRB's list of seven "common objects we love that define us as Americans" at P25: "Opportunity. Security. Liberty. Dignity. Respect. Honor. And, yes, the truth." That espoused love of the truth was then placed in another oppositional juxtaposition with the lies and falsehoods that typified DJT's four years in office (see Chapter 8): "Recent weeks and months have taught us a painful lesson. There is truth and there are lies. Lies told for power and for profit" (P25), with a double-p alliteration and a there-there repetition. Employing battleground imagery and a double-d alliteration, JRB went on to ask his audience "to defend the truth and to defeat the lies" (P25).

At P26, JRB asked his audience: "not to turn inward, to retreat into competing factions, distrusting those who don't look like you do, or worship the way you do, or don't get their news from the same sources you do," alluding to difference in appearance and religion, while acknowledging the influence of the media. JRB's call to focus on commonalities rather than differences paved the way for more comparing and contrasting pairs, and another example of lexical density, in which a great deal of meaning is expressed within relatively little language. At P27, JRB was able to compact four pairs of differences into one sentence of fewer than 20 words: civil vs uncivil conflict, the differences between the political parties supported, areas inhabited, and lastly differences in attitudes and inclinations: "We must end this uncivil war that pits red against blue, rural versus urban, conservative versus liberal."

The main recurring theme in P28 to P31 was Strength, in terms of making the USA a stronger country and a more powerful country, but also a more peaceful one:

> if we are this way, *our country will be stronger*, more prosperous, more ready for the future (P28) . . . America has been tested and *we have come out stronger for it* (P30) . . . We will lead not merely by *the example of our power* but by *the*

> *power of our example.* We will be a strong and trusted partner for *peace, progress, and security* (P31)

A number of linguistic moves and metaphors can be seen in those paragraphs, including the idea of passing a test, of setting a good example, and of being a trustworthy ally, incorporating an example-power/power-example inversion, as well as multiple p-word repetition and alliteration: [power-power] + [peace-progress]. At P29, JRB repeated his call for unity: "My fellow Americans... We must set aside the politics and finally face this pandemic as one nation. One nation... We will get through this, together. Together." Starting with the now-familiar "my fellow Americans," JRB followed that with another call for unity, this time in the form of setting aside political differences, in effect, attempting to de-politicize the COVID-19 health crisis, in the way that it had been politicized under the previous US government administration (Viglione, 2020), incorporating a double-p power-pandemic pairing.

As we discussed earlier, in the opening first quarter of the BIA, at P11 out of a total of 40 paragraphs, JRB called on: "every American to join me in this cause. Uniting to fight the common foes we face: Anger, resentment, hatred. Extremism, lawlessness, violence. Disease, joblessness and hopelessness." In the last quarter of the BIA, at P33, a similar list was reiterated in connection with the notion of being tested: "Folks, this is a time of testing. We face an attack on our democracy and on truth. A raging virus. Growing inequity. The sting of systemic racism. A climate in crisis. America's role in the world" (P33). An attack-defend construction is used again here, followed by a description of COVID-19 as "raging," which can mean severe and extremely serious but which can also allude to anger itself. "Growing inequity" and "[t]he sting of systemic racism" is another echo or callback, this time to P13 (analyzed earlier), where JRB described: "a constant struggle between the American ideal that we are all created equal and the harsh, ugly reality that racism, nativism, fear, and demonization have long torn us apart. The battle is perennial and victory is never assured" (P13). In both places, P13 and P33, warist discourse of the attack-defend, battle-victory kind were employed by JRB. However, as we discussed in Chapter 7, fighting against something undesirable, such as racism and climate change, is considered to be positive. Lastly, at P33, the use of the sentence-initial "Folks" is easy to overlook, as a way of addressing people in general. However, 'folks' can also mean: "the persons of one's own family" and even "a group of kindred tribes forming a nation," making 'folks' a more influential way of speaking to an audience than may be consciously realized by the audience at the time.

As we saw earlier, in the 500+ words and 11 paragraphs from P9 to 19, which make up more than 20% of this Address, the central theme of the BIA was Unity. At P34, as JRB approached the conclusion, the same theme was proposed and promoted again, using the pronoun 'we', together with other linguistic devices and language moves:

> Now we're going to be tested. Are we going to step up? All of us?
>
> It's time for boldness, for there is so much to do. And, this is certain. I promise you.
>
> We will be judged, you and I, by how we resolve these cascading crises of our era.
>
> Will we rise to the occasion is the question? Will we master this rare and difficult hour?
>
> Will we meet our obligations and pass along a new and better world for our children?
>
> I believe we must—I'm sure you do as well—I believe we will.
>
> And when we do, we'll write the next great chapter in the history of the United States of America, the American story (P34)

Between P6 and P32, JRB emphasized the importance of the American people coming together, using the 'we will' formulation, especially in the sentence-initial position, at least ten times, as the following excerpts show:

P6: *We will* press forward with speed and urgency

P8:. . . *we will* defeat [the rise in political extremism, white supremacy, domestic terrorism]

P16: If we do that [unite] I guarantee you, *we will not* fail.

P29: My fellow Americans, in the work ahead of us, *we will* need each other . . . *We will* need all our strength to persevere through this dark winter . . . *We will* get through this, together.

P30: *We will* repair our alliances and engage with the world once again.

P31: *We will* lead not merely by the example of our power but by the power of our example . . . *We will* be a strong and trusted partner for peace, progress, and security.

P32: *We will* honor them [the 400,000 Americans who had died from COVID-19 by January 2021] by becoming the people and nation we know we can and should be.

At P34, in those 120 words, which took about 40 seconds to say, between the 17th and 18th minute of the 21-minute address, JRB used an inverted form of the recurring 'we will' to ask the question 'will we': "Will we rise to the occasion... Will we master this rare and difficult hour? Will we meet our obligations?" P34 ended with a we-must + we-will pairing, a contracted form, 'we'll' and a story book/next chapter metaphor.

Concluding Statements

In the closing paragraphs, JRB came full circle, connecting the end of the BIA with the beginning, by offered his "fellow Americans... a sacred oath" (P37) which included his triple-defense promise to "defend the Constitution... defend our democracy... defend America [and to].... give my all in your service, thinking not of power, but of possibilities" (P37), employing a not-of-A but-of-B structure together with negative-positive power-possibility pairing. The metaphor of chapters and story books was followed up at P38, with more contrasting pairs and more alliterative rhythms: "And together, we shall write an American story of hope, not fear. Of unity, not division. Of light, not darkness. An American story of decency and dignity. Of love and of healing. Of greatness and of goodness." Regarding the [light = good] vs [dark = bad connotation], on the one hand, "Of light, not darkness" may have been a simple statement of literal illumination, or the lack thereof. However, it is at least as likely that that light-darkness contrast was influenced by the biblical equating of lightness with goodness and darkness with badness. For example: "For how can righteousness and lawlessness be partners? What fellowship does light have with darkness?" (2 Corinthians, 6:14) is one of a number of such [light = good] vs. [dark = bad] statements.

As a person of color myself (mostly brown), such dichotomous and dualistic connotations are problematic. However, from an NPL perspective, that is not to say that phrases such as "Of light, not darkness" should not be said—as we saw in Chapter 3, NPL is not about 'politically correct' policing of language use. But NPL is about becoming (much) more consciously aware of how the language we use—and the language used by the world's most powerful people—has the power to shape our understanding, on the intellectual, head level, and our emotional responses, on the affective, heart level.

In the penultimate paragraph, P39, JRB continued to weave a narrative thread with his repeated references to story-telling: "May this be the story that guides us... The story that tells ages yet to come that we answered the call of history... That democracy and hope, truth and justice, did not die on our watch but thrived" (P39). As we can see, the notion of defending espoused core values, such as "hope, truth and justice," against attack appears again, as another way of connecting the ending and the beginning of the BIA. At the end of P39, JRB made a reference to being "Sustained by faith, Driven by conviction," concluding with the standard God-bless-America ending, to which soldiers were added this time: "May God bless America and may God protect our troops" (see Chapters 6 and 7). That closing came from the unofficial anthem of the USA, written by the Russian-born Jewish-American composer, Irving Berlin (1888–1989), the opening line of which is: "God bless America, land that I love" (McCollum, 2019). The song was first written in 1918, but was left to languish in an old suitcase for 20 years, before seeing the light of day in 1938 (McCollum, 2019). In conclusion, as one of the earliest points made in this book was about the importance of names and naming, the composer changed his name from 'Israel Beilin' to 'Irving Berlin'—to avoid the anti-Semitism that was growing in America, and elsewhere, at that time.

To briefly recap, the BIA illustrated the importance of explicitly recognizing and publicly acknowledging existing injustices and inequities as an essential prerequisite before attempting to redress those imbalances. In this case, the imbalances included four centuries of US slavery, and the resulting on-going systemic and institutionalized racism, a global climate crisis and a global pandemic, among other pressing issues, including the growing number of White supremacists and domestic terrorists in the USA. The solutions proposed by JRB revolved around the central idea of the people of the USA setting aside their differences, focusing on their commonalities, and coming together, to work together.

Suggestions for Further Reading

To complement the NPL analysis of the words spoken by JRB during the BIA, it can be revealing to read (extracts from) some of the books written by JRB. For example, in 2017, he published an autobiographical book, *Promise Me, Dad: A Year of Hope, Hardship, and Purpose* (Flatiron Books).

For an earlier perspective on his life and work, JRB's 2008 book, *Promises to Keep: On Life and Politics* (Random House) is a useful resource, especially as that book was published shortly before JRB became the 47th Vice President of the USA, serving under BHO from 2009 to 2017.

One of the most recent biographies of JRB (probably with many more to come during his presidency) is by the National Book Award winning author, Evan Osnos, and titled *Joe Biden: American Dreamer* (2020, Scribner).

A number of newspapers published commentaries on the BIA, including *The Washington Post.* And shortly after the BIA, Cergy Paris Université professor, Jérôme Viala-Gaudefroy, published a piece, 'Joe Biden's Inaugural Speech: A Return to Normalcy?' in which professor Viala-Gaudefroy pointed out that:

> Joe Biden's speech was 'normal' insofar as its main theme was clearly unity. It stood in stark contrast to Donald Trump's 'American carnage' address, which pitted the establishment against 'the people' and mentioned the government only in negative terms. While Trump made no mention of citizenship or collective responsibility, Joe Biden was particularly remarkable for his *intentional use of collective words and expressions* related to governing, democracy and the responsibility of citizens (emphasis added)

https://theconversation.com/joe-bidens-inaugural-speech-a-return-to-normalcy-154124

13

The New Peace Linguistics

Looking Back, Looking Forward

NPL: Looking Back: A Brief Recap of Some of the Main Points

We have covered a lot of ground over the last 100,000 words or so. And if you have made it this far on the long and winding path towards the possibility of a more peaceful world, with the help of NPL, my heartfelt thanks to you for making it this far. Given all that we have covered, it would be helpful here to present a brief recap of some of the main points and recurring themes in this book. This recap is not designed to address every point, as that would be cumbersome and needlessly repetitious, but instead to serve as a memory-jogging reminder of points that I hope will stay with you after you turn the last page. From the first four, Part I chapters, which are the foundation on which the rest of the book is built, some important points to remember going forward are:

The New Peace Linguistics and The Role of Language in Conflict, pages 233–244

i. Language is a powerful, human-made tool and like any such tool, it can be used for constructive or destructive purposes. And because meaning is co-constructed between the parties communicating with each other, the recipient of the message can choose how they respond.
ii. Language is a two-way street, i.e., language not only *reflects* our perceptions of the world within us, between us and around us, but language also *shapes* those perceptions too. Those perceptions determine how we (choose to) respond.
iii. Language is not neutral. Therefore, what we call things matters. For example, if an image of an armed soldier is captioned 'terrorist', we cannot help responding differently to exactly the same image if it was captioned 'freedom fighter.'
iv. Language can help or language can hinder. The world today may or may not be more or less embroiled in conflicts, armed and otherwise, than in previous times. However, we are certainly living through a time of great and global tensions, exacerbated by the COVID-19 global pandemic, which highlighted the inequities between the 'haves' and the 'have nots.' Language can help bridge those divides or language can push us further apart.
v. Language is everywhere, all that time. That has been true since the earliest human languages were created, but with the exponential expansion of the Internet, mobile media devices and (anti)social media, we may well be living through one of the most language-intense periods of human history.
vi. Words have consequences and words can be weaponized. By the same token, words can be used to make peace. Indeed, without words, peace may not be possible, as all negotiations are based on language. No language, no negotiation.
vii. The *idea* of PL has been around for decades. Unfortunately, the *practice* of PL lay largely dormant for a long time, until recently, when the 'L' in 'PL' was made the focus. It is possible that the lack of linguistic analyses may be one of the reasons for PL still being almost completely unheard of in language education and peace studies. From PL a New PL was developed, paying particular attention to the language of those who have the power to start wars or to bring peace.
viii. For the purposes of this book, 'scientific' and 'systematic' do not mean the same thing, especially in relation to gender and race, and NPL is based on in-depth, systematic linguistic analyses.
ix. In recent years, the PL focus on giving advice to English language teachers and learners about using positive language and avoiding negative language has shifted from that to a New

Peace Linguistics (NPL), based on in-depth, systematic analyses of the language of the world's most powerful people—as it is they much more than us that have the power to bring peace or to start wars. That is not say that we as individuals are powerless, as discussed in the point immediately below.

x. Intra-personal peace, i.e., peace within ourselves, may be an essential starting point, but it not enough to bring about world peace. While everyone one of us has the potential—as well as the duty—to do what we can to make the world a more peaceful place, only a fraction of a percentage of the world's population has the power to bring about peace on a global scale.

xi. A central premise and basic tenet of NPL is that there can be language without conflict, but there cannot be conflict without language, as conflicts usually begin with language, and likewise peace is usually achieved through language.

xii. Applied Linguistics matters because Language matters. Peace Linguistics matters because Peace matters. And the New Peace Linguistics matters because NPL may help bring about more peace, or at least help there to be less conflict.

xiii. Although NPL is positioned firmly within the disciplinary knowledge domain of applied linguistics, it should be recognized as a distinct branch, and not as some peripheral area of interest, subsumed within other areas of applied linguistics.

xiv. NPL is not about Political Correctness or about being the Language Police, as that kind of correctness has been shown to be unhelpfully prescriptive and unenforceable. Instead, NPL aims to help raise awareness of the language we use and the language of others—not the language we and others *should* or *should not* use—in relation to how the language used can lead to more or less peaceful or conflicted outcomes.

xv. This book on NPL may not necessarily and not directly lead to the world being a more peaceful place, as there does not appear to be any single book throughout human history that has ever been published that has been able to bring about World Peace. Indeed, some of the world's most widely read books, all of which preach peace, have been used for centuries to justify war.

xvi. As this book appears to be the first book published under the title of 'Peace Linguistics', and it is certainly the first book ever to be published on the New Peace Linguistics, it should be read as a first attempt, and as nothing is ever done 100% all right first time, there will be points and positions that need to be adjusted over time. That is a normal and natural part of the growth and development of a new field.

From the three Part II chapters, which are based on NPL analyses of spoken texts presented by George W. Bush, Colin L. Powell, and Barack H. Obama, some important NPL aspects of language use are:

a. In terms of military might, for better and for worse, the USA is the most powerful country in the world—at least for now. Therefore, the words of the presidents of the USA have the greatest potential to bring about peace or to start wars (to end large-scale armed conflicts or to continue the never-ending wars)
b. Pronouns are powerful; perhaps more influential in shaping our thoughts than we are consciously aware of. Pronouns can be used to include or to exclude people who are different from the majority, i.e., the language of 'othering'. That kind of language can be used to present differentness as dangerous, rather than presenting differentness as a positive aspect of societies and as an essential prerequisite for the benefits of diversity to be realized.
c. Language may exist without 'othering', but 'othering' cannot exist without language. Othering' can be contrasted with 'Ouring', in which inclusive pronouns are used in ways that emphasize the similarities between people, rather than their differences. Instead of an Us-vs-Them mindset, in 'ouring' those pronouns are used to promote a sense of 'we're all in this together', especially during trying times.
d. Beware the false dichotomy! For example, when a world leader says, "Either you are with us or you are with the terrorists," a potentially catastrophic false dichotomy is created which is doomed to result in untold (and avoidable) deaths. Tolerance for ambiguity can be difficult to develop, but it is the gray area, between back-and-white, where most of human life takes place.
e. The Internet, (anti)social media, and 24/7 news coverage, around the clock and around the world, have not helped with the problems of information overload and the spread of misinformation. Therefore, it behooves us to be critical and even skeptical sometimes about who is telling us what about whom. For example, when a secretary of state tells their government—and the rest of the world—that a war is necessary, based on false premises. Apologies cannot bring back needlessly lost lives. Worse still, language used to deny responsibility and blame others adds insult to injury (and death).
f. NPL Practitioners (of whom there may be as few as only one in the world who self-identifies as such, at the time of writing, but we hope many more will soon follow) pay attention to some specific features of language used by people in power to communicate

with their audiences (who generally have considerably less power). Those features include: compacting meaning, i.e., squeezing a lot of meaning into relatively little language, using language that may distance some audience members but draw others in, as well as the use of narrative structures, rhythmic structures, and strategic omissions or 'language substitutions' as a specialized form of euphemism.

g. NPL Practitioners also pay attention to some other features of language used by people in power, including echoing or 'calling back' to previous texts in the same genre, such as US presidential inaugural addresses. Other features of interest are the use medical and military metaphors, warist discourse and re-representations of history. However, as discussed earlier, there are different kinds of warist discourse, and an important question is: How to honor the dead for having made the ultimate sacrifice without glorifying killing?

h. NPL goes deep, i.e., far below the surface of the apparent and obvious meanings, because language is layered, which makes it necessary to peel away the skin, to see what lies at the heart of the message. An example of NPL's deep-dive approach is the deconstruction of a single paragraph from the OFA text (in Chapter 7). From that one paragraph of spoken text many features of NPL interest were identified, including references to:
   - military might
   - democratic ideals
   - citizens and citizenship
   - terrorism and torture
   - civil liberties
   - expanding democracy and human rights
   - extremism, sectarianism and authoritarianism
   - freedom and the rule of law
   - the likelihood of war

As we saw in the four Part III chapters based on NPL analyses of spoken and written texts by the 45th US President, DJT exposed himself to the world, via (anti)social media and other forms of media, on a scale that was unprecedented. His language was generally characterized as being full of falsehoods, deeply divisive, and feeding off the fear and anger, hatred and suspicion that grew as a result of his relentless verbal attacks on everyone who disagreed with him or who challenged him. Although such a stream of angry, accusatory language did a great deal of damage—up to and including US citizens killing each other, because of a disagreement about an election result—DJT provided a treasure trove of language for NPL practitioners to work with. Unfortunately, any examples of potentially positive uses of language—of language that might bring about more peaceful and less violent outcomes—appear to have been buried under piles of language that did quite the opposite. Consequently, the language of DJT became a series of object lessons and a set of exemplars of language use that NPL practitioners can analyze to see where, when and how language is being used in potentially destructive and damaging ways. Here then is a reminder of the language strategies used by DJT, uncovered and laid bare as a result of NPL analyses:

From an NPL analysis of the South Carolina Commentary:

- Appealing to the 'losers', i.e., those who feel they have lost everything they value
- Cries for attention' (narcissism)
- Claims of greatness
- Claims of superiority (genetic, educational, etc.)
- Misrepresentations of the self/the speaker (deliberate or accidental)
- Self-aggrandizing claims
- The myth of 'the self-made man'
- Presenting insults as compliments
- Negative stereotyping based on race, ethnicity
- Labeling entire cultures and civilizations 'killers'

From an NPL analysis of the Rose Garden Speech:

- Alluding to being at war, including trade wars
- Taking extreme positions, to polarize groups, to an extent that prevents discussion
- Scapegoating/blaming others to avoid having to take/share responsibility for problems/challenges
- Claiming to be disrespected, and therefore having to fight to (re)gain that respect
- Claiming to be taken advantage of, treated unfairly, and stolen from
- Lying, repeating the same lies, and expanding on those lies by exaggerating
- Manufacturing crises and feeding off the fear created by those crises
- Presenting a Winning vs. Losing mutually exclusive dichotomy, in which there are only winners and losers

- Appealing to those who have lost, for example, their jobs, their homes, etc.
- Describing people and places as 'infestations' and 'invasions'
- Invoking images of mythical, satanic beast, such as 'monsters' to refer to 'the Other'

The analysis of the RGS also found examples of using language to: i) present invalid arguments; ii) to cast 'the other' as infections, infestations and as monstrous aliens from a hostile planet; to repeat the same story, again and again and again, in attempting to make lies seem like the truth; to make 'winners' out of 'losers' by promising victory over 'the Other'

From an NPL analysis of the Letter from DJT to KJU:

- Semiotic mixed messages
- Self-aggrandizing
- Egocentric expressions
- Dissing and Disrespecting
- Turning the tables
- Emphatic discourse markers
- Exaggerating
- Threatening and accusatory warnings
- Fake charm
- Content-free, garrulous verbiage

From an NPL analysis of DJT's Foreign Policy Statement on 'Standing with Saudi Arabia'

- Making excuses
- Appealing to supporter self-interest
- Obfuscating versus Communicating
- Scaring the audience and Feeding off the Fear
- Over-Dramatizing and Over-Emphasizing
- Exaggerate figures to distort facts
- Heroizing the in-group, while demonizing the out-group
- Using descriptors such as 'defense contractors', rather than 'mercenaries'
- Claiming to be defending one thing, e.g. 'Democracy', while actually protecting something else, e.g., oil supplies and arms sales
- Claiming that war is not only good for, but a vital part of, an economy—as long as the war is somewhere else
- Blaming the victim through the use of 'reverse innuendo'

- Making 'non-statements' and 'false promises'
- Using 'doublespeak' and 'doublewrite'

Any time any of the 40-plus DJT language strategies above are used, that is of concern to an NPL practitioner, as such strategies can be taken as a warning sign that the audience may be being manipulated rather than communicated with, in ways that make a less peaceful outcome more likely.

From an NPL analysis of the JRB's Inaugural Address:

- Acknowledging historical injustices
- Accepting that those injustices have led to present-day inequities that must be addressed
- Recognizing the need to counter the rise of political extremism, especially that which is race-based
- Committing to take measures to address the global, climate crisis
- Committing to take measures to address the global, COVID-19 pandemic crisis
- Calling for unity, for people to work together, and for people to set aside their differences
- Giving examples of the benefits of uniting
- Warning of the dangers of long-lasting disunity

From an NPL perspective, the above points from the BIA are examples of language being used in ways that make a more peaceful outcome more likely.

Looking Forward: Hopes for the Future of NPL

Sir Edmund William Gosse (1849–1928) was an English poet, author and lecturer in English literature at the University of Cambridge in England. One of his best-know works is the poem *May Day*, from which the oft-quoted openings lines are:

> "The past is like a funeral gone by,
>
> The Future comes like an unwelcome guest"

That may be a reminder of the perils of predicting the future, which is one reason why this chapter is not titled, for example, 'The Future of the New Peace Linguistics'. There are other reasons too. For example, in his book on text analysis, Robert Grant quoted the film producer Samuel Goldwyn's (1879–1974) witty remark that "'Only a fool would make predictions—especially about the future'" (Grant, 2010, p. 287). And while making predictions about the past may be silly, it is much safer. There is also the line from the American management educator, Peter Drucker (1909–2005), to whom is attributed the seemingly obvious but succinctly put observation that: The only thing we know about the future is that it will be different—presumably, different from before, and different from now. Personally, I prefer the evocative directional analogy, also attributed to Drucker: "Trying to predict the future is like trying to drive down a country road at night with no lights while looking out the back window" (cited in Newman, 2009, p. 53), i.e., foolhardy and potentially dangerous.

Writing from the World Economic Forum's annual meeting in Davos, Switzerland in 2015, one of the attendees, Martin Sonnenschein, posted a piece in which he described predicting the future as "a fool's game." With refreshing honesty, Sonnenschein wrote that: "I have a confession to make. I have no idea how the future will look—and neither does anyone else" (Sonnenschein, 2015). He described his confession as a "resignation [that] might seem out of place at the World Economic Forum's Annual Meeting, the aim of which is to assess recent global developments to find out where they're heading." Sonnenschein also wrote that: "An honest look back at looking forward shows that predictions have always been a fool's game," and referring to "the Ukraine crisis" and "the terror of ISIS," he observed that: "History offers infinite testimony that tomorrow is unknowable" which makes "the act of forecasting... an expression of human frailty" (Sonnenschein, 2015). However, he concluded on a cautiously encouraging note: "But acknowledging our inability to foresee the unforeseeable should not discourage us from thinking about what lies ahead." Having, then, established the apparent foolishness of attempting to see into the future (unless you are the Oracle of Delphi), let me go ahead and do just that—briefly and tentatively—but in a way that is more hopeful than predictive, especially as NPL is a new field. Given that newness, this chapter will, then, be a brief look at areas that I hope and believe will inform future work in the field of NPL going forward.

My first hope is that the texts analyzed in NPL field become more diverse—a word that has come to mean many different things to many different people. By 'diverse texts' I mean NPL analyses of texts written and/or said by people who are not political world leaders, but who may be leaders in their local communities, or who may not even consider themselves to be leaders. Any time that one person uses language to communicate with another, there is the risk of communication breakdown, which has the potential to lead to conflict. That conflict can grow rapidly and exponentially to involve other people and places, with the possibility of eventually escalating all the way to violent, armed encounters. Therefore, in future, spoken and written texts from a more diverse group of speakers and writers could be analyzed using NPL approaches.

The reasons that most of the texts analyzed in this book are from presidents of the USA were explained in Chapter 6, i.e., partly based on analyses of the most powerful people in the world, according to, for example, ten years of the *Forbes* annual survey. Some areas of Peace Studies may focus on Peace and Love, and the relationships between them. Not NPL. NPL is about the power of language as it used by the people in power—because they are the ones who have the most power to end large-scale, armed conflicts or to bring about world peace. Therefore, their spoken and written texts belong in a special category, and merit special attention. However, anyone may be in a position of power relative to someone else, such as an employer-employee, parent-child, teacher-student relationship. In that case, NPL can help avoid those kinds of one-to-one communications breakdowns, that can escalate from a small flame to a raging wildfire, with alarming speed and intensity, by looking at how the language being used may be fanning those flames. That kind of understanding may then result in a de-escalation of the conflict, and increase the likelihood of a more peaceful outcome.

Although a detailed a discussion of the complex questions regarding the relationships between sex/gender and power is beyond the scope of this book, it is important to note the disparities. For example, of the 90 slots in the *Forbes* list of the top-ten most powerful people in the world over a ten-year period (2009 to 2018; no list in 2017) just *10* of the *90* slots were occupied by women, and those 10 slots were occupied by just three women (Ewalt, 2018). As the Chancellor of Germany for more than 15 years (since 2005) Angela Merkel was listed seven times (ranked 4th in 2011; 2nd in 2012; 5th in 2013 and 2014; 2nd in 2015; 3rd in 2016; and 4th in 2018). Merkel (b. 1954), who was awarded a doctoral degree for her work on quantum chemistry in 1986, served as Germany's Minister of Women and Youth from 1991–1994, and as Minister for the Environment from 1994 to 1998. Shortly after DJT was elected, *The Times of Israel* described Merkel as "the leader of the free world" (December, 2016).

One of the other two women was Sonia Gandhi, ranked 9th in 2010; the Italian-born Indian politician, a member of the Nehru–Gandhi family, and former president of the Indian National Congress, who remained in office for a record-breaking 19 years (1998–2017). In 1998, the *New York Times* reporter, John Burns wrote that: "At 51, Mrs. Gandhi has added an astonishing new chapter to the story of the Nehrus and the Gandhis, the family that has done more to write the political history of India in the 20th century than any other," making the texts of those two families good examples of the power of language used by people in power, in the world's largest democracy (Frayer & Khan, 2019). The third woman to occupy one of the 90 slots in the *Forbes* list of the top-ten most powerful people in the world, between 2009 and 2018, was Janet Yellin, who was ranked 6th in 2014. Yellen started her professional life in the early 1970s, as an assistant professor in the Department of Economics at Harvard University. In 2014, Yellen was nominated by President Obama to be the first woman to be the Chair of US Federal Reserve; a post she held for four years, until 2018. After being elected President, JRB named Yellin as his nominee for US Treasury Secretary. She was confirmed and is the first woman ever to hold that post in the US government.

In addition to political, military and business leaders, it would be revealing to apply NPL analyses to the texts of those who oversee some of the largest economic institutions in the world. An example would be Christine Lagarde, who is a French lawyer and politician who served as Chair and Managing Director of the International Monetary Fund, from 2011 to 2019. She has also been serving as the President of the European Central Bank since 2019. Another example is Kristalina Georgieva, who has been serving as the Managing Director of the International Monetary Fund since 2019.

Another area for future NPL studies is the texts of those leaders whose first languages are not English, as most of the world's leaders do not use English as their first language. Although they are likely to have a good command of English, for diplomatic purposes, English may be a second, third, fourth, etc. language for them. For example, Jiayu Wang (2017) analyzed President Xi Jinping's political discourse, which Wang concluded, "legitimizes the Chinese Communist Party (CCP) as China's ruling Party through representations of political ideologies" (p. 413). Wang examined 97 texts, including President Xi's speeches, interviews and correspondence from when he became president, in November 2011, to September 2015, from which Wang selected 17 texts for in-depth study. Based on those analyses, Wang concluded that the CCP's political ideologies are: "framed as values that are at once stable and keep on changing, being adapted and Sinicized... represented as moral values with an authoritative nature that guides both the state and the society" (p. 430). According to Wang, the representations "subliminally utilize the political culture of statecraft, rationalization or 'zhengming', and the Marxist and Chinese cultural dialectics of 'change'" (p. 430) in order to substantially legitimize the CCP's status as China's ruling party.

Yet another area of NPL that could be expanded upon is longitudinal studies, of the kind presented in Chapters 6 and 7, i.e., the NPL analyses of President Barack Obama's (first) inaugural speech, given in 2009, and his farewell speech, given eight years later, at the end of his second term, in

2017. Also, in Chapter 5, another longitudinal NPL analysis was presented, showing how then-Secretary of State Colin Powell's language changed between 2003, when he regretted helping to start a war that was largely fought under false pretenses, and 2016, by which time he was denying all responsibility and/or claiming to be proud of his role in starting that war.

Lastly, an additional area of potential development in the NPL field would be a clearer articulation of the relationship between the areas of using language peacefully (as in Gomes de Matos' work), peace language approaches (as in the work of Oxford and her colleagues), and NPL with a focus on the 'L'. Chronologically, those relationships could be presented as a timeline, starting with using language peacefully, then peace language approaches, including 'peace languaging' (Johnson & Murphey, 2018), then NPL. Alternatively, the relationships could be represented as a Venn Diagram, with each of the three approaches occupying one of three main circles, with a small central area of overlap between all three. That small central area could then be surrounded by three other larger areas showing two-part overlaps, in this case, between: i.) using language peacefully and peace language approaches; ii.) between using language peacefully and NPL; and iii.) between peace language approaches and NPL.

In conclusion, here are ten possible areas for future development in the field of NPL. Analyses of the texts of:

i. women leaders
ii. leaders of color
iii. women leaders of color
iv. other under-represented groups, such as leaders in the LGBTQ community
v. military leaders
vi. leaders of the world's most influential economic institutions
vii. leaders of the world's largest businesses
viii. leaders who do not use English as their first language/L1/mother-tongue
ix. longitudinal NPL studies of the same leader, whose texts change over time
x. clearer articulation of relationships between using language peacefully, peace language approaches, and NPL.

Needless to say, we hope there are many more potential areas of NPL growth, which we are looking forward to following closely and carefully in the years ahead.

APPENDIX A

Books on Linguistics and Applied Linguistics, Peace Studies, and Peace Education

As mentioned in Chapter 1, earlier drafts of this manuscript included separate chapters on Linguistics, on Applied Linguistics, and on Sociolinguistics, as well as chapters on Discourse Analysis, on Text Analysis and Rhetoric, and on Peace Studies, Peace Research and Peace Education. However, as there are already many comprehensive texts available on each of those areas, we decided to focus this first book on aspects of PL and NPL that have not been published on before. Therefore, instead of separate chapters on the areas listed above, this appendix gives details of a dozen books on Linguistics and Applied Linguistics, and on Peace Studies and Peace Education (six in each of those two main areas).

These are books I have recommended to people working in Peace Studies and Peace Education, who have had limited exposure to Linguistics and Applied Linguistics, and vice versa, i.e., people working in Linguistics and Applied Linguistics, who have had limited exposure to Peace Studies and

The New Peace Linguistics and The Role of Language in Conflict, pages 245–249

Peace Education, as one of the goals of this book is to help bridge those two domains. These books received positive feedback from people in those two groups, and the books represent a wide range of breadth and depth of coverage of the material, from those new to these fields, to those with some years of experience already. In addition to these books, there are materials on Linguistics and Applied Linguistics, Peace Studies and Peace Education that are freely available, for example, from professors who have made their course notes available online. There are also videos of lectures and presentation on platforms such as YouTube that also cover material that is presented on such courses.

Linguistics and Applied Linguistics

Linguistics: A Complete Introduction: A Teach Yourself Guide by David Hornsby. First edition published in 2014 by McGraw-Hill Education. [300 pages, 13 chapters]

This self-study guide starts with chapters titled 'Think like a linguist' and 'A brief history of linguistic thought', then moves on to chapters on structural linguistics, speech sounds and sound systems, morphology, syntax and grammar, as well as syntax, semantics and language variation. The last two chapters cover multilingualism and language planning, and language change.

A Concise Introduction to Linguistics by Bruce Rowe and Diane Levine. Fifth edition published in 2018 by Routledge. [350 pages, 14 chapters]

This book starts by considering the nature of communication, comparing and contrasting human and non-human communication. That is followed by chapters on phonetics and phonology, morphology, syntax and semantics, sociolinguistics and linguistic anthropology, language acquisition, sign language, writing systems, non-verbal communication, and historical linguistics.

Linguistics: An Introduction by William McGregor. First edition published in 2015 by Bloomsbury Academic. [400 pages, 16 chapters]

This book is divided into three parts, starting with 'Language: System and Structure', includes chapters on phonetics, phonology, morphology and syntax. Part Two, 'Language: A Human Phenomenon', which has chapters on sociolinguistics, psycholinguistics and language acquisition. The last part, 'Language: Uniformity and Diversity', includes chapters on sign languages, writing, language change, and languages of the world.

For the Love of Language: An Introduction to Linguistics by Kate Burridge and Tonya N. Stebbins. First edition published in 2016 by Cambridge University Press. [450 pages, 18 chapters]

This is a more comprehensive text than the three above, starting with questions such as 'What is language?' and 'What is a word?' In addition to the usual chapters on morphology, semantics, phonetics, phonology and syntax, there are also chapters on 'Language as a social fact: Variation and change' (Part 4); 'Language that roles up its sleeves: Language at work' (Part 5); and 'Language is the dress of thought: Language, mind and world' (Part 6).

Linguistics: An Introduction to Language and Communication by Adrian Akmajian, Ann Farmer, Lee Bickmore, Richard Demers and Robert Harnish. Seventh edition published in 2017 by Massachusetts Institute of Technology. [530 pages, 12 main chapters]

This is the most detailed and in-depth of the books in this section. It is divided into two main parts. Part One contains chapters on 'The structure of human language' and 'What is language?' as well as chapters on morphology, phonetics, phonology, sentence structure, linguistic meaning, language variation and language change. Part Two includes chapters on 'Communication and cognitive science', pragmatics, speech production and acquisition, child language acquisition, and language and the brain.

Cambridge Introduction to Applied Linguistics edited by Susan Conrad, Alissa Hartig and Lynn Santelmann. Published in 2021 by Cambridge University Press. [400 pages, 26 chapters].

This is one of the most recent books to be published in this area, written by more than 30 contributing authors from around the world. The chapters most relevant to NPL are those in Section 5, on 'Language Rights, Power, and Ideology', including chapters on 'Activist Applied Linguistics', by Janet Cowal and Genevieve Leung, on 'Legal Issues and Forensic Linguistics', by Keith Walters, and on 'Media Discourse and Ideology' by Winnie Cheng and Phoenix Lam.

Peace Studies and Peace Education

The Anatomy of Peace: How to Resolve the Heart of Conflict by The Arbinger Institute. Second edition published in 2015 by Berrett-Koehler Publications. [250 pages, 24 chapters]

The first of the book's four parts, 'The heart of peace', includes chapters on 'Peace in war time' and 'The pattern of conflict'. Part Two, 'From peace to war', has chapters on 'The need for war' and 'The path to war'. The third part of the book reverses the direction, i.e., 'From war to peace', with chapters on 'Apologies' and 'Surrendering'. The last part is on 'Spreading peace'.

Invitation to Peace Studies by Houston Wood. First edition published in 2016 by Oxford University Press. [250 pages, 13 chapters]

The first part of this book, 'The global peace network' leads with discussions of 'Peace concepts, disputes and confusions' and 'Peace networks:

benefits and challenges.' Part Two, 'From violence to non-violence', includes chapters on 'Interstate war and peace' and 'Non violent power, methods and strategies'. The three chapters in the third and final part, 'Disciplinary perspectives' are: 'Peace psychology', 'The sociology of violence' and 'Inner and outer peace'.

Peace and Conflict edited by David Backer, Ravinder Bhavnani and Paul Huth. First edition published in 2016 by Routledge. [210 pages, 17 chapters]

Notable chapters include Chapter 2, by Karsten Donnay and Ravi Bavnani, on 'The cutting edge of research on peace and conflict'; Chapter 3, on 'Armed conflict 1946–2014', and Chapter 10, by Jason Quinn and Madhav Joshi, on 'Global trends in the implantation of interstate peace agreements'. The text is supported by more than eighty figures, as well as tables and other visual support.

Researching Terrorism, Peace and Conflict Studies: Interaction, Synthesis and Opposition edited by Ioannis Tellidis and Harmonie Toros. First edition published in 2015 by Routledge. [230 pages, 12 chapters]

The two main parts of the book are 'Theoretical debates' and 'Case studies.' The former includes chapters titled, 'Towards critical peace research', 'Critical theory and terrorism' and 'Processes of disengagement from political violence'. Part Two includes chapters on 'Peacebuilding in Colombia', 'The case of Northern Ireland' and 'Terrorism, violence and conflict in the digital age'. A concluding chapter looks at the relationships between terrorism studies and peace studies.

Routledge Companion to Peace and Conflict Studies edited by Sean Byrne, Thomas Matyók, Imani Michelle Scott and Jessica Senehi. Published in 2020 by Routledge. [500 pages, 41 main chapters]

This is the most detailed and in-depth of these books, in this section. The 41 chapters are divided into eight parts: I: Peace and Conflict Studies Praxis (Theory and Practice); II: Structure-Agency, Social Justice, Nonviolence, and Relationship Building; III: Gender, Masculinity and Sexuality; IV: Partnership and Allies in Racial, Ethnic, and Religious Peacebuilding; V: Culture and Identity; VI: Critical and Emancipatory Peacebuilding; VII: International Conflict Transformation and Peacebuilding; and VIII: Global Responses to Conflict.

Conflict Resolution after the Pandemic: Building Peace, Pursuing Justice edited by Richard Rubenstein and Solon Simmons. Published in 2021 by Routledge. [130 pages, 14 chapters]

The COVID-19 global pandemic changed everything for everyone, and this relatively slim volume is one of the newest books on the topic. Part One, which focuses on 'Conflict resolution in a period of social crisis', starts with a chapter on 'Big peace: an agenda for peace and conflict studies after the coronavirus catastrophe' by Solon Simmons. And Part Two, which is about 'Global political conflicts after the pandemic', concludes with a chapter on 'The coming moral conflict between the United States and China', by Gao Qing.

APPENDIX B

Official Transcripts

Official transcripts of the texts analyzed in this book can be found at the US Government websites below.

Notes

1. When governments change, the new administration sometimes archives—or even deletes from their official record—the texts of the leader of the previous administration. If that happens with any of the White House Archive links below, newspapers across the USA and around the world carried transcripts of all of these speeches and written texts, sometimes with minor differences between the transcripts reported in different media sources.
2. The official government transcripts sometimes differ from the transcripts reported in the media. However, the former may not necessarily be more accurate than the latter, for example, when the speaker departs from the official, prepared text and goes 'off-script.'

The New Peace Linguistics and The Role of Language in Conflict, pages 251–252

3. The paragraph numbers of the text analyzed used throughout this book are approximations, as some transcripts, for example, show every pause by the speaker as the end of a paragraph, even if the statements that follow are clearly a continuation of the of the previous thought.
4. There is no official government transcript for the 'South Carolina Commentary' (Chapter 8)

Chapter 5: Selected Speeches of President George w. Bush: 2001–2008
https://georgewbush-whitehouse.archives.gov/infocus/bushrecord/documents/selected_speeches_george_w_bush.pdf

Chapter 6: President Barack Obama's Inaugural Address [January 2009]
https://obamawhitehouse.archives.gov/blog/2009/01/21/president-barack-obamas-inaugural-address

Chapter 7: President Obama's Farewell Address to the Nation [January 2017]
https://obamawhitehouse.archives.gov/blog/2017/01/07/weekly-address-president-obamas-farewell-address-nation

Chapter 9: Presidential Proclamation on Declaring a National Emergency Concerning the Southern Border of the United States [February 2019]
https://trumpwhitehouse.archives.gov/presidential-actions/presidential-proclamation-declaring-national-emergency-concerning-southern-border-united-states/

Chapter 10: Letter to Chairman Kim Jong Un [May 2018]
https://trumpwhitehouse.archives.gov/briefings-statements/letter-chairman-kim-jong-un/?utm_source=link&utm_medium=header

Chapter 11: Statement from President Donald T. Trump on Standing with Saudi Arabia [November 2019]
https://trumpwhitehouse.archives.gov/briefings-statements/statement-president-donald-j-trump-standing-saudi-arabia/

Chapter 12: President Joseph Biden's Inaugural Speech [January 2021]
https://www.whitehouse.gov/briefing-room/speeches-remarks/2021/01/20/inaugural-address-by-president-joseph-r-biden-jr/

References

Aalai, A. (2012, April 9). Sport as warfare? *Psychology Today*. https://www.psychologytoday.com/nz/blog/the-first-impression/201204/sports-warfare?amp

Abdo, H. (2017, May 23). How the Aramco IPO will make history and transform Saudi Arabia's economy. *The Conversation*. https://theconversation.com/how-the-aramco-ipo-will-make-history-and-transform-saudi-arabias-economy-75759

Adversary. (2021). *Cambridge Advanced Learner's Dictionary*. https://dictionary.cambridge.org/dictionary/english/adversary?a=british

Aitchison, J. (1996). *The seeds of speech: Language origin and evolution*. Cambridge University Press.

Albert., A., & Maizland, L. (2020, January 23). The Rohingya crisis. *Council on Foreign Relations*. https://www.cfr.org/backgrounder/rohingya-crisis

Alterman, E. (2020). *Lying in state: Why presidents lie—And why Trump is worse*. Basic Books.

Anderson, W.K.Z. (2017). (De)coding whiteness: Rhetorical refinement of coded rhetoric by white nationalist women appropriated by US politicians. *Rhetoric Review, 36*(4), 263–273.

Appelbaum, S.H. (2021, January 6). Trump's dangerous narcissism may have changed leadership forever. *The Conversation*. https://theconversation.com/trumps-dangerous-narcissism-may-have-changed-leadership-forever-151184

Ashley, S. (2015). Making the case for war: A comparative analysis of CNN and BBC coverage of Colin Powell's presentation to the United Nations Security Council. *Media, War and Conflict, 8*(1), 120–140.

The New Peace Linguistics and The Role of Language in Conflict, pages 253–279

Baker, B. (2004, June 10). Language littered with alliteration. *Daily Press.* https://www.dailypress.com/news/dp-xpm-20040610-2004-06-10-0406090256-story.html

Baker, S. (2020, January 19). The most powerful countries on earth in 2020, ranked. *Business insider.* https://www.businessinsider.com/worlds-most-powerful-countries-2020-ranked-us-news-2020-1

Barron, J. (2019, September 11). Remembering Those Lost 18 Years Ago. *The New York Times.* https://www.nytimes.com/2019/09/11/nyregion/september-11-tribute-ceremony.html

Barton, F.D. (2018). *Peace works: America's unifying role in a turbulent world.* Rowman & Littlefield.

BBC Bitesize. (2019). Paragraphs. https://www.bbc.com/bitesize/guides/z2c2xnb/revision/3

BBC Ethics Guide. (2014). Just War: Introduction. http://www.bbc.co.uk/ethics/war/just/introduction.shtml#:~:text=A%20war%20is%20only%20a,in%20which%20they%20were%20fought.

BBC World News. (2011, December 14). Iraq war in figures. https://www.bbc.com/news/world-middle-east-11107739

BBC World News. (2017, April 19). MS-13 gang: The story behind one of the world's most brutal street gangs. https://www.bbc.com/news/world-us-canada-39645640

Beaucham, Z. (2017, August 14). Trump loves saying "radical Islamic terrorism." He has a tough time with "white supremacy." *Vox.* https://www.vox.com/world/2017/8/14/16143634/trump-charlottesville-white-supremacy-terrorism-islamism

Bebout, L. (2021, January 6). Trump tapped into white victimhood—Leaving fertile ground for white supremacists. *The Conversation.* https://theconversation.com/trump-tapped-into-white-victimhood-leaving-fertile-ground-for-white-supremacists-150587

Bergengruen, V, & Hennigan, W. J. (2019, August 8). 'We Are Being Eaten from Within.' Why America Is Losing the Battle Against White Nationalist Terrorism. *Time.* https://time.com/5647304/white-nationalist-terrorism-united-states/

Beschloss, M. (2018). *Presidents of War.* Crown Publishing.

Besheer, M. (2020, December 4). WHO Chief Urges Investment, Preparation for Next Pandemic. *VOA (Voice of America) News.* https://www.voanews.com/covid-19-pandemic/who-chief-urges-investment-preparation-next-pandemic

Bethune, B. (2018, May 8). How Shakespeare explains Donald Trump's rise to power. *Maclean's.* https://www.macleans.ca/culture/books/how-shakespeare-explains-donald-trumps-rise-to-power/

Bhalla, J. (2013, May 8). It is in our nature to need stories. *Scientific American.* https://blogs.scientificamerican.com/guest-blog/it-is-in-our-nature-to-need-stories/

Billman, J.C. (2019, January 30). Donald Trump may believe he's a genius, but Nancy Pelosi is way better at this game than he is. *Orlando Weekly*. https://www.orlandoweekly.com/orlando/donald-trump-may-believe-hes-a-genius-but-nancy-pelosi-is-way-better-at-this-game-than-he-is/Content?oid=23604402

Blake, A. (2019, February 15). Trump's national emergency press conference. *The Washington Post*. https://www.washingtonpost.com/politics/2019/02/15/trumps-bewildering-national-emergency-press-conference-annotated/

Blair, O. (2016, November 19). Barack Obama meets six-year-old boy who wrote letter offering his home to Syrian refugee. *The Independent*. https://www.independent.co.uk/news/people/barack-obama-six-year-old-boy-letter-white-house-meeting-video-syria-omran-daqneesh-aleppo-a7426466.html

Blinken, A., & Kagan, R. (2019, January 4). 'American first' is only making the world worse. Here's a better approach. *Brookings*. https://www.brookings.edu/blog/order-from-chaos/2019/01/04/america-first-is-only-making-the-world-worse-heres-a-better-approach/

Bloody (2021). *Cambridge Advanced Learner's Dictionary*. https://dictionary.cambridge.org/dictionary/english/bloody?q=bloody_1

Bouie, J. (2013, January 8). Is Obama Aloof? Sure. Does it Matter? No. *The American Prospect*. https://prospect.org/power/obama-aloof-sure.-matter-no./

Braddock, K. (2021, January 12). At impeachment hearing, lawmakers will deliberate over a deadly weapon used in the attack on Capitol Hill—President Trump's words. *The Conversation*. https://theconversation.com/at-impeachment-hearing-lawmakers-will-deliberate-over-a-deadly-weapon-used-in-the-attack-on-capitol-hill-president-trumps-words-153074

Brandes. S. D. (1997). *Warhogs: A History of war profits in America*. University Press of Kentucky.

Brown, G., & Yule, G. (1983). *Discourse analysis*. Cambridge University Press.

Braudy, L. (2016, October 28). Why we'll always be obsessed with—and afraid of—Monsters. *The Conversation*. https://theconversation.com/why-well-always-be-obsessed-with-and-afraid-of-monsters-65080

Bredart, S., Brennen, T., & Valentine, T. (1997). Dissociations between the processing of proper and common names. *Cognitive Neuropsychology*, *14*(2), 209–217.

Breslow, J. M. (2016, May 17). Colin Powell: U.N. Speech "Was a Great Intelligence Failure." *PBS Frontline*. https://www.pbs.org/wgbh/frontline/article/colin-powell-u-n-speech-was-a-great-intelligence-failure/

Brock-Utne, B. (2003). The language question in Africa in the light of globalisation, social justice and democracy. *International Journal of Peace Studies*, *8*(2), 67–87.

Brodie, J. (2018). *Contemporary inequalities and social justice in crisis times*. University of Toronto Press.

Brown, J. (2018, January 4). What the science suggests so far about the impact of platforms such as Facebook, Twitter or Instagram on your mental well-being. *BBC Future.* https://www.bbc.com/future/article/20180104-is-social-media-bad-for-you-the-evidence-and-the-unknowns

Burns, A. (2019, April 15). Pete Buttigieg's campaign kickoff: Full speech, annotated. *The New York Times.* https://www.nytimes.com/2019/04/15/us/politics/pete-buttigieg-speech.html

Burns, J. F. (1998). Sonia Gandhi, the 'foreigner,' startles the political pundits. *The New York Times, Archives.* https://www.nytimes.com/1998/02/27/world/sonia-gandhi-the-foreigner-startles-the-political-pundits.html

Busby, E. (2019, January 9). Racist school bullying has risen in areas that voted for Trump in presidential election, study finds. *The Independent.* https://www.independent.co.uk/news/world/americas/us-politics/racist-bullying-school-trump-presidential-election-virginia-study-republican-democratic-a8719191.html

Byman, D. (2019, August 5). Right-wingers are America's deadliest terrorists. *Slate.* https://slate.com/news-and-politics/2019/08/right-wing-terrorist-killings-government-focus-jihadis-islamic-radicalism.html

Cabral, S. (2021, February 17). Capitol riots: Did Trump's words at rally incite violence? *BBC World News.* https://www.bbc.com/news/world-us-canada-55640437

Cady, D. (2010). *From warism to pacifism: A moral continuum* (2nd ed.). Temple University Press.

Cage, J. (1939). *Silence: Lectures and writings.* Wesleyan University Press.

Carroll, L. (1871). *Through the looking glass.* Macmillan.

Carstarphen, M. G., Welch, K. E., Anderson, W. K. Z., Houck, D. W., McPhail, M. L., Frank, D. A, & Corrigan, L. M. (2017). Rhetoric, race, and resentment: Whiteness and the new days of rage. *Rhetoric Review, 36(*4), 255–347.

Cary, M. (2011, 28 June). Homeless turn to Twitter for food, shelter. *CNN* (*Cable News Network*). http://www.cnn.com/2011/TECH/social.media/06/28/homeless.twitter.help/index.html

Cathey, L. (2020, August 12). Weaponizing religion: Trump's attacks on Biden's faith, calling him 'against God'. *ABC news (American Broadcasting Network).* https://abcnews.go.com/Politics/weaponizing-religion-trumps-attacks-bidens-faith-calling-god/story?id=72240325

Cathey, L. (2021, January 20). Legacy of lies: How Trump weaponized mistruths during his presidency. *ABC news (American Broadcasting Network).* https://abcnews.go.com/Politics/legacy-lies-trump-weaponized-mistruths-presidency/story?id=75335019

Charteris-Black, J. (2014). *Analysing political speeches: Rhetoric, discourse and metaphor.* Palgrave Macmillan.

Chatterjee, P. (2004). *Iraq, Inc.: A profitable occupation.* Seven Stories Press.

Chatterjee, P. (2010). *Halliburton's army: How a well-connected Texas oil company revolutionized the way America makes war.* Nation Books.

Churchwell, S. (2018). *Behold America: The entangled history of "America First" and "the American Dream."* Basic Books.

Cillizza, C. (2019, February 18). The 47 most outrageous lines from Donald Trump's wild national emergency declaration. *CNN.* https://www.cnn.com/2019/02/18/politics/donald-trump-emergency-declaration-wall/index.html

Clark, C. (2017, March 15). Ranked: The 23 most powerful nations on earth. *Business Insider UK.* http://uk.businessinsider.com/the-most-powerful-nations-on-earth-2017-3

Clyne, M. (1987). The role of linguistics in peace and conflict studies. *Australian Review of Applied Linguistics, 10*(1), 76–97.

Clyne, M. (2000). Lingua Franca and Ethnolects in Europe and beyond. *Sociolinguistica, 14,* 83–89.

Coats, T. N. (2017, October). The first white President. *The Atlantic.* https://www.theatlantic.com/magazine/archive/2017/10/the-first-white-president-ta-nehisi-coates/537909/

Cohen-Wade, A. (2016, April 6). Donald Trump performs Shakespeare's soliloquies. *The New Yorker.* https://www.newyorker.com/humor/daily-shouts/donald-trump-performs-shakespeares-soliloquies

Colbert, S. (2018). *Whose boat is this boat? Comments that don't help in the aftermath of a hurricane.* Simon & Schuster.

Cole, D., & Subramaniam, T. (2020, September 3). Trump on Covid death toll: 'It is what it is'. *CNN.* https://www.cnn.com/2020/08/04/politics/trump-covid-death-toll-is-what-it-is/index.html

Collomb, J-D. (2014). The ideology of climate change denial in the United States. *European Journal of American Studies, 9*(1), 1–21.

Communicate. (2021). *Cambridge Advanced Learner's Dictionary.* https://dictionary.cambridge.org/dictionary/english/communicate

Communication. (2021). *Cambridge Advanced Learner's Dictionary.* https://dictionary.cambridge.org/dictionary/english/communication?a=british

Commentary. (2021). *Cambridge Advanced Learner's Dictionary.* https://dictionary.cambridge.org/dictionary/english/commentary?a=british

Condone. (2021). *Cambridge Advanced Learner's Dictionary.* https://dictionary.cambridge.org/dictionary/english/condone

Conflict. (2021). *Cambridge Advanced Learner's Dictionary.* https://dictionary.cambridge.org/dictionary/english/conflict?q=conflict_1

Contest. (2021). *Cambridge Advanced Learner's Dictionary.* https://dictionary.cambridge.org/dictionary/english/contest?q=contest_1

Conclave. (2021). *Cambridge Advanced Learner's Dictionary.* https://dictionary.cambridge.org/dictionary/english/conclave

Cook, K. J., & Stambaugh, P. M. (1997). Tuna memos and pissing contests: Doing gender male dominance on the internet. In C. R. Ronai, B. A. Zsembik, & J. R. Feagin (Eds.), *Everyday sexism in the third millennium* (pp. 62–83). Routledge.

Corder, J. (1982). Editorial. *Rhetoric Review, 1*(1), 1–8.

Coxall, B., Robins, L., & Leach, R. (2003). Political ideologies: The battle of ideas. In *Contemporary British Politics* (pp. 50–72). Palgrave Macmillan.

Crespi, J. A. (2009). *Voices in revolution: Poetry and the auditory imagination in modern China.* University of Hawaii Press.

Crilly, R. (2017, March 24). Donald Trump finding out that winning as president does not come easy. *The Telegraph.* https://www.telegraph.co.uk/news/2017/03/24/donald-trump-finding-winning-president-does-not-come-easy-asdealmaker/

Crystal, D. (1999). *The Penguin Dictionary of Language.* Penguin Publishers.

Crystal, D. (2003). *Dictionary of Linguistics and Phonetics* (5th ed.). John Wiley & Sons.

Crystal, D. (2004). *Creating a World of Languages.* Introductory Speech, 10th Linguapax Congress, Barcelona.

Curtis, A. (2006). A brief introduction to critical race theory, narrative enquiry, and educational research. In A. Curtis & Romney, M. (Eds.), *Color, race and English language teaching: Shades of meaning* (pp. 1–10). Lawrence Erlbaum Associates.

Curtis, A. (2017a). Back from the battlefield: Resurrecting peace linguistics. *TESL Reporter, 50* (1), 20–34. http://lir.byuh.edu/index.php/Issue1/article/view/969/922

Curtis, A. (2017b). Whatever happened to peace (linguistics)? *The English Connection, 21*(3), 23–24. https://koreatesol.org/sites/default/files/pdf_publications/TECv21n3Autumn2017_0.pdf

Curtis, A. (2017c). Diversity and inclusion in another world: Beyond rhetoric to reality. *TESOLers For Social Responsibility Newsletter.* http://newsmanager.commpartners.com/tesolsris/issues/2017-09-21/9.html

Curtis, A. (2017d). *Methods and methodologies for language teaching: The criticality of context.* Palgrave.

Curtis, A. (2018a). Introducing and defining peace linguistics. *The Word, 27*(3), 11–13. http://www.hawaiitesol.wildapricot.org/resources/Documents/Word/2018%20May.pdf

Curtis, A. (2018c, May 3). Peace Linguistics Immigration, and Weaponizing Words. Keynote Presentation, University of Malta. https://hawaiitesol.org/wp-content/uploads/2021/09/2018-May.pdf

Curtis, A. (2018d). Individual, Institutional and International: Three aspects of intercultural communication. In A. Curtis & R. Sussex (Eds.), *Intercultural communication in Asia: Education, language and values* (pp. 21–36). Springer.

Curtis, A. (2018f). Re-defining peace linguistics: Guest editor's introduction. *TESL Reporter, Special Issue: From Peace Language to Peace Linguistics, 51*(2), 1–9.

Curtis, A. (2018g). The new peace linguistics: Guest editor's concluding comments. *TESL Reporter, Special Issue: From Peace Language to Peace Linguistics, 51*(2), 101–107.

Curtis, A., & Tarawhiti, N. (2018h). Peace linguistics in the language classroom. *TESL Reporter, Special Issue: From Peace Language to Peace Linguistics, 51*(2), 77–95.

Curtis, A., & Gomes de Matos, F.C. (2018i) Interview with Professor Francisco Cardoso Gomes de Matos. *TESL Reporter, Special Issue: From Peace Language to Peace Linguistics, 51*(2), 96–100.

Curtis. A. (2018j, November 14). A linguistic look at the world's most prolific liar. *IAFOR: The Academic Platform.* https://think.iafor.org/a-linguistic-look-at-the-worlds-most-prolific-liar/

Curtis, A., & Oxford, R. L. (2021). Applying peace linguistics: What peacebuilders can learn from the languages of hurt, hate and harm. In R. L. Oxford, M. M. Olivero, M. Harrison, & T. Gregersen (Eds.), *Peacebuilding in language education: Innovations in theory and practice* (pp. 214–227). Multilingual Matters.

Daté, S., V. (2020, January 15). The Ministry of Untruth: What Donald Trump's unending stream of lies has done to our White House, our country and us. *Huffpost Canada.* https://www.huffingtonpost.ca/entry/trump-untruth-lies-false_n_5e0bac46e4b0843d360c94ea?ri18n=true

Dearden, L. (2018, 11 May). Racism has become more acceptable since Brexit vote, United Nations warns. *The Independent.* https://www.independent.co.uk/news/uk/home-news/brexit-racism-religious-intolerance-united-nations-special-rapporteur-a8348021.html

de Castillo, C. K. (2019, April 7). Calgary survivor recalls murder of his family as world marks 25th anniversary of Rwandan genocide. *Global News.* https://globalnews.ca/news/5139724/calgary-rwanda-genocide-anniversary-survivor-family-murder/

Dedaić, M. (2003). Introduction: A peace of word. In M. N. Dedaić., & D. N. Nelson. (Eds.), *At war with words* (pp. 1–26). Mouton de Gruyter.

Dedaić, M. N., & Nelson, D. N. (2003). *At war with words.* Mouton de Gruyter.

Demby, G., & Marisol, M. (2020, November 18). The white elephants in the room. *NPR (National Public Radio).* https://www.npr.org/2020/11/17/935910276/the-white-elephants-in-the-room

Detrow, S. (2016, April 21). Show's Over? Trump Pledges to Be 'So Presidential You Will Be So Bored'. *NPR.* https://www.npr.org/2016/04/21/475126907/shows-over-trump-pledges-to-be-so-presidential-you-will-be-so-bored

DeZalia, R. A. P. (2014). Being Rwandan: The use of language, history, and identity in post-genocide Rwanda. In S. Moeschberger & R. A. P. DeZalia (Eds.) *Symbols that bind, symbols that divide* (pp. 157–180). Springer.

DiAngelo, R. (2011). White fragility. *International Journal of Critical Pedagogy, 3*(3), 54–70.

Dixon, R. M. W. (1965). *What is language? A new approach to linguistic description.* Longmans.

Dixon, R. M. W. (2010). *I am a linguist.* Brill.

Do a number on sb. (2021). *Cambridge Advanced Learner's Dictionary.* https://dictionary.cambridge.org/dictionary/english/do-a-number-on-sb

Dog Whistle. (2021). *Merriam-Webster.* https://www.merriam-webster.com/dictionary/dog%20whistle

Domingo, M. (2012). Linguistic layering: social language development in the context of multimodal design and digital technologies. *Learning, Media and Technology, 37*(2), 177-197.

Dollard, J., Miller, N. E., Doob, L. W., Mowrer, O. H., & Sears, R. R. (1939). *Frustration and aggression.* Yale University Press.

Donmall, G. (1992). Language awareness: Wat is dat? *Language Awareness, 1*(1), 1–3.

Donohue, W.A. (2011). The identity trap: The language of genocide. *Journal of Language and Social Psychology, 31*(1), 13–29.

Drew, K. (2020, January 15). U.S. suffers greatest global decline in trust. *US news and world report.* https://www.usnews.com/news/best-countries/articles/2020-01-15/us-trustworthiness-rating-dives-in-2020-best-countries-report

Dreyfuss, E. (2017, November 2). Want to make a lie seem true? Say it again. And again. And again. *Wired.* https://www.wired.com/2017/02/dont-believe-lies-just-people-repeat/

Drucker, P. F. (1966). *The effective executive.* HarperCollins.

Easwaran, E. (1994). *Take your time: How to find patience, peace, and meaning.* Nilgiri Press.

Editors. (1957). *Journal of Conflict Resolution, 1*(1), 1–2. [no article title]

Engelhardt, T. (2010). *The American way of war: How Bush's wars became Obama's.* Haymarket Books.

Engelhardt, T. (2011). *The United States of fear.* Haymarket Books.

Engelhardt, T. (2018). *A nation unmade by war.* Haymarket Books.

Engelhardt, T. (2020, February 14). Our forever wars in 6 questions: After 18-plus years of seemingly endless conflict, our government owes us answers. *The Nation.* https://www.thenation.com/article/world/forever-war-six-questions/

Eschholz, P. A., Rosa, A. F., & Clark, V. P. (Eds.). (1974). *Language awareness* (2nd ed.). St. Martin's Press.

Ewalt, D. M. (2018, May 8). The world's most powerful people 2018. *Forbes.* https://www.forbes.com/powerful-people/list/

Fairclough, N. (2001). *Language and power.* Pearson Education.

Fairclough, N. (2003). 'Political correctness': The politics of culture and language. *Discourse & Society, 14*(1), 17–28.

Fairclough, I., & Fairclough, N. (2012). *Political Discourse Analysis.* Routledge

Falk, D., & Hildebolt, C. (2017). Annual war deaths in small-scale versus state societies scale with population size rather than violence. *Current Anthropology, 58*(6), 805–813.

Falsehood. (2021). *Cambridge Advanced Learner's Dictionary.* https://dictionary.cambridge.org/dictionary/english/falsehood

Fanatic. (2021). *Cambridge Advanced Learner's Dictionary.* https://dictionary.cambridge.org/dictionary/english/fanatic

Fascism. (2021). *Cambridge Advanced Learner's Dictionary.* https://dictionary.cambridge.org/dictionary/english/fascism?a=british

Farndale, N. (2012, October 30). Colin Powell on why he doesn't regret a thing. *The Telegraph.* https://www.telegraph.co.uk/culture/9630719/Colin-Powell-on-why-he-doesnt-regret-a-thing.html

Fayazi, N. (2017, December). *Iran: Is it really the leading state-sponsor of terrorism? (Occasional Paper 72).* Institute for Global Dialogue.

Fields, C. D. (1998). Black scientists: A history of exclusion. *Black Issues in Higher Education, 15*(3), 12–16.

Fraga, K. (2018, February 1). "My fellow Americans": A brief history of the state of the union. *History First.* https://history-first.com/2018/02/01/my-fellow-americans-a-brief-history-of-the-sotu/

Fraley, J. (2021, January 8). 'The Dissident' chronicles assassination of Jamal Khashoggi. *WTOP News.* https://wtop.com/entertainment/2021/01/review-the-dissident-chronicles-assassination-of-jamal-khashoggi/

Frank, D. A., & McPhail, M. L. (2005). "Barack Obama's address to the 2004 Democratic National Convention: Trauma, compromise, concilience, and the (im)Possibility of racial reconciliation. *Rhetoric & Public Affairs, 8,* 571–93.

Fractenberg, B. (2018, July 30). Trump keeps White supremacist donations to 2020 campaign. *Forward.* https://forward.com/news/406833/trump-keeps-white-supremacist-donations-to-2020-campaign/

Frayer, L., & Khan, F. L. (2019, April 11). Polls open in the world's largest democracy. *NPR (National Public Radio).* https://www.npr.org/2019/04/11/712107668/polls-have-opened-in-the-worlds-largest-democracy-fun-facts-on-india-s-election

Friedersdorf, C. (2012, January 27). What Americans mean when they say they're conservative. *The Atlantic.* https://www.theatlantic.com/politics/archive/2012/01/what-americans-mean-when-they-say-theyre-conservative/252099/

Friedrich, P. (2007). English for peace: Toward a framework of peace sociolinguistics. *World Englishes, 26*(1), 72–83.

Friedrich, P. (2012a). (Ed.). Communicative dignity and a nonkilling mentality: An interview with and suggestions by Francisco Gomes de Matos. In P. Friedrich (Ed.), *Nonkilling linguistics: Practical applications* (pp. 157–164). Honolulu, HI: Center for Global Nonkilling.

Friedrich, P. (2012b). (Ed.). *Nonkilling linguistics: Practical applications.* Honolulu, HI: Center for Global Nonkilling. http://w.nonkilling.org/pdf/nklinguistics.pdf

Friedrich, P. (2016). World Englishes and peace linguistics: Their contribution to English for diplomatic purposes. In P. Friedrich (Ed.), *English for diplomatic purposes* (pp. 94–108). Bristol.

Frisk, A. (2018, July 12). Donald Trump again says he's a 'very stable genius' at NATO summit. *Global News Canada.* https://globalnews.ca/news/4327555/donald-trump-very-stable-genius-nato/

Fuelner, E. J. (2016, June 1). The last full measure. *The Heritage Foundation.* https://www.heritage.org/defense/commentary/the-last-full-measure

Funk, N. C., & Said, A. A. (2004). Islam and the West: Narratives of conflict and conflict transformation. *The International Journal of Peace Studies, 9*(1), 1–28.

Gallo, C. (2012, July 2). Thomas Jefferson, Steve Jobs, and the Rule of 3. *Forbes.* https://www.forbes.com/sites/carminegallo/2012/07/02/thomas-jefferson-steve-jobs-and-the-rule-of-3/#6f4da8131962

Galtung, J. (1969). Violence, peace, and peace research. *Journal of Peace Research, 6*(3), 167–191.

Galtung, J. (1985). Twenty-five years of peace research: Ten challenges and some responses. *Journal of Peace Research, 22*(2), 141–158.

Galtung, J. (2006). Peace studies: A ten-point primer. In A. Hunter (Ed.), *Peace studies in the Chinese century: International perspectives* (pp. 15–20). Ashgate.

Gandhi, S. (2018, March 9). Speech at India Today Conclave 2018. *India Today.* https://www.dailyo.in/politics/sonia-gandhi-india-today-conclave-2018-congress-party-reimagining-india-bjp-constitution/story/1/22740.html

Gardiner, A. H. (1932). *The theory of speech and language.* Oxford University Press.

Garrard, P. (2016). On the linguistics of power (and the power of linguistics). In P. Garrard & G. Robinson (Eds.) *The intoxication of power* (pp. 135–154). Palgrave Macmillan.

Gasparri, L., & Marconi, D. (2015). Word meaning. In E. N. Zalta (Ed.), *The Stanford encyclopedia of philosophy* (Summer 2015 ed.). https://plato.stanford.edu/entries/word-meaning/

Gay, W. C. (1997). Nonsexist public discourse and negative peace: The injustice of merely formal transformation. *The Acorn,* pp. 45–52.

Gay, W. C. (1998). Exposing and overcoming linguistic alienation and linguistic violence. *Philosophy & Social Criticism, 24*(2–3), 137–156.

Gay, W. C. (1999). The language of war and peace. In L. Kurtz (Ed.), *Encyclopedia of violence, peace, and conflict* (Vol. 2, pp. 303–312). Academic Press.

Gellman, L. (2010, April 27). Feeding the beast – Our addiction to anger and fear. *The Huffington Post.* https://www.huffingtonpost.com/larry-gellman/feeding-the-beast–our-ad_b_476852.html

Gillis, C. (2017, May 17). Trump vs Nixon: A look at how the two presidents compare. *Macleans.* https://www.macleans.ca/politics/washington/trump-vs-nixon-a-look-at-how-the-two-leaders-compare/

Gillum, R. M. (2018). *Muslims in a Post-9/11 America: A survey of attitudes and beliefs and their implications for U.S. national security policy.* University of Michigan Press.

Gilmore, S. (2017, May 23). The definitive list of every person Donald Trump has called a loser. *Maclean's.* https://www.macleans.ca/news/world/the-definitive-list-of-every-person-donald-trump-has-called-a-loser/

Gjelten, T. (2020, November 8). 2020 faith vote reflects 2016 patterns. *NPR (National Public Radio)*. https://www.npr.org/2020/11/08/932263516/2020-faith-vote-reflects-2016-patterns

Gkonou, C., Olivero, M. M., & Oxford, R.L. (2021). Empowering language teachers to be influential peacebuilders: Knowledge, competencies and activities. In R. L. Oxford, M. M. Olivero, M. Harrison, & T. Gregersen (Eds.), *Peacebuilding in language education: Innovations in theory and practice* (pp. 29–42). Multilingual Matters.

Glanton, D. (2018, December 3). Donald Trump may just be worse than Richard Nixon. *The Chicago Tribune.* https://www.chicagotribune.com/news/columnists/glanton/ct-met-dahleen-glanton-trump-nixon-corruption-20181130-story.html

Godula, G. Cheval, S., Cockerell, J., & Baritello, S. (2020, November 12). US presidential election: A turbulent transfer of power. *France 24 news.* https://www.france24.com/en/tv-shows/inside-the-americas/20201112-us-presidential-election-a-turbulent-transfer-of-power

Golshan, T. (2017, January 11). Donald Trump's unique speaking style, explained by linguists. *Vox.* https://www.vox.com/policy-and-politics/2017/1/11/14238274/trumps-speaking-style-press-conference-linguists-explain

Golshan. T. (2019, February 15). Trump keeps highlighting 'angel moms' to make the case for his immigration agenda. *Vox.* https://www.vox.com/2019/2/5/18213132/trump-angel-moms

Gomes de Matos, F. (1982). Toward a human-improving applied linguistics. *The Linguistic Reporter, 5*(1).

Gomes de Matos, F. (1986). A gap in ESL pedagogy: Learners' rights. *TESOL Newsletter, 20*(2), 9.

Gomes de Matos, F. (1992). Using foreign languages for communicative peace. *FIPLV World News, 59*(25), 1–2.

Gomes de Matos, F. (2000). Harmonizing and humanizing political discourse: The contribution of peace linguists. *Peace and Conflict: Journal of Peace Psychology, 6*(4), 339–344.

Gomes de Matos, F. (2012). LIF PLUS: The life-improving force of peaceful language use. In P. T. Coleman & M. Deutsch (Eds.), *Psychological components of sustainable peace* (pp. 121–129). Springer.

Gomes de Matos, F. (2014). Peace linguistics for language teachers. *Documentação de Estudos em Lingüística Teórica e Aplicada, 30*(2), 415–424.

Gomes de Matos, F. (2018). 16 Planning Uses of Peace Linguistics in Second Language Education. In C. S. Chua (Ed.), *Un(intended) language planning in a globalising world: Multiple levels of players at work* (pp. 290–300). Gruyter.

Graham, R. (2018, June 1). Church of the Donald. *Politico.* https://www.politico.com/magazine/story/2018/04/22/trump-christian-evangelical-conservatives-television-tbn-cbn-218008

Granek, L. (2014). Mourning Sickness: The Politicizations of Grief. *Review of General Psychology, 18*(2), 61–68.

Grant, R. M. (2010). *Contemporary strategy analysis: Text and cases.* Wiley.

Graves, K. (2020, September 10). Women's Political Participation After 1920: Myth and Reality. *National Women's History Museum.* https://www.womenshistory.org/articles/womens-political-participation-after-1920-myth-and-reality

Green, J. (2021, January 19). It's Time to Turn the Page on the Trump-Shakespeare Comparisons. *The New York times.* https://www.nytimes.com/2021/01/19/theater/trump-shakespeare-comparisons.html

Greenblatt, S. (2018). *Tyrant: Shakespeare on politics.* W. W. Norton & Company.

Gregerson,T., & MacIntyre, P. D. (2021). The nonverbal channels of peacebuilding: What teachers, trainers and facilitators need to know. In R. L. Oxford, M. M. Olivero, M. Harrison, & T. Gregersen (Eds.), *Peacebuilding in language education: Innovations in theory and practice* (pp. 43–60). Multilingual Matters.

Grice, H. P. (1975). Logic and conversation. In P. Cole & J. L. Morgan (Eds.), *Syntax and semantics, volume 3, speech arts* (pp. 41–58). Academic Press.

Groom, N., & Littlemore, J. (2011). *Doing applied linguistics: A guide for students.* Routledge.

Gross, J. (2021, January 20). Far-Right Groups Are Behind Most U.S. Terrorist Attacks, Report Finds. *The New York times.* https://www.nytimes.com/2020/10/24/us/domestic-terrorist-groups.html

Guasco, M. (2017, September 13). The Misguided Focus on 1619 as the Beginning of Slavery in the U.S. Damages Our Understanding of American History. *The Smithsonian magazine.* https://www.smithsonianmag.com/history/misguided-focus-1619-beginning-slavery-us-damages-our-understanding-american-history-180964873/

Gyatso, T. (2018). Inner peace and tranquility as basis for world peace. *World Peace Council.* https://www.worldpeacecouncil.net/news/1825-inner-peace-and-tranquility-as-basis-for-world-peace

Hall, S. (2019, August 28). Beyond 1619: Slavery and the Cultures of America. *US Library of Congress.* https://blogs.loc.gov/folklife/2019/08/beyond-1619/

Haller, M. H. (1963). *Eugenics: Hereditarian attitudes in American thought.* Rutgers University Press.

Hancock, J.T., Curry, L.E., & Goorha, S. (2008). On lying and being lied to: A linguistic analysis of deception in computer-mediated communication. *Discourse Processes,* 45(1), 1–23.

Harding, S. (1991). *Whose science? Whose knowledge? Thinking from women's lives.* Cornell University Press.

Harpaz, B. J. (2016, April 18). Trump and Wharton: A complicated relationship. *The Seattle Times.* https://www.seattletimes.com/nation-world/trump-and-wharton-a-complicated-relationship/

Harper, D. (2021). Conflict. *Online Etymology Dictionary.* https://www.etymonline.com/word/conflict

Harper, D. (2021). Kill. *Online Etymology Dictionary.* https://www.etymonline.com/word/kill

Harper, D. (2021). Language. *Online Etymology Dictionary.* https://www.etymonline.com/word/language

Harper, D. (2021). Lie. *Online Etymology Dictionary*. https://www.etymonline.com/word/lie

Harris, S., Miller, G., & Dawsey, J. (2018, November 16). CIA concludes Saudi crown prince ordered Jamal Khashoggi's assassination. *The Washington Post*. https://www.washingtonpost.com/world/national-security/cia-concludes-saudi-crown-prince-ordered-jamal-khashoggis-assassination/2018/11/16/98c89fe6-e9b2-11e8-a939-9469f1166f9d_story.html

Hart, R. P. (1984). *Verbal style and the presidency: A computer-based analysis*. Academic Press.

Harwood, W. (2011). *Dictionary of contemporary mythology* (3rd ed.). World Audience Publishers.

Hauser, M. D., Chomsky, N., & Fitch, W. T. (2002). The faculty of language: What is it, who has it, and how did it evolve? *Science 22, 298*(5598), 1569–1579.

Head, N. (2012). Transforming conflict: Trust, empathy, and dialogue. *International Journal of Peace Studies*, 17(2), 33-55.

Heer, J. (2017, September 23). The post-literate American presidency. *The New Republic*. https://newrepublic.com/article/144940/trump-tv-post-literate-american-presidency

Heidegger, M. (1971). *On the way to language* (1st ed.). Harper & Row.

Herman, E. S. (1987). U.S. sponsorship of international terrorism: An overview. *Crime and Social Justice, 27/28*, 1–31.

Herman, P. C. (2021, January 8). Shakespeare and the catastrophic end of Donald Trump's presidency. *Times of San Diego*. https://timesofsandiego.com/opinion/2021/01/08/shakespeare-and-the-catastrophic-end-of-donald-trumps-presidency/

Herrman, J. (2017, March 14). If everything can be 'weaponized,' what should we fear? *The New York Times*. https://www.nytimes.com/2017/03/14/magazine/if-everything-can-be-weaponized-what-should-we-fear.html

Hesson, T., Cooke, K., & Hosenball, M. (2020, September 29). U.S. intelligence reports warn of extremist threat around election. *Reuters*. https://www.reuters.com/article/us-usa-election-extremists-idUSKBN26K2J7

Hill, C., Corbett, C., & St. Rose, A. (2010). *Why so few? Women in science, technology, engineering, and mathematics*. American Association of University Women.

Hogenboom, M. (2015, July 3). Humans are nowhere near as special as we like to think. *BBC Earth*. http://www.bbc.com/earth/story/20150706-humans-are-not-unique-or-special

Holden, A. (2009, March 9). How war is big business. *The Telegraph*. https://www.telegraph.co.uk/culture/books/bookreviews/4943411/How-war-is-big-business.html

Holmes, J. (2016, December 1). A Trump Surrogate Drops the Mic: 'There's No Such Thing as Facts'. *Esquire*. https://www.esquire.com/news-politics/videos/a51152/trump-surrogate-no-such-thing-as-facts/

Holmes, J. (2019, May 8). Trump lost a billion dollars in business, which seems bad for a businessman president. *Esquire*. https://www.esquire.com/news

-politics/a27405708/donald-trump-lost-1-billion-new-york-times-tax-returns/

Holtgraves, T., & Lasky, B. (1999). Linguistic power and persuasion. *Journal of Language and Social Psychology, 18*(2), 196–205.

Hutton, C. (1999). *Linguistics and the Third Reich: Mother-tongue fascism, race and the science of language.* Routledge.

Israeli, L. (2011).'The Other'—A threat or a resource? Polar interpretations of two children's stories: 'The ugly duckling' by H.C. Andersen and 'Raspberry Juice' by H. Shenhav. *Journal of Peace Education, 8*(1), 1–17.

Janicki, K. (2015). *Language and conflict: Selected issues.* Palgrave Macmillan.

Jaworski, A. (1993). *The power of silence: Social and pragmatic perspectives.* Sage.

Jenkins, N. (2017, December 11). President Trump brags he was a top student at Wharton. Here's what it said about his tax bill. *Time.* http://time.com/5058855/donald-trump-wharton-tax-analysis/

Johnson, K. R., & Murphey, T. M. (2018). Promoting students' trajectories of agentive, reflective, and peace-making-languaging in TEFL classes and beyond. *TESL Reporter, Special Issue: From Peace Language to Peace Linguistics, 51*(2), 34–52.

Jones, J. O. (2003, November). The man who wrote the Pledge of Allegiance. *The Smithsonian Magazine.* https://www.smithsonianmag.com/history/the-man-who-wrote-the-pledge-of-allegiance-93907224/

Jones, S. (2019, August 7). White supremacists are right about one thing: Donald Trump is their president. *Philadelphia Inquirer.* https://www.inquirer.com/opinion/el-paso-shooting-white-supremacist-president-trump-statement-20190807.html

Joyce, C., & Lynch, O. (2016). "Doing peace": The role of ex-political prisoners in violence prevention initiatives in Northern Ireland. *Studies in Conflict & Terrorism, 40*(12), 1072–1090.

Juneau, T. (2018, November 21). 'A pile of lies, BS and nonsense': Professor debunks Trump's comments. *Middle East Eye.* https://www.middleeasteye.net/fr/news/pile-lies-bs-and-nonsense-canadian-professor-debunks-trumps-statement-721103980

Kagge, E. (2017). *Silence: In the age of noise.* Pantheon Books.

Karaman-Kepenekci, Y. (2010). An analysis on children's rights in stories recommended for children in Turkey. *Journal of Peace Education, 7*(1), 65–83.

Karni, A. (2019, April 1). Trump lives by ratings. He won't like this one. *The New York Times.* https://www.nytimes.com/2019/04/01/us/politics/trump-e-score-rating.html

Kellett, P. M. (2007). *Conflict dialogue: Working with layers of meaning for productive relationships.* SAGE.

Kendrick, L. (1983). Rhetoric and the rise of public poetry: The career of Eustache Deschamps. *Studies in Philology, 80*(1), 1–13.

Keppel, B. (1995). *The work of democracy.* Harvard University Press.

Keskin, T. (Ed.). (2018). *Middle East Studies after September 11: Neo-Orientalism, American Hegemony and Academia.* BRILL.

Kessler, G., Kelly, M., Rizzo, S., & Ye Hee Lee, M. (2021, January 20). In four years, President Trump made 30,573 false or misleading claims. *The Washington Post.* https://www.washingtonpost.com/graphics/politics/trump-claims-database/?utm_term=.27babcd5e58c&itid=lk_inline_manual_2&itid=lk_inline_manual_2

Kevles, D. J. (1995). *In the name of eugenics: Genetics and the uses of human heredity.* Harvard University Press.

Khan, R. (2010, March 26). War and peace in Quran and Bible. *Al Jazeera.* https://www.aljazeera.com/program/riz-khan/2010/3/26/war-and-peace-in-quran-and-bible

Khouri, RG. (2016, October 12). The frighteningly high human and financial costs of war. *Al Jazeera.* https://www.aljazeera.com/indepth/opinion/2016/10/frighteningly-high-human-financial-costs-war-syria-afghanistan-161010085529971.html

Kich, M. (2015, November 21). The great divide: Political rhetoric and political reality. *Academe.* https://academeblog.org/2015/11/21/the-great-divide-political-rhetoric-and-political-reality-2/

Kill. (2021). *Cambridge Advanced Learner's Dictionary.* https://dictionary.cambridge.org/dictionary/english/kill?q=kill_1

Kircher, R., & Fox, S. (2019) Attitudes towards multicultural London English: Implications for attitude theory and language planning, *Journal of Multilingual and Multicultural Development, 40*(10), 847-864.

Klein, E. (2015, November 13). Republicans think America is doing terribly, but it isn't. *Vox.* https://www.vox.com/2015/11/13/9727132/republicans-economy

Koschorke, A., & Kaminskij, K. (Eds.). (2017). *Tyrants writing poetry.* Central European University Press.

Kruse, M. (2018, September 18). Trump has no fear: 'Makes Nixon look like a cream puff'. *Politico.* https://www.politico.eu/article/donald-trump-has-no-fear-makes-nixon-look-like-a-cream-puff/

Kruse, M., & Weiland, N. (2016, May 5). Donald Trump's Greatest Self-Contradictions. *Politico* https://www.politico.com/magazine/story/2016/05/donald-trump-2016-contradictions-213869

Kulis, S., Chong, Y., & Shaw, H. (1999). Discriminatory organizational contexts and black scientists on postsecondary faculties. *Research in Higher Education, 40*(2), 115–148.

Kurtzleben, D. (2016, October 1). *Trump and the testosterone takeover of 2016.* NPR (National Public Radio). https://www.npr.org/2016/10/01/494249104/trump-and-the-testosterone-takeover-of-2016

Kurtzleben, D. (2020, October 28). Trump has weaponized masculinity as President. *NPR (National Public Radio).* https://www.npr.org/2020/10/28/928336749/trump-has-weaponized-masculinity-as-president-heres-why-it-matters

Labov, W. (1982). Objectivity and commitment in linguistic science: The case of the Black English Trial in Ann Arbor. *Language in Society, 11*(2), 165–201.

Lakoff, G., & Johnson, M. (1980). *Metaphors we live by.* University of Chicago Press.

Language. (2021). *Cambridge Advanced Learner's Dictionary.* https://dictionary.cambridge.org/dictionary/english/language?a=british

Language. (2021). *Macmillan Dictionary.* https://www.macmillandictionary.com/dictionary/american/language

Language. (2021). *Merriam-Webster online dictionary.* https://www.merriam-webster.com/dictionary/language

Language. (2021). *Oxford Living Dictionaries.* https://en.oxforddictionaries.com/definition/us/language

Lankiewicz, H., & Wąsikiewicz-Firlej, E. (Eds.). (2014). *Languaging experiences: Learning and teaching revisited.* Newcastle upon Tyne, UK: Cambridge Scholars Publishing.

Lederach, J. (2003). *Little book of conflict transformation: Clear articulation of the guiding principles by a pioneer in the field.* Oxford University Press.

Levin, B. (2019, April 29). Trump has told more than 10,000 lies since being inaugurated. *Vanity Fair.* https://www.vanityfair.com/news/2019/04/trump-has-told-more-than-10000-lies-since-being-inaugurated-washington-post

Lexical density. (2021). *Macmillan Dictionary.* https://www.macmillandictionary.com/dictionary/british/lexical-density

Lie. (2021). *Cambridge Advanced Learner's Dictionary.* https://dictionary.cambridge.org/dictionary/english/lie?q=lie_1

Linguistic. (2021). *Cambridge Advanced Learner's Dictionary.* https://dictionary.cambridge.org/dictionary/english/linguistic

Linguistics. (2021). *Cambridge Advanced Learner's Dictionary.* https://dictionary.cambridge.org/dictionary/english/linguistics

Lipka, M. (2017, August 9). Muslims and Islam: Key findings in the U.S. and around the world. *Pew Research.* http://www.pewresearch.org/fact-tank/2017/08/09/muslims-and-islam-key-findings-in-the-u-s-and-around-the-world/

Lithgow, J. (2020). *Trumpty Dumpty wanted a crown: Verses for a despotic age.* Chronicle Prism Press.

Loofbourow, L. (2016, October 20). Welcome to Trumplandia, where feelings trump facts. *The Week.* https://theweek.com/articles/656455/welcome-trumplandia-where-feelings-trump-facts

Lopez, G. (2020, August 13). Donald Trump's long history of racism, from the 1970s to 2020. *Vox.* https://www.vox.com/2016/7/25/12270880/donald-trump-racist-racism-history

Lyons, J. (1968). *Introduction to theoretical linguistics.* Cambridge University Press.

Lopez, G. (2017, November 29). Trump is still reportedly pushing his racist "birther" conspiracy theory about Obama. *Vox.* https://www.vox

.com/policy-and-politics/2017/11/29/16713664/trump-obama-birth-certificate

Lord of War. (2005). IMDB (Internet Movie Database). https://www.imdb.com/title/tt0399295/

Maass, A. (2017, February 9). Nothing can be changed until it is faced. *Socialist Worker.* https://socialistworker.org/2017/02/09/nothing-can-be-changed-until-it-is-faced

Macias, A.M. (2020, November 14). 'It's time to come home'—Acting Pentagon chief wants to end America's wars in the Middle East. *CNBC.* https://www.cnbc.com/2020/11/14/acting-pentagon-chief-says-wars-must-end-in-first-address.html

Mahalingappa, L., Rodriguez, T. L., & Polat, N. (2021). Promoting peace through social justice pedagogies for immigrant Muslim communities: Using critical language awareness in second language classrooms. In R. L. Oxford, M. M. Olivero, M. Harrison, & T. Gregersen, *Peacebuilding in language education: Innovations in theory and practice* (pp. 162–176). Multilingual Matters.

Mann, M. (2004). *Fascists.* Cambridge University Press.

Mason, J., & Charbonneau, L. (2013, September 27). Obama, Iran's Rouhani hold historic phone call. *Reuters.* https://www.reuters.com/article/us-un-assembly-iran/obama-irans-rouhani-hold-historic-phone-call-idUSBRE98Q16S20130928

Mathews, A. (2011, February 24). The victim identity. *Psychology Today.* https://www.psychologytoday.com/ca/blog/traversing-the-inner-terrain/201102/the-victim-identity

May, S. (2005). Language rights: Moving the debate forward. *Journal of Sociolinguistics, 9*(3), 319–347.

McAndrews, F.T. (2015, August 3). Home Is Where the Heart Is, but Where Is 'Home'? *Psychology Today.* https://www.psychologytoday.com/us/blog/out-the-ooze/201508/home-is-where-the-heart-is-where-is-home

McCarthy, D. (1933). Language development. In C. Murchison (Ed.), *The International University series in psychology. A handbook of child psychology* (2nd ed., pp. 329–373). Atheneum Publishers.

McCarthy, N. (2021, January 11). End of The Road for Trump's Twitter Account. *Statista.* https://www.statista.com/chart/19561/total-number-of-tweets-from-donald-trump/

McCollum, S. (2019, September 17). God Bless America: The story behind the song. *The Kennedy Center.* https://www.kennedy-center.org/education/resources-for-educators/classroom-resources/media-and-interactives/media/music/story-behind-the-song/the-story-behind-the-song/god-bless-america/

McCutcheon, C., & Mark, D. (2014). *Dog whistles, walk-backs, and Washington handshakes: Decoding the jargon, slang, and bluster of American political speech.* University Press of New England.

McGrath, T. (2014, December 8). The US is now involved in 134 wars or none, depending on your definition of 'war'. *The World.* https://www.pri.org/stories/2014-09-16/us-now-involved-134-wars-or-none-depending-your-definition-war

McPhail, M. L., & Frank, D. A. (2017). Racing the Trump card: Rhetorics of whiteness and the politics of adaptive resistance after Obama. *Rhetoric Review, 36*(4), 282–293.

Miller, J. F., & Chapman, R. S. (1981). The relation between age and mean length of utterance in morphemes. *Journal of Speech, Language, and Hearing Research, 24*(2), 154–161.

Mintz, S. (n.d.). *Historical Context: American Slavery in Comparative Perspective.* The Gilder Lehrman institute for American history. https://www.gilderlehrman.org/history-resources/teaching-resource/historical-context-american-slavery-comparative-perspective

Molloy, T., & Graham, T. (2008). Jaw Jaw is better than war war. *Trusts & Trustees, 14*(10), 674-675.

Murphy, B. (2018, September 6). After that truly shocking transcript, here's the 1 question every leader must answer now. *Inc.* https://www.inc.com/bill-murphy-jr/woodward-trump-fear-book-washington-post.html

Myers, D. (2017, November 7). For irreligious evangelicals, Christianity is about politics—Not God. *Quartz.* https://qz.com/1122117/what-does-it-mean-to-be-evangelical-how-the-right-wing-hijacked-christian-identity/

Nahai, G. (2014, January 23). On being Persian. *The Huffington Post.* https://www.huffingtonpost.com/gina-nahai/on-being-persian_b_4098419.html

Nahari, G., Ashkenazi, T., Fisher, R. P., Granhag, P. A., Hershkowitz, I., Masip, J., Meijer, E. H., Nisin, Z., Sarid, N., Taylor, P. J., Verschuere, B., Vrij, A. (2019). 'Language of lies': Urgent issues and prospects in verbal lie detection research. *Legal and Criminal Psychology, 24*(1), 1–23.

Ndahiro, N. (2019, April 13). In Rwanda, we know all about dehumanizing language. *The Atlantic.* https://www.theatlantic.com/ideas/archive/2019/04/rwanda-shows-how-hateful-speech-leads-violence/587041/

Neate, R., & Tuckman, J. (2015, July 6). Donald Trump: Mexican migrants bring 'tremendous infectious disease' to US. *The Guardian.* https://www.theguardian.com/us-news/2015/jul/06/donald-trump-mexican-immigrants-tremendous-infectious-disease

Newman, E. (2009). The future possibility of talent management technology. In A. Schweyer, E. Newman & P. De Vries (Eds.) *Talent management technologies* (pp. 53–69). AuthorHouse.

Nguyen, T. (2019, February 15). Trump's "national emergency" speech was a rambling mess. *Vanity Fair.* https://www.vanityfair.com/news/2019/02/donald-trump-national-emergency-declaration-wall

Nilsen, A. B., Fylkesnes, S., & Mausethagen, S. (2017). The linguistics in othering: Teacher educators' talk about cultural diversity. *Reconceptualizing Educational Research Methodology, 8*(1), 40–50.

Niose, D. (2011, March 13). Is the religious right seeking to banish the inclusive motto? *Psychology Today*. https://www.psychologytoday.com/us/blog/our-humanity-naturally/201103/e-pluribus-unum-becomes-controversial

Novak, M., Adams, P., & Shaw, E. (2015). *Social Justice isn't what you think it is.* Encounter Books.

Nowrasteh, A. (2019, May 7). Terrorists by Immigration Status and Nationality: A Risk Analysis, 1975–2017 (Policy Analysis No. 866). *The Cato Institute.* https://www.cato.org/publications/policy-analysis/terrorists-immigration-status-nationality-risk-analysis-1975-2017

Nunan, D. (2013). *What is this thing called language?* (2nd ed.). Palgrave Macmillan.

Paschal, O. (2019, February 15). President Trump's speech declaring a national emergency. *The Atlantic.* https://www.theatlantic.com/politics/archive/2019/02/trumps-declaration-national-emergency-full-text/582928/

Oddo, J. (2014). *Intertextuality and the 24-hour news cycle: A day in the rhetorical life of Colin Powell's U.N. address.* Michigan State University Press.

O'Grady, S. (2016, April 15). Rwandan who called Tutsis 'cockroaches' in 1992 gets life sentence. *Foreign Policy.* https://foreignpolicy.com/2016/04/15/rwandan-who-called-tutsis-cockroaches-in-1992-gets-life-sentence/

Oliker, O. (2017). Is Putinism a thing? Putinism, populism and the defence of liberal democracy. *Survival: Global Politics and Strategy, 59*(1), 7–24.

Olivero, M. M., Harrison, M., & Oxford, R. L. (2021). Peacebuilding through classroom activities: Inner, interpersonal, intergroup, intercultural, international and ecological peace. In R. L. Oxford, M. M. Olivero, M. Harrison, & T. Gregersen (Eds.), *Peacebuilding in language education: Innovations in theory and practice* (pp. 245–271). Multilingual Matters.

O'Mealy, J. H., & Lyons, L. E. (Eds). (1998). *Language, linguistics, and leadership: Essays in honour of Carol M. K. Eastman.* University of Hawaii Press.

Orr, D. (2008). The politics of poetry. *Poetry, 192*(4), 409-418.

Outpost. (2021). *Cambridge Advanced Learner's Dictionary.* https://dictionary.cambridge.org/dictionary/english/outpost

Oxford, R. L. (1990). Styles, strategies, and aptitude: Connections for language learning. In T. S. Parry & C. W. Stansfield (Eds.), *Language aptitude reconsidered* (pp. 67–125). Prentice-Hall.

Oxford, R. L. (1992). Research on second language learning strategies. *Annual Review of Applied Linguistics, 13,* 174–187.

Oxford, R. L. (1996). What have we learned about language learning strategies around the world? In R. L. Oxford (Ed.), *Language learning strategies around the world: Cross-cultural perspectives* (pp. 247–281). University of Hawaii Press.

Oxford, R. L. (2013). *The language of peace: Communicating to create harmony.* Information Age Publishing.

Oxford, R. L., & Crookall, D. (1988). Learning strategies. In J. B. Gleason (Ed.), *You can take it with you: Helping students maintain foreign language skills beyond the classroom* (pp. 23–49). Prentice-Hall.

Oxford, R. L., & Jin, J. (Eds.). (2011). *Transformative eco-education for human and planetary survival.* Information Age Publishing.

Oxford, R. L., Gregersen, T., & Olivero, M. M. (2018). The interplay of language and peace education: The language of peace approach in peace communication, linguistic analysis, multimethod research, and peace language activities. Peace linguistics in the language classroom. *TESL Reporter, Special Issue: From Peace Language to Peace Linguistics, 51*(2), 10–33.

Oxford, R. L. (2021). From hate speech to empathy: Lesson for language educators and society. In R. L. Oxford, M. M. Olivero, M. Harrison, & T. Gregersen (Eds.), *Peacebuilding in language education: Innovations in theory and practice* (pp. 196–213). Multilingual Matters.

Oxford, R. L., & Curtis, A. (2021). Exploring peace language: Hope, help and harmony. In R.L. Oxford, M.M. Olivero, M. Harrison, & T. Gregersen (Eds.), *Peacebuilding in language education: Innovations in theory and practice* (pp. 228–241). Multilingual Matters.

Oxford, R.L., Olivero, M. M., Harrison, M., & Gregersen, T. (2021). *Peacebuilding in language education: Innovations in theory and practice.* Multilingual Matters.

Paige G. D. (1970). *1950: Truman's decision: The United States enters the Korean War.* Chelsea House.

Pandey, A. (2004). Constructing otherness: A linguistic analysis of the politics of representation and exclusion in freshmen writing. *Issues in Applied Linguistics, 14*(2), 153–184.

Paige G.D. (1970). *1950: Truman's decision: The United States enters the Korean War.* Chelsea House.

Pardi, P. (2012, April 10). Argument proves that philosophy doesn't exist. *Philosophy News.* https://www.philosophynews.com/post/2012/04/10/Argument-Proves-That-Philosophy-Doesnt-Exist.aspx

Patriot. (2021). *Cambridge Advanced Learner's Dictionary.* https://dictionary.cambridge.org/dictionary/english/patriot?a=british

PBS Frontline. (2014). Rwanda: A historical chronology. https://www.pbs.org/wgbh/pages/frontline/shows/rwanda/etc/cron.html

Peace. (2021). *Cambridge Advanced Learner's Dictionary.* https://dictionary.cambridge.org/dictionary/english/peace?q=peace_1

Pennebaker, J. W. (2011). *The secret life of pronouns: What our words say about us.* Bloomsbury Press.

Pettersson, T., & Eck, K. (2018). Organized violence, 1989–2017. *Journal of Peace Research, 55*(4), 535–547.

Pigliucci, M. (2014, July 16). Neil deGrasse Tyson and the value of philosophy. *The Huffington Post.* https://www.huffingtonpost.com/massimo-pigliucci/neil-degrasse-tyson-and-the-value-of-philosophy_b_5330216.html

Pirani, B.M., & Smith, T.S. (2016). *Embodiment and cultural differences.* Cambridge Scholars.

Polletta, F. (2015). Characters in political storytelling. *Storytelling, Self, Society, 11*(1), 34–55.

Prado, J., Uguralp-Cannon, G., Green, J. M., Harrison, M., & Smith, L. F. (2021). Seeking connection through difference: Finding the nexus of transformative learning, peacebuilding and language teaching. In R. L. Oxford, M. M. Olivero, M. Harrison & T. Gregersen (Eds.), *Peacebuilding in language education: Innovations in theory and practice* (pp. 110–126). Multilingual Matters.

Rabin, A., & Tan, R. (2017, February 15). Was Trump really a top student at Wharton? His classmates say not so much. *The Daily Pennsylvanian.* https://www.thedp.com/article/2017/02/trump-academics-at-wharton

Ramm, B. (2017, October 25). Why tyrants love to write poetry. *BBC Culture.* https://www.bbc.com/culture/article/20171025-why-tyrants-love-to-write-poetry

Rapoza, K. (2019, January 14). China is losing the trade war. *Forbes.* https://www.forbes.com/sites/kenrapoza/2019/01/14/china-is-losing-the-trade-war-in-nearly-every-way/#227dc0e17f03

Rathie, S. (2018a, July 28). Dehumanizing metaphors lead to dehumanizing policies. *Psychology Today.* https://www.psychologytoday.com/ca/blog/words-matter/201807/dehumanizing-metaphors-lead-dehumanizing-policies

Rathie, S. (2018b, December 17). Do we need a common enemy? *Psychology Today.* https://www.psychologytoday.com/ca/blog/words-matter/201812/do-we-need-common-enemy

Reilly, K. (2019, February 27). Donald Trump criticized Obama's grades. But his lawyer threatened Trump's alma maters not to release his own grades. *Time.* http://time.com/5540152/donald-trump-michael-cohen-academic-records/

Resistance. (2021). *Oxford English Dictionary.* https://www.lexico.com/en/definition/resistance

Reston, M., & Liptak, K. (2021, January 9). The day America realized how dangerous Donald Trump is. *CNN Politics.* https://www.cnn.com/2021/01/09/politics/donald-trump-dangerous-capitol-riot/index.html

Robertson, C. (2020, April 24). How reader behavior is changing during the COVID-19 crisis. *BookBub.* https://insights.bookbub.com/reader-behavior-changing-covid19-crisis/

Rosenman, S. (1938). *The public papers of Franklin D. Roosevelt: The year of crisis, 1933.* Random House.

Rothkopf, D. (2018, February 5). Who's worse, Trump or Nixon? *The L.A. Times.* https://www.latimes.com/opinion/op-ed/la-oe-rothkopf-watergate-trump-20180205-story.html

Rothman, J. R., & Sanderson, S. (2018). Language and peace: Using global issues in the English language classroom to create a more sustainable dialogue. *TESL Reporter, Special Issue: From Peace Language to Peace Linguistics, 51*(2), 53–76.

Roy, A. (2003). *War talk.* South End Press.

Rucker, P., & Leonnig, C. (2020). *A very stable genius: Donald J Trump's testing of America.* Penguin Press.

Rozsa, M. (2018, November 20). Washington Post slams Trump for "statement smearing Jamal Khashoggi and giving Saudi Arabia a pass". *Salon.* https://www.salon.com/2018/11/20/washington-post-slams-trump-for-statement-smearing-jamal-khashoggi-and-giving-saudi-arabia-a-pass/

Sapir, E. (1929). The status of linguistics as a science. *Language, 5*(4), 207–214.

Scarborough, R. (2015, September 13). Iran responsible for deaths of 500 American service members in Iraq. *The Washington Times.* https://www.washingtontimes.com/news/2015/sep/13/iran-responsible-for-deaths-of-500-us-service-memb/ [Note: This link needs to be fixed or changed]

Schäffner, C., & Wenden, A. L. (Eds.). (1995). *Language and peace.* Hardwood Publishers.

Schiebinger, L. (2000). Has feminism changed science? *Signs, 25*(4), 1171–1175.

Schmidt-Radefeldt, J. (1977). On so-called 'rhetorical' questions. *Journal of Pragmatics, 1*(4), 375–392.

Schumacher, H. (2020, December 31). Is this the most powerful word in the English language? *BBC Culture.* https://www.bbc.com/culture/article/20200109-is-this-the-most-powerful-word-in-the-english-language#:~:text='The'%20tops%20the%20league%20tables,of%20every%20100%20words%20used

Schwarz, J. (2018, February 6). 15 years ago, Colin Powell lied to the United Nations. *The Intercept.* https://theintercept.com/2018/02/06/lie-after-lie-what-colin-powell-knew-about-iraq-fifteen-years-ago-and-what-he-told-the-un/

Seipel, B. (2018, October 3). Trump: People 'would be so bored' if I acted presidential. *The Hill.* https://thehill.com/homenews/administration/377793-trump-people-would-be-so-bored-if-i-acted-presidential

Seltzer, L.F. (2014, February 6). Don't confuse revenge with justice: Five key differences. *Psychology Today.* https://www.psychologytoday.com/ca/blog/evolution-the-self/201402/don-t-confuse-revenge-justice-five-key-differences

Shetterly, M. L. (2016). *Hidden figures: The story of the African-American women who helped win the space race.* HarperCollins.

Silberstein, S. (2004). *War of words: Language, politics and 9/11.* Routledge.

Silberstein, C., Doyle, A., Eastman, C. M. K., & Watkins, E. (1998). Talking Peace, Waging War: Mining the language of leadership. In J. H. O'Mealy (Ed.), *Language, linguistics, and leadership: Essays in honour of Carol M. K. Eastman* (pp. 1–18). University of Hawaii Press.

Shear, M. D., Haberman, M., Confessore, N., Yourish K., Buchanan, L., & Collins, K. (2019, November 2). How Trump reshaped the presidency in over 11,000. *The New York Times.* https://www.nytimes.com/interactive/2019/11/02/us/politics/trump-twitter-presidency.html

Sheerin, J. (2021, March 6). Who truly was the most dishonest president? *BBC World News.* https://www.bbc.com/news/world-us-canada-56246507

Shih, C-F. (2003). Language and ethnic politics in Taiwan. *International Journal of Peace Studies, 8*(2), 89–102.

Simon, A. (2018, June 19). People are angry President Trump used this word to describe undocumented immigrants. *Time.* https://time.com/5316087/donald-trump-immigration-infest/

Simpson, D. (1992). Lying, liars and language. *Philosophy and Phenomenological Research, 52*(3), 623–639.

Smarmy. (2021). *Cambridge Advanced Learner's Dictionary.* https://dictionary.cambridge.org/dictionary/english/smarmy

Summit. (2021). *Cambridge Advanced Learner's Dictionary.* https://dictionary.cambridge.org/dictionary/english/summit?q=summit_1

Smith, A. (1978). The myth of the self-made man in English Canada, 1850–1914. *Canadian Historical Review, 59*(2), 189–219. https://muse.jhu.edu/article/571391/pdf

Smith, C. (2016, March 10). *The white nationalists who support Donald Trump. ABC News (American Broadcasting Network).* https://abcnews.go.com/Politics/white-nationalists-support-donald-trump/story?id=37524610

Sparks, K. (2021, January 12). Trump's Terrible fall from Triumph: A Story about a sore loser. *University of Birmingham (UK) Research Perspectives.* https://www.birmingham.ac.uk/research/perspective/trumps-terrible-fall-from-triumph.aspx

Spinelli, D. (2015, August 19). Trump flaunts Wharton degree, but his college years remain a mystery. *The Daily Pennsylvanian.* https://www.thedp.com/article/2015/08/donald-trump-wharton-classmates

Soldier. (2021). *Cambridge Advanced Learner's Dictionary.* https://dictionary.cambridge.org/dictionary/english/soldier

Sonnenschein, M. (2015, January 23). Predicting the future: a fool's game? *World Economic Forum.* https://www.weforum.org/agenda/2015/01/predicting-the-future-a-fools-game/

Sorell, T. (2013). *Scientism: Philosophy and the infatuation with science.* Routledge.

Stafford, T. (2014, July 29). Psychology: Why bad news dominates the headlines. *BBC Future.* http://www.bbc.com/future/story/20140728-why-is-all-the-news-bad?ocid=twfut

Stanton, G. (2017, November 20). Call it genocide. *The Daily Star.* https://www.thedailystar.net/opinion/politics/call-it-genocide-1493548

Stetka, B. (2017, November 9). Steven Pinker: This Is history's most peaceful time—New study: 'Not so fast'. *Scientific American.* https://www.scientificamerican.com/article/steven-pinker-this-is-historys-most-peaceful-time-new-study-not-so-fast/

Strawhand, J. (2012, May 26). A history of weaponized language. *The Huffington Post.* https://www.huffpost.com/entry/weaponized-language_b_1380788

Sundvall, S. (2018). Without a world: The rhetorical potential and 'dark politics' of object-oriented thought. *Philosophy & Rhetoric, 51*(3), 217–244.

Sung, M. (2018, June 5). Watch Trump straight up lie about reading the letter from Kim Jong-un. *Mashable.* https://mashable.com/2018/06/01/trump-letter-north-korea-kim-jong-un-lie/#zaVCNi6oIiqG

Swain, E. (2019, March 3). It's still open: Will the Guantánamo Bay prison become a 2020 issue? *The Intercept.* https://theintercept.com/2019/03/03/guantanamo-bay-carol-rosenberg-intercepted/

Tanaka, G. (2005). Storytelling and peace education. *Journal of Peace Education, 2*(1), 93–97.

TARDIS. (2021). *Oxford Living Dictionaries.* https://en.oxforddictionaries.com/definition/us/Tardis

Tauber, A.I. (2010). *Freud, the reluctant philosopher.* Princeton University Press.

Tekingunduz, A. (2018, October 16). Are private military contractors any different from mercenaries? *TRT World.* https://www.trtworld.com/americas/are-private-military-contractors-any-different-from-mercenaries-20680

Tharoor, I. (2016, April 3). Donald Trump repeats stereotype about Iranians when attacking Obama. *The Washington Post.* https://www.washingtonpost.com/news/worldviews/wp/2016/04/03/donald-trump-repeats-stereotype-about-iranians-when-attacking-obama/

The Times of Israel. (2016, December 3). Merkel: From austerity queen to 'leader of free world'. https://www.timesofisrael.com/merkel-from-austerity-queen-to-leader-of-free-world/

Thomas, P. L. (2017). *Trumplandia: Unmasking post-truth America.* Garn Press.

Thomas, R. Z. (201 Tharoor, I. (2016, April 3). Donald Trump repeats stereotype about Iranians when attacking Obama. *The Washington Post.* https://www.washingtonpost.com/news/worldviews/wp/2016/04/03/donald-trump-repeats-stereotype-about-iranians-when-attacking-obama/

Tope, D., Pickett, J. T., Cobb, R. J., & Dirlam, J. (2014). Othering Obama: Racial attitudes and dubious beliefs about the nation's first black president. *Sociological Perspectives, 57*(4), 450–469.

Trump, M. L. (2020). *Too much and never enough: How my family created the world's most dangerous man.* Simon & Schuster.

Trump, D. J. (2011). *Time to get tough: Making America great again!* Regnery Publishing.

Tsaousides, T. (2015, November 19). 7 things you need to know about fear. *Psychology Today.* https://www.psychologytoday.com/ca/blog/smashing-the-brainblocks/201511/7-things-you-need-know-about-fear

Turley, J. (2014, January 11). Big money behind war: the military-industrial complex. *Al Jazeera.* https://www.aljazeera.com/indepth/opinion/2014/01/big-money-behind-war-military-industrial-complex-20141473026736533.html

Tyrant. (2021). *Cambridge Advanced Learner's Dictionary.* https://dictionary.cambridge.org/dictionary/english/tyrant

Valania, J. (2019, September 14). Fact-checking all of the mysteries surrounding Donald Trump and Penn. *Philadelphia Life.* https://www.phillymag.com/news/2019/09/14/donald-trump-at-wharton-university-of-pennsylvania/

Valet, V. (2019, October 15). The World's Most Reputable Countries 2019. *Forbes.* https://www.forbes.com/sites/vickyvalet/2019/10/15/the-worlds-most-reputable-countries-2019/?sh=7430585c4cb8

van Dijk, T. A. (1993). *Elite discourse and racism.* SAGE.

van Dijk, T.A. (2006). Ideology and discourse analysis. *Journal of Political Ideologies, 11*(2), 115–140.

van der Valk, I. (2003). Racism, a threat to global peace. *International Journal of Peace Studies, 8*(2), 45–66.

Ventura, L. (2018, June 12). The most peaceful countries in the world 2018. *Global Finance.* https://www.gfmag.com/global-data/non-economic-data/most-peaceful-countries

Vercellone, C. (2020, March 9). Who were the largest major arms exporters in the last 5 years? *Defense News.* https://www.defensenews.com/2020/03/09/who-were-the-largest-major-arms-exporters-in-the-last-5-years/#:~:text=WASHINGTON%20%E2%80%94%20The%20United%20States%20was,Peace%20Research%20Institute%20think%20tank

Vigilant. (2021). *Cambridge Advanced Learner's Dictionary.* https://dictionary.cambridge.org/dictionary/english/vigilant

Viglione, G. (2020, November 3). Four ways Trump has meddled in pandemic science – and why it matters. *Nature.* https://www.nature.com/articles/d41586-020-03035-4

Wakefield, C. (2012). *Negotiating the inner peace treaty: Becoming the person you were born to be.* Balboa Press.

Wang, J. (2017). Representations of the Chinese Communist Party's political ideologies in President Xi Jinping's discourse. *Discourse & Society, 28*(4), 413–435.

Ward, A. (2019, 5 April). Saudi Arabia is detaining American activists 6 months after Khashoggi's murder. *Vox.* https://www.vox.com/world/2019/4/5/18296866/saudi-arabia-mohammed-bin-salman-women-activists-drive

Waterfield, R., & Yunis. H. (2018). *Aristotle: The Art of Rhetoric.* Oxford University Press.

Watson, C. (2012). *My missile is bigger than yours: A gender analysis of decision making by the executive committee of the United States National Security Council during the Cuban missile crisis* [Master's thesis, Geneva Centre for the Democratic Control of Armed Forces].

Wee, L. (2015). Adding insult to injury. *Pragmatics and Society, 6*(1), 1–21.

Wehner, P. (2019, September 9). Trump is not well: Accepting the reality about the president's disordered personality is important—Even essential. *The Atlantic.* https://www.theatlantic.com/ideas/archive/2019/09/donald-trump-not-well/597640/

Wei, M., & Zhou, Y. (2021). International faculty and international students in universities: Their roles in fostering peace across languages and cultures. In R. L. Oxford, M. M. Olivero, M. Harrison, & T. Gregersen (Eds.), *Peace-building in language education: Innovations in theory and practice* (pp. 146–161). Multilingual Matters.

Weir, K. (2017). Why we believe alternative facts: How motivation, identity and ideology combine to undermine human judgment. *APA Monitor, 48*(5) https://www.apa.org/monitor/2017/05/alternative-facts

Weisman, S. R. (2005, September 9). Powell calls his U.N. speech a lasting blot on his record. *The New York Times.* https://www.nytimes.com/2005/09/09/politics/powell-calls-his-un-speech-a-lasting-blot-on-his-record.html

Wenden, A. L. (2003). Achieving a comprehensive peace: The linguistic factor. *Peace & Change, 28*(2), 169–201.

Wenden, A. L. (2007). Educating for a critically literate civil society: Incorporating the linguistic perspective into peace education. *Journal of Peace Education, 4*(2), 163–180.

Weyers, S. (2017). *Happiness now! A guided journey: Unleash motivation and take action to experience greater peace, meaning and joy.* Eudokima.

White, R. C. (2011, March 4). *Honest Abe reminds us of the power of words. NPR (National Public Radio).* https://www.npr.org/2011/03/04/134162178/150-years-later-lincolns-words-still-resonate

Widdowson, H. G. (2000). On the limitations of linguistics applied. *Applied Linguistics, 21*(1), 3–25.

Wiese, H. (2015). "This migrants' babble is not a German dialect!": The interaction of standard language ideology and 'us'/'them' dichotomies in the public discourse on a multiethnolect. *Language in Society, 44*(3), 341–368.

Williams, M. (2018, 10 May). Is Iran really 'the world's leading state sponsor of terror'? *Channel Four News.* https://www.channel4.com/news/factcheck/is-iran-really-the-worlds-leading-state-sponsor-of-terror

Wilson-Hartgrove, J. (2018). *Reconstructing the gospel: Finding freedom from slaveholder religion.* InterVarsity Press.

Wilson, J. R. (2020a). *Shakespeare and Trump.* Temple University Press.

Wilson, J. R. (2020b, April 23). *10 scenes from Shakespeare that fit Donald Trump's presidency: Streaming now.* Market Watch. https://www.marketwatch.com/story/10-scenes-from-shakespeare-that-fit-donald-trumps-presidency-streaming-now-2020-04-17

Winchester, S. (2005). *The professor and the madman: A tale of murder, insanity, and the making of the Oxford English Dictionary.* Oxford University Press.

Woodward, B. (2018). *Fear: Trump in the Whitehouse.* Simon & Schuster.

Woodward, B. (2020). *Rage.* Simon & Schuster.

Woodward, C., & Riechmann, D. (2021, January 9). No surprise: Trump left many clues he wouldn't go quietly. *Yahoo News Canada.* https://ca.news.yahoo.com/no-surprise-trump-left-many-063529108.html

Word. (2021). *Cambridge Advanced Learner's Dictionary.* https://dictionary.cambridge.org/dictionary/english/word?a=britis

Word. (2021). *Urban Dictionary.* https://www.urbandictionary.com/define.php?term=Word

Word of the Year 2016. (n.d.). *Oxford Languages.* https://languages.oup.com/word-of-the-year/2016/

Wright, S. (Ed.). (1998). *Language and conflict: A neglected relationship.* Multilingual Matters

Wright, A., Betteridge, D., & Buckby, M. (2006). *Games for language learning* (3rd ed.) Cambridge University Press.

Yglesias, M. (2019, July 18). Trump's racist tirades against "the Squad," explained: Is there a method to the madness? *Vox.* https://www.vox.com/2019/7/15/20694616/donald-trump-racist-tweets-omar-aoc-tlaib-pressley

Young, L. (2017, October 11). What happens to North Korea's aid money. *Global News.* https://globalnews.ca/news/3797235/north-korea-aid-money/

Zarefsky, D. (2007). Making the case for war: Colin Powell at the United Nations. *Rhetoric and Public Affairs, 10*(2), 275–302.

Zelazko, A. (2020, March 16). How long did the Flu pandemic of 1918 last? *Encyclopedia Britannica.* https://www.britannica.com/story/how-long-did-the-flu-pandemic-of-1918-last

Zimmer, B. (2015, September 16). "I'm going to have to science the shit out of this". *Strong Language.* https://stronglang.wordpress.com/2015/09/16/im-going-to-have-to-science-the-shit-out-of-this/

Zimmer, B. (2019, July 29). What Trump talks about when he talks about infestations: The frightening political history of the word 'infest'. *Politico.* https://www.politico.com/magazine/story/2019/07/29/trump-baltimore-infest-tweet-cummings-racist-227485

Zurcher, A. (2018, May 24). Analysing Trump's letter to Kim Jong-un. *BBC World News.* https://www.bbc.com/news/world-us-canada-44233641

About the Author

After working in UK hospitals, as a clinical, medical biochemist, Dr. Andy Curtis finally found his true passions: teaching and learning; languages and cultures. That journey, from science to science education to language education to applied linguistics, has enabled him to take a uniquely interdisciplinary approach that breaks down barriers and builds bridges between disconnected domains of knowledge. From 2015 to 2016, he served as the 50th President of the TESOL International Association, and in 2016, he received one of the Association's 50-at-50 Awards, when he was voted one of the Fifty Most Influential Figures in the Field, over the last 50 years. Dr. Curtis has (co) authored and (co)edited 200 articles, book chapters and books, presented to 50,000 language educators in 100 countries, and his work has been read by 100,000 language educators in 150 countries. He is an online professor at Anaheim University, and he is based in Ontario, Canada.

The New Peace Linguistics and The Role of Language in Conflict, page 281

About the Author

www.ingramcontent.com/pod-product-compliance
Lightning Source LLC
LaVergne TN
LVHW052256200926
848481LV00002B/383